CORNER
football + society
VOL. 1

PUNCH 2019

- 5 — Claudiu Revnic — Escape to Victory
- 9 — Corneliu Porumboiu — As Long as Something is Being Filmed There Will Be Some Kind of Ideology Behind It
- 14 — Ion Dumitrescu — The Third Game. An Outplay
- 24 — Cat Năstăsoiu — Colosseum
- 29 — Bogdan Ghiu — The Current State of the Stadium
- 42 — James Montague — Five Years a Slave
- 46 — Ștefan Tiron — What It Means to Lose Your Head
- 49 — Florin Flueras — One–One
- 53 — Vasile Mihalache — The Taming of the Body
- 58 — Alexandra Pirici — The Body as Technology for Spectacle in Contemporary Football
- 63 — Alexandra Pirici & Jonas Lund in conversation with Harry Thorne and Moritz Hollinger — Gaming the Score
- 74 — Ion Dumitrescu — Opera Cup
- 81 — Irina Costache — With Love, on Women's Football
- 84 — Young Hopes
- 86 — Pompiliu Nicolae-Constantin — Anti-System Supporterism
- 93 — Powerpuff interview — Watch the Game, Don't Stare at Me!
- 98 — Christopher Johnson — Against Modern Football.jpg
- 102 — Ion Dumitrescu — A Plant for Processing the Irrational
- 106 — Matei Sâmihăian — Don't Run. Hooligans on E
- 110 — Cosima Opârtan — Casual Terrace Style

CORNER VOL. 1

119 Ben Shave
Supporters - the Heart of the Game

121 Mihnea Anțilă
Minor Football

125 A Guide
How to Make Your Own Football Team

126 Ovidiu Țichindeleanu
Football Dispatches about the End of the World, Immigrants, and History in Images

130 Florin Poenaru
F.C. Refugees

134 Anamaria Pravicencu
Haunted Swimming

137 Octav Avramescu
A Few Years Ago Exactly or the First Winter

143 Claudiu Revnic
Ethnicity and Community vs. Nationalism and Fantasy

151 Florin Oprea
Performers & Performance

158 Andrei Mihail
Now It's for Money

163 Petrică Mogoș
The New Old Teams

171 Violeta Beclea-Szekely
I Don't Think Sport Belongs to Anyone

183 Declan Clarke
The System Against the System - Holland v USSR in Euro 88

205 Matei Bejenaru
Solidarność

210 Anca Verona Mihuleț
La Mano de Dios

214 Anca Verona Mihuleț
Symbolic Language and Social Behaviour. An Interview with Dumitru Graur

222 V. Leac
Horoscope

INDEX

4

Enric Fort Ballester
Kleine Skizze für grosse aktionen, 2013
Pigment ink on paper, 297 × 210 mm

Escape to Victory,

or why football always has and always will disappoint us

Claudiu Revnic

I used to watch *Escape to Victory* as a kid with my dad or uncle, both rabid football fans with different allegiances, my dad being a Universitatea Craiova supporter and my uncle a Rapid București fan. My dad had seen the film at the cinema, during a time where most films shown in theatres were either too old or too heavily censored; at the end of the day this film was as American as they come, with European and South American football players standing in for Fred Astaire and Ginger Rogers. My uncle had seen it on a bootleg video-tape, where it shared storage space with the Chuck Norris oeuvre *Operation Delta Force*. When I watched it myself at the age of 12, after the intense praise of both of these men, I was profoundly delighted. And that feeling haunts me every time I see it. It is one of those things that confirmed the myth of the brilliant football player in many a spectator.

Seen as mere entertainment, *Escape To Victory* is stupendous. In the director's chair we have John Huston, the cinematic maestro of lost causes and quixotic debacles. In goal, we have Rocky as a keeper, with Italo-American flair and razor-sharp glances at full speed. We have Pelé as the main striker and stand-up comedian de chance and Michael Caine as an officer and a coach in a fantasy football match up against the Nazis. For me, this film serves up those two passions; an heirloom, passed on like a grandfather clock; the obsession for football and the fetish for all things WWII. It was also a no-holds barred jubilation of football heroism and pet peeves of the European male. Though inspired by the true, and ultimately tragic, experience of Ukrainian team FC Start, that garnered outstanding victories against a German dream team in a series of events aimed at glorifying the German übermensch exceptionalism, *Escape to Victory* is a fantasy film with fashionably historically accurate sets and spirit-gliding theme music. It is precisely that fairy tale we run to from today's "all about the money", "on steroids" or "dirty" game and makes us drool with nostalgia over the "great" football of yesteryear.

The film is otherwise the epitome of the way we over-glorify football and of the way we perceive great football players: accomplished athletes, oozing with fool-proof sports ethics, fair play and high morals. Houston's opus takes everything to slightly hyperbolic realms. We have these fantastic footballers that basically, more or less directly, fight against the Nazis. The film instils an instant nostalgia for the football of the 1960s and the 1970s. The footballing legends of those times, undisputed champions and performers of the shifty and ambiguous milieu of the Cold War, play WW2, this unequivocal moment of triumph of good against evil. Houston, more or less overtly, bestows this mantra of nobleness over the game and more importantly over a generation of players that have fundamtented the fascination people have for the game that Pepsi and Coca-Cola so restlessly like to sponsor. This in return bespells the notion that great players can only be dignified, righteous, battle-born and anti-fascist. In the full throttle of amazing dribbles and suspenseful scenes of sabotage we neglect the fact that, phenomenal players like Ardiles and Pelé, were in fact used as poster boys for the fascist military regimes of Argentina and Brazil respectively and for their underlying value systems. Football is a sports-narrative experience that we have incorporated as a mythology and as a validation form for the human spirit. This is why football shall always disappoint us and shall always lie to us, without really wanting to.

Escape to victory is a David vs. Goliath story where an impromptu squad of allied prisoners from a POW camp are more or less obliged to take part in a, not exactly, friendly match against a German representative team. The film reveals just how much we go for stories where the underdogs jubilantly triumph with modesty and determination. We rejoice rampantly when a modest squad wins the Premier League, even if the owner is a millionaire, putting the plans of the sacred and the holy on hold, or when a team almost sprung out of the fjords of a country with a population of 300,000, defeats teams that are practically subscribed to success. These exceptions nurture the confirmation that there is something sacred to football. And then we get disappointed by the success of the usurper to the throne of football glory that is Cristiano Ron-

Escape to Victory

aldo and we overlook the fact that his multiple Balon D'Or wins are due to him training harder than most players, that is when he is not projecting his Ferraris onto tunnel walls while speeding. We expect of football players a standard of etiquette and morals than what we don't even expect of film stars.

We are lying to ourselves when we look at football as anything else than a spectacle. This is one of the reasons why Jorge Luis Borges had a deep disdain for the game: its power to lie and transform athletes into remote controlled marionettes meant to stir the population according to the needs and wants of military regimes. In a short story written together with friend and collaborator Adolfo Bioy Casares, Borges describes how a die-hard football fan finds out that all of the matches are rigged and they are in fact little more than theatre, with actors instead of players and with sports commentators that read from a script, and even then he vows to continue to support his team, promising its owner never to reveal the big secret. Borges was in fact to write this inspired by the way South American dictators were using the fans' passion for the game to certify their status as champions of the people or to consolidate their nationalistic rhetoric. In the '60s, in all its glory, Pelé's image was used by the military dictatorship on massive posters spread all over Brazil's major cities with a slogan reading "Nothing can stop this country now." Another military regime from the region used its status as host of the 1978 World Cup, won by an Argentinian squad of which Ardiles took part as well, to detract attention from the torture and decimation of political prisoners that went on in its detention centres, which were situated metres away from the stadiums where people cheered for the victorious. Football was also the sugar cane used to implant nationalism deep in post-89 Romania, with a deadly concoction of eternal disappointment, self-teasing and pleasure of being lied to.

I still indulge in watching this film, but now at the age of 30, I can enjoy it as a football fan's Rocky, a sort of hybrid between *The Great Escape* and *Star Wars*. I am not being the least bit ironic when I use these comparisons. I enjoy the sabotage scenes as much as I do with *The Guns of Navarone*, and I rejoice watching the splendidly choreographed game scenes like I did at the '94 World Cup when Romania beat Columbia in one of the most surprising up-turns in the tournament's history. I understand how we all grew up with these nauseating expectations from the players we admired and I understand how we continue to lie to ourselves and kid ourselves that football is anything more than sports entertainment.

image: John Huston, *Escape to Victory* (1981), film still ©Lorimar Film Entertainment

Claudiu Revnic

Corneliu Porumboiu
The Second Game, 2014, film still

As long as something is being filmed there will be some kind of ideology behind it

> Nowadays the spectator is also a referee and a coach. He must take part in it.

Interview with Corneliu Porumboiu

Corner: What do the identities of the two teams you were talking about in the beginning of the film mean today?

Corneliu Porumboiu: I understand Steaua has the most supporters in Romania, over 90% and this is due to winning the Champions Cup and continuity of performance. Its presence in newspapers is also great. My impression is they lost themselves somehow, maybe younger policemen would relate to Dinamo, but I don't think so, now the team is left with representing the neighbourhood. I believe it took time for these identities to be lost, especially after '89, since the generation of today's supporters was born after this date. At Steaua there was an impression that "everyone is with Steaua" and yet they played very good football all the time.

Is it preferred that private investors manage the teams?

Yes, at least partly. If you ask me, football is important to the community, but I don't know how important it is to get subsidised with a lot of public money, maybe there are other things to be done in the country.

What football team are you supporting?

When I was a kid I used to root for Dinamo. I also had a nickname, around the block I was called Orac, after one of Dinamo's players. Then I rooted for Vaslui, but now Vaslui is gone. I don't have a favourite team anymore and I haven't actually watched the games for a while now.

Is football a perishable product?

> Very much so. Football as well as film are for immediate consumption. A small part of consumers are interested in football in its various aspects.

The match presented in the film does not have the dynamics of an ordinary football game, it looks like a choreography.

> It's interesting because you discover another type of football. It's spectacular in another form. The pitch is absolutely impractical, they play with ambition until the very last breath, the game is of a high quality, it doesn't become rough, it's at the limit. Due to the weather, it looks like a choreography. In the end you don't even know where the ball is. It takes on another dimension, the game is more than what you see.

What place did footballers occupy in society? What about referees or the fans?

> It wasn't a *star system*. They were known, but not that well known. There wasn't this kind of over-the-air press. You saw them, you knew them, you sometimes saw stickers or stamps. There was no major impact in the media or society. Back then, the press didn't allow for alternatives. There was a famous legend with Duckadam who lost the use of his arm because he was shot by Valentin Ceaușescu, who was reportedly jealous of him. The communist system gave privileges, but couldn't give money. In a real market, players like them would make a lot more money. When they won the Champions Cup they gave them each an ARO car, but some were broken. A footballer told me that they gave him an ARO, he tried to sell it. He met with a shepherd from Sibiu for the deal and they got arrested by the police. In Vaslui, there was local pride because my father was from there. He was a director of the Public Food Supply, we had an apartment in a better housing block, he travelled to international matches because he was a FIFA referee, we had a VHS player. All the fans that appear in the movie are silent, it's weird. Lots of military and policemen surround the pitch, the spectators are an amorphous mass. The aesthetics or the way a football match is filmed has changed in the imagination of a certain type of society. There aren't many shots with the players either. If you look at a match in the Romanian champi-

As long as something is being filmed ...

onship today, there are still frames from above and and others are cropped. At an international level it's completely something else, it is filmed with probably 30 cameras, the filming covers the position of the spectator, of the pitch, the spectator positioned in the stands. Today a lot is being shot from ground level, from the coach's position. You're replacing the coach, seeing the match from his level. Nowadays the spectator is also a referee and a coach. You have to attend. At the time there were few replays, and they didn't doubt the referee either.

How do you describe the directing of the match? How do you think it has evolved?

Currently UEFA and FIFA are promoting an anti-narrative aesthetic, certain messages are not filmed, very hard fouls are avoided. As long as something is being filmed there will be a kind of ideology behind it. The match was filmed with a certain aesthetic and behind there was a certain kind of political vision. Now football is a product that makes immense amounts of money. It tries to not get parasitised by other messages. They're emphasising the spectacular, replays and slow-motion shots in which the players become heroes: heroes selling a product. Unconsciously, everyone is talking about the who is the best, Messi or Ronaldo. From my point of view, it's a forced thing, it's something that preoccupies many people. You have the impression that it's built to entertain from the outside. Now

Interview with Corneliu Porumboiu

all of them are part of this world, each one participates in it. The matches are also filmed in the same way. It's a huge industry. The spectator must be there.

What changes did you make to the original version?

The tape is from Mircea Lucescu. It had no sound and I didn't cut any of it. Those who made the show Replay, Marian Olaianos and Marius Mitran, no longer found cassettes with matches in the TVR archive. The tape was made directly in the transmission cart, it did not pass through the studio. Lucescu used to re-watch the matches for tactical analysis. I remember not understanding anything from the match when I saw it on TV.

How would you film a match?

Like *The Second Game*, from a distance.

How did you see the match?

At home, I had to explain whether it was offside or not. I was the referee in front of the TV.

How would you describe your experience as a footballer?

I played at a children's and juniors' level for a few years, I was a central midfielder. It was important, I had a pretty rigorous schedule and that helped me later on, it gives you a certain kind of seriousness and responsibility. I haven't been playing sports for years, my vitality feeds on what's left from what I did as a kid. Whether I feel like writing or not, I come to the office and I write 2-3 pages. I played between the ages of 8 and 10 and then between 14 and 16. I even didn't like it that much, I wasn't passionate about it. It was the time that college was coming, I had to decide and it was clear that I was not going to do this anymore. Dad told me that I was a Division B player, at most a weak player on a bad team in Division A. You had to give up a lot of things, be super passionate about it, you definitely need sacrifice. It disciplined me, it made me more curious. The team or the people were from many different backgrounds, each with his own story and that opened my eyes.

What did it mean for you to be the son of a famous referee?

When I was playing football, they made me be the referee. They asked me all the time, even if I was playing, I was a sort of an authority. Many in the town came and asked me if my dad supported Dinamo or Steaua.

As long as something is being filmed ...

When was the last time you played football?
> About two years ago I used to go to Piața Muncii to play. I played with some guys from the Prefecture who used to hit you and foul you when you didn't have the ball. There are a lot of people who are frustrated and put everything at stake. They are desperate to win.

Do you watch other sports?
> I played squash, pelota and tennis. I watch a lot of sports, that's why I didn't even install sports channels, because I'd watch TV all day.

Tell us about a football film you like.
> *Escape to Victory* with Stallone and Pelé. When the Germans are playing with the prisoners' team during World War II. Boxing, athletics or baseball are easier. Team sports are dramatically more difficult, in football there are many characters. What can you choose? More likely a coach or a player. It's a matter of space and ratio with eleven players.

How was the film perceived?
> *The Second Game* was borderline experimental. I promoted it in the *Gazeta Sporturilor* and in the *Dilema Veche*. It was only screened in cinemas in certain areas, in the provinces I don't think it was seen at all. People were pretty disappointed at Union cinema, they didn't expect to see something like this, they wondered if it was an actual film. People were expecting a classic narrative. Romanians are more shy, there is no real culture of dialogue. In Berlin it worked very well. The match itself is a document, I like football at this level too.

> image: Corneliu Porumboiu, The Second Game, 2014, film still ©42KM FILM

The Third Game. An Outplay

Ways of navigating the past

Ion Dumitrescu

Once upon a time in Romania, 1988 was the future. An Orwellian one. Perceived today through a recorded game of football, it looks murky, gloomy, while we know that in those totalitarian years football and gymnastics were *the* national discharge channels for its subjects.

Before the Revolution, sports were a regular outlet for the people. Generally, sport success stories functioned as a *meta*-link between the citizens of a reduced or condensed society of spectacle. In the midst of dystopia, the athletic triumphs of the 'Nation' were an energising breath of fresh air for the people. Nadia Comăneci in the seventies, the European Champions League Cup of 1986 won by Steaua București, other gold medallists of Romanian gymnastic teams - the only reasons to watch TV.

In Corneliu Porumboiu's film *Al Doilea Joc* (*The Second Game*, 2014), we have access to that pre-revolution reality through 'the eyes' of TV cameras, the soundless original live broadcast of a Dinamo București - Steaua București match, the eternal derby of the eighties.

The game starts without preamble. The re-run broadcast is a time-tunnel that induces a diffuse ambiance in which multiple dimensions are pulsating on the screen. Through a dense snowfall one glimpses fragments of a (partly) bygone world. The match becomes a vehicle, a back-in-time transporter, like listening to Electrecord (music label) records of the eighties, or diving in TVR archives. By immersing in pop cultures, one can trace remains and snapshots of a mental ecology. Behind The Iron Curtain public cultural products sometimes revealed a point of intersection between people's aspirations and official propaganda; compressed paradigms and affects, some long extinct while others latently present to this day. Watching the film, we initially face an emotional confusion, gritted in uncontrollable nostalgia –witnessing the birth of the 'Golden Generation' national football team overlapping with Ceaușescu's noir 'Golden Age'.

The game begins only if the ball bounces and the visibility is reasonable.

After a more alert dialogue between the director and his father (the actual referee of the 1988 game) in the beginning of the film, silence gradually sets in. Comments become sparse, monosyllabic, referring strictly to irrelevant moments of the game. The snow is now falling abundantly, some small splatters of blood on the shirt of No. 11's (Cămătaru, Dinamo) are beginning to appear and the rhythm of the film/match, while lively, becomes sluggish, disintegrating into invisibility and chaos.

The images fade in a canvas of snow and mud; coherence and conventions are dissolving. The players disappear sporadically, as micro agents of the situation, leading to the dismantling of the game's rules and conventions. Coaches are barely visible through the curtain of snow, and in the stands, a compact swarm of black-umbrellas hide the trembling fans. Multiple psycho-affective layers are feeding our experience.

Arriving at the limits of cinematic language, there is still more to be said. Diverting moving images towards literature, political commentary and realist speculation. An outplay. We can fill in the silent gaps with text, pre-analyses, observations, and aimless digressions; with thoughts orbiting a sphere with its centre nowhere. For Porumboiu, *The Second Game* seems a gateway to conceptual art territory. The director is transgressing cinema conventions.

A work between visual genres, at the edge of a certain approach and the opening to another kind of art hybrid. Through its time setting – a particular moment in 1988 broadcasted on TVR and resurrected by Porumboiu from a VHS tape without sound – the film produces a secondary discourse at the limits of apprehension, beyond 'minimalism'. *The Second Game* becomes performative and it is conceived as a conceptual manoeuvre: transferring an object/event from its conventional reality to another. A football game in a cinema theatre: the entire 90 minutes of a broadcast football match projected in a different space of representation. While the gesture is essentially in the lineage of Duchamp's work, the director's recontextualisation is infused with a strong personal dimension – the relationship between father (protagonist as arbiter) and son (director), a 64-year-old Adrian Porumboiu seeing himself as a young man at the peak of his referee career.

But there is a precedent to Corneliu Porumboiu's approach. In *Football as Never Before* (Hellmuth Costard, 1971), the cameras are following George Best during a Manchester United - Coventry match. FANB is one of first conceptual visual works that aims to survey the football spectacle from another angle, showing us a different perspective. While using some of the same mechanics later employed by Porumboiu, the 1971 film aims to de-structure the sport's conventions of representation. Observing the same reality but turning the 16mm camera onto other points of interest. Neither focused on the ball, nor on who is playing. Who scores or the score time-line is of little importance. The montage strictly follows George Best, capturing the myth in its subliminal construction. The protagonist himself is blurred, he becomes ethereal, a pop spectre and a pretext for a singularity to shine. Hellmuth Costard extracts from this grand show another dimension of its aesthetics, the potential of the ultimate experience, a niche divorced from the actual match; disregarding the main competition he is focused on the fascination.

We gradually enter a trance, we are led, as if hypnotised, from the 19th century entrails of Old Trafford, out into the sun-lit open pitch, and outside of the game itself. We are in the stadium but we grasp a different viewpoint, a different cut of the game.

The trance, the hypnotic, and even dizziness, are present in another recent and already famous film, this time featuring Zinedine Zidane, made under the same conceptual circumstances as *Football as Never Before*. In *Zidane: A 21st Century Portrait*, directed by Douglas Gordon and Philippe Parreno, we follow a non-eventful game where the football star doesn't even display some the extraordinary qualities that made him famous. We are rather watching a monotonous game until an absurd outburst of violence perturbs the end of the match. The process of mythologising is again in view here but we see yet another angle, the "humanity" of the professional player, his moment of weakness that rapidly slips into an irrational act.

Football and the production of unknown

At halftime we're switching to speculative philosophy – denying our subjectivity, intellectually fighting against 'experience'. Football becomes the symbol of an ecstatic world as we perceive it, the alpha child of global sports, or a phenomenological trap. Unlike other sports originating in Great Britain, mostly invented by the aristocracy, football evolved in the 19th century within industrial urban communities, with teams coagulating in neighbourhoods with a proletarian and bourgeois fan base. It seems a mysterious and privileged process, the one that prompted football in the epicentre of global sports addiction at the end of the 20th century; an ultra-profitable factory producing trained and consistent heroes and staggering social ascension shortcuts. The heart of sport entertainment. Yet perhaps this process is not so mysterious. The more "the end of history" was pushed forward in the west, the faster the expansion, accumulation, and 'economic growth' became. In late, post-Fordism capitalism, communities have disintegrated (have been de-territorialised), while the number of foreign players allowed in a team has improved multi-culturalism. Football clubs are now on the stock market. Manchester United is in bad shape but is increasingly profitable. Javier Mascherano (FC Barcelona) lamented the situation in an interview; in England, club managers are too often not able to attend matches because they reside at thousands of kilometres away, on different continents. European football clubs act as incubators for globalisation.

Furthermore, football has proven it has the extra-dose of unpredictability necessary to maintain the nourishing tensions inside the global monopoly (the end of competition), produced by the acceleration of mergers and the obligatory diversity. The production of the unknown is packaged and sold as mega-spectacle. Nowadays, however, football is progressively mathematically measurable. The market pushes the game towards a type of posthuman professionalisation, producing bodies and minds for a new era of sports. Young players become professional as fast as possible, maximising performance at all costs, in tune with the neoliberal economic model. Fabregas was Arsenal's captain at only 19.

Ion Dumitrescu

In contemporary sports one can sense how the artificial is rationalised: Let the bots play! We can foresee teams of androids singing the sponsor/corporation's anthem instead of the national one, as imagined in the dystopian society of Rollerball (Normal Jewison, 1975), where citizens are equipped with 'privilege cards'. But bots also break down and become obsolete.

You would think football stands no chance in the universe of the 'realists'. It is so fundamentally correlational, from the glorification of 'experience', common to all sports, to the game itself, which makes no sense without teams, histories, subjects as spectators. It is the perfect trap for the 'model of the self'. Football consolidates an illusion of a world built for us, it hooks you to your own world, the nemesis of realist speculation.

The game re-represented in *The Second Game* induces a different impression, one of dissolution – an overflowing spectacle of a different kind, drifting towards decomposition, it lacks effervescence or any kind of urgency. The film seems an exercise doomed to an absolute irrelevance. The experience is more alienating than correlational. Adrian Porumboiu mentions a number of times throughout the film that football is 'perishable', stored in the present it has almost no value. In football, "like in art", he claims, nobody is interested in the past. Great players are quickly forgotten. The former international referee insists on the futility of his son's attempt to look back at that game, and turn it into a film: "Nobody will watch it."

The FIFA anomaly

The more progressive and anti-racist FIFA's messages become, the more authoritarian/corporate it behaves. An epiphany of capitalism 2.0 and 3.0, when the subject's resistance is integrated in the market. FIFA allows the highest-bidding countries to organise world cups. In Brazil a series of protests erupted because of the absurd expenses. In South Africa, an entire infrastructure was built and now lies in neglect, abandoned as it is impossible to sustain. On the other hand, women's football has gained momentum, competitions are being increasingly mediatised. Nike ends an endorsement for a homophobic boxer Manny Pacquiao. MoMA together with Volkswagen organise exhibitions rousing eco-pollution awareness and the need to reduce greenhouse gasses. The FBI is arguing with Apple about citizens' right to privacy. We are living in the contradictions prophesied by 1980s cyberpunk writers. Third world countries are being coerced by global football interests just like multinational companies coerce a nation-state. Until last year's huge scandals, FIFA's top 11 leadership seemed to have won all games. Now the whole board is under investigation, while some small-time bureaucrats have already ended up be-

The Third Game. An Outplay

hind bars. Sepp Blatter stated that he will wait out his 8-year ban and shall not quit his position. He seems unstoppable, displaying the winner mentality till the end. Meanwhile, stadiums in Qatar are rising triumphantly amidst the inaudible cries of thousands of Nepalese workers, treated like androids in Automata (Gabe Ibáñez, 2014). The 'king of sports' is coming apart, the betting overdose and corruption are now visibly manifesting. Ultra-visible. In the end, club bosses (Becali, Borcea, Copos, etc.) involved in player-transfer scandals, were the involuntary avant-garde. The great outernational corruption particularised by Romania in late 2000s was a paradoxical echo, one that preceded the collapse of the international football elite. An anastrophe. Even Mourinho started losing. In 2016 he is a man without a team, just like Robert Duvall in *Network* (Sidney Lumet, 1976), 'a man without a corporation'.

The International Association of Athletic Federations (IAAF) has also been 'shaken' by structural dysfunctionalities piercing through the surface of the on-going mega-live shows, involving the most virtuoso bodies in the world. Powerful characters like Lamine Diack and Lord Coe are stampeded by journalists and are now publicly contested. The marriage between anti-corruption and media; the ingurgitation and regurgitation of sensationalism within radical populist realms. Sports as the entertainment division of the military-industrial complex, spilling beyond its designated bounds into the core of global subjects.

The need for theoretical reform is already performed by right-wing accelerationists. FIFA made their move too quickly. Over-grown and opulent, the football international edifice is exposed to the global speculative corruption, in sync with the speed of algorithmic finance. It became obese, full of amazing, addictive football players.

The Narco Race

Football is the epitome of mass activities living almost exclusively out of spectacle. Absolute professionalisation is the road to sport excellence. Germany's national team had its own all-inclusive basecamp built for the 2014 World Cup in Brazil. A 10-million-euro investment, that helped exponentially in winning the cup. The "Mannschaft" case proved beyond doubt that technology improves performance. From nutrition, physique, muscular and technique metrics, everything can now be displayed as a chart while meta-data is gathered for further optimisation. The Football Industry keeps up with the latest break-through studies in cognitive sciences, neurology and analytics. In the same time all sport disciplines have intensified their technological research efforts in order to minimise risk, not only to increase performance. The expo-

Ion Dumitrescu

nential growth of investments in sports has created a universe populated by techno-biologically engineered athletes. It's no longer about 1% talent and 99% work, but 50% talent (DNA) and 50% technological enhancement.

In cycling, doping is routine. A sport where competition has been being transferred to the field of chemistry long ago; red blood cells increase; uncharted steroids and other methods are in use for quite some time. A race for oxygenation, as seen in *The Program* (2015), Stephen Frears's film about Lance Armstrong's mega-scam. The race between how efficient the substances can be hidden in the body and how fast sport institutions are able to detect them. Doping should in fact be legalised. The free market should do its thing. Let the spectacle of drug deregulation begin! No more substance restrictions! May the best biochemist win! Take the Formula 1 model, one company provides the engine, another the design, another the tyres, and now a pharma sport department is showcasing the drug. The multiple levels of contemporary competition.

The best way to illustrate the absolute deregulation that neoliberalism preaches, is to use sports. Perhaps soon we will have genetic mutations: genetically modified athletes. In this plausible future cyclists would have developed disproportionate legs in rapport to the torso. A teratologic gallery will be featured at the starting line: giants with emaciated heads, humanoids with exstrophied lungs, and other bio-hybrid athletes, each tagged with its pharmaceutical logo.

When Lance Armstrong admitted to his fraud, the world of cycling was put in a delicate position. The history of the sport became volatile. Hierarchies of the past became loose. For instance, we don't really know what happened with the Tour de France between 1999 and 2006. Fundamental parts of the cycling tradition are erased.

Transition and beyond infinity

Coming back to the hypnotic stasis of the 1988 match between Dinamo and Steaua, one realises how unprepared people were for the 1989 revolution, and how difficult it was to anticipate the imminent change. The stream of thoughts inevitably jumps into the '90s, when both teams sold most of their players to Western leagues. The beginnings of privatisation, then hundreds of thousands of workers were left without jobs, then falling victims to pyramid schemes like Caritas, FNI, and others; massive waves of people leaving the country, for work, study, or to steal.

Public fund draining and bureaucratic anarchy. In the first 10 years of post-89, more than a million people went abroad. While in Romania, suitcases filled with cash were being passed around between various powerful individuals and institutions; times when corruption was not perceived as such, it was the status quo. The end of the 2000s saw many of the Romanian football bosses and protagonists in prison – including former Barcelona star Gică Popescu – together with a few dozen politicians and mayors. In the '90s the underground mixed with the above-ground. Football club managers didn't walk away unscathed by the post-revolution decade. The 'transition', a.k.a. the never-ending phase of primitive capitalism, proved in the end to be unkind to its winners. Recently, I got to "admire" once again the Dinamo București stadium's official executive box/booth, built around the early 2000s by Dinamo owners: a DIY-like plastic structure excrescence built on top of the old official executive box. The image functions like a metonymy for the contribution of club managers to the development of Romanian football.

After the 2008 crash, a new transition began, the last one, endless. In the wake of the National Anticorruption Agency crackdown, Romanian football breathes heavily, re-grouping in the ruins of former glory. When we look back, in 1988, things seemed much calmer, albeit hiding desperation. The totalitarian system was readable, sometimes exposed through football club rivalries: Steaua (Army's team) vs. Dinamo (Police's team). A symmetrical world, predictable, at the peak of its stagnation. A perimeter of meaning none of whose subjects foresaw its inevitable demise.

Ion Dumitrescu

Ion Dumitrescu
The Executive Box of Dinamo Stadium, 2016, photograph

DID YOU KNOW?

... in heraldry, supporters are figures placed on either side of a shield, imagined as supporting it. These figures can be animals, humans, or, less commonly, plants or objects, real or fictional.

... in 2014, DC Comics (1934) sued Valencia CF (1919) for copying the Batman logo (1939).

... Neymar's shin pads are printed with a photo of himself and his boy.

... PSG asked musician M.I.A. to stop broadcasting the video of her song Borders', where she wears a shirt of the team on which the sponsor Fly Emirates has been replaced with 'Fly Pirates'.

... Totti, the symbol of AS Roma, published a book with all the jokes made about him. *All the Totti Jokes* has sold hundreds of thousands of copies, and the profits were donated to an elderly support programme from Rome and to a UNICEF program for homeless children in the Congo.

.... for the 2006 World Cup, Rirkrit Tiravanija, the artist who uses cooking in his practice, made a recipe book for the matches' half time break. It contains 16 dishes that can be prepared and eaten within 15 minutes.

... in a press conference, Lassana Diarra, who plays for Olympique de Marseille, had to publicly refute claims that he had enrolled as a jihadist in Syria after such rumours had been spread on the internet.

... at a ceremony in Abu Dhabi, representatives of Real Madrid unveiled a personalised card for the clients of the national bank of the United Arab Emirates that contains the club's logo minus the Christian cross.

- the national women's football team of Norway is the first women's team to receive the same compensation as the men's team.
- team Lazio's ultras made stickers showing Anne Frank wearing the t-shirt of their rival AS Roma. The outcome: the team's president Claudio Lotito will send 200 ultras each year on an education visit to Auschwitz, and, before each Serie A match parts of Anne Frank's diary will be read and the referees will hand the teams' captains a copy of the book together with a copy of Primo Levi's *I sommersi e i salvati*.
- Jabulani, the official ball of the 2010 World Championship, was designed by the Loughborough University Sports Technology Institute. Many players complained that it is difficult to control, as it is too round.
- Turkey launched an investigation into Galatasaray SK after the team's fans displayed a giant poster showing Rocky Balboa accompanied by the caption: 'Stand up. They look big because you are kneeling.' Supporters of the Turkish government believe it was a reference to a sermon held by Fethullah Gülen.
- players of Hertha Berlin knelt during the anthem before a game with Schalke 04. The gesture was one of solidarity with Colin Kaepernick and other NFL players, who did a similar thing during the US anthem in protest against police brutality, also seen as a gesture of resistance against the Trump administration.
- FC Barcelona took part in the general strike in Catalonia as a sign of solidarity with the citizens.
- Sepp Blater is no longer FIFA's president.
- Sleaford Mods sponsored a kids' football team. The Seven Sisters AFC U9 will play with the band's name on their t-shirts.
- the president of Beitar Ierusalim, the most nationalist team in Israel, stepped down after declaring he would never sign a Muslim player.

COLOSSEUM

Cat Năstăsoiu

In the early '80s, in Buzău, on an autumn day, a good friend whispered to me in a conspiratorial tone: "My bro is playing a film [VHS] on Saturday evening, five *lei* to get in. Are you in? Dunno the address yet." For me, this was going to be a memorable premiere for various reasons. First, because I gained access to a group of spectators for illicit viewings of films "on v-h-s", and second, because I could see a VHS player for the first time ever. Moreover, this would be my first time watching a movie starring Bruce Lee and, little did I know back then, Chuck Norris too.

Illicit viewings took place in friends of friends' apartments, without sharing details about who they were or the relationships between them. Windows were covered with indigo carbon copy paper, to make sure the flicker of the TV's light could not be seen from the street. The whole scene was a mix of emotions and adrenaline, a combination of enthusiasm and anticipation of a kind of entertainment the like of which we had not experienced before. This emotional complex was boosted also by the fear of getting snitched on by some neighbour and getting caught while illegally viewing a banned and novel show. The movie was *The Way of the Dragon*, released in 1972, and its synopsis went like this: Bruce Lee arrives in Rome to help out some relatives at a restaurant, a family business. The plot is centered around the pressure a mob union inflicts on his family to sell the property where they were running their business. When Bruce Lee becomes a threat to the syndicate, their bosses hire martial arts experts from Japan and Europe to eliminate him. Just as expected, Tang, the character played by Lee, beats the hell out of every fighter sent to execute him, which determines the mobsters to eventually hire Chuck Norris, aka Colt, an American fighter, obviously an expert in martial arts as well, to defeat Tang. And because the movie takes place in Rome, there couldn't be a more fitting place for the final confrontation than the Colosseum. The ancient amphitheatre, having witnessed so many gladiator fights, was going to host once more, in modern times, a confrontation between two 'gladiators', this time of the big screen.

Even now I recall the tension filling the apartment room of the communist block where, squeezed in front of the black and white television set, five to seven teenagers watched every single move of the two fighters. We would clench teeth, grabbing the edge of our seats, cheer quietly, while involuntary gestures that mimicked skilful hits would burst spastically from our bodies in our attempt to support Bruce Lee in his fight against the blonde American.

If a fight scene 'on screen' between two fictional characters could generate such an emotional repertoire, I can only imagine what an extraordinary impact live gladiator fights in the ancient Colosseum had on a viewer. I'd have to multiply the number of viewers from that night in the apartment room by ten thousand and imagine the space from the TV expanding to a stadium's scale. The proportions are overwhelming as it is, both in regards to the number of people, and the emotional charge generated in this context, admittedly an imaginary one.

Emperor Vespasian, in whose times the Colosseum's construction started, came to the throne of the Roman Empire after Nero, who had left Rome in a deep social and political turmoil. To distract attention from the critical problems that the Empire was facing, Vespasian, the founder of the Flavian dynasty, commissioned the construction of an amphitheatre where gladiator games would come to take place, drawing in large crowds the citizens of the Roman capital.

These citizens had free access to the shows. It was the right of citizens to join banquets offered by the popular rich aristocrats, enjoying in this way the entertainment shows that were part of them. In order to collect social capital, the prominent figures of Rome made a duty out of maintaining the appropriate clientele and entourage. The entertainment, the games, or *panem et circenses* (bread and circus), as the Romans would refer to them, were a popular way of obtaining this social capital, which had its end goal in consolidating political backing.

On a much bigger scale, in comparison to Rome, games were funded first of all by the Emperor. It is thought that at least one in twenty Roman citizens participated at the games organised in the Colosseum.

It is estimated that, in 69 BC, Rome counted a population of about a million people. Amfiteatrum Flavium, as it was named initially, hosted on average around 65 thousand spectators, full capacity reaching around 85 thousand. An amphitheatre is different from a theatre, where spectators are seated facing the stage, through its oval or circular shape, while the stage is the arena, located in the centre. The gazes of 65 thousand viewers, focused on the middle of the arena where the action took place, devoured with intense emotion the entertainment of the games, making them forget their personal concerns, as well as those of the empire. At first, gladiator games were religious rituals, but shortly their sacred character was forgotten. Its place was taken over by huge theatrical productions, with ever mounting costs which went hand in hand with people's increasing appetite for spectacle. The most popular *ludi* (public games) were the circus shows or the arena races, but the most remarkable productions would go as far as enacting naval battles, which involved flooding the arena, or the Silvae shows, where animals populated an elaborate scenography – for example, in a landscape of forests and rocks dramatic takes on well-known mythological tales would be enacted. Against all expectations, gladiator fights were not so frequent and were rather associated with *venatio*, shows where wild animal hunting scenes would be enacted, and which would sometimes involve the execution of convicted criminals.

The social importance held by the gladiator games determined legal regulation and the organising of an annual schedule for these *ludi*. Line-up, script, production, show, stars, circus, focus, audience, all these are common ingredients of mass-media, of TV productions or of a blockbuster. In fact, beyond the legendary battles with their heroic protagonists, the Colosseum was a media infrastructure, built and conceived to attract and maintain the interest of the audience away from society's issues. During the games, the famous amphitheatre hosted an audience of more than 5% of Rome's population. The emotional intensity surpassed almost any personal or social matter, with eyes fixated on the centre of the amphitheatre, watching the gladiators' every move, the animals' every jump, hit, or dodge that could be fatal, or merely a delay of the ending. They would cheer, mumble with satisfaction or disillusionment. The sounds must have been unheard of for the citizen who participated for the first time to this show – they were clenching teeth, jumping off their seats, mimicking fighting gestures, a kind of air fight. By mimicking or anticipating, judgments were cast with total disregard to the final consequences, which could mean continued life or, in most cases, death. The audience, having free access to the Colosseum, received, by paying with their presence, a power that many couldn't afford the luxury of: escape from immediate reality and access to the state of being a spectator.

Both fighters take off their clothing, exhibiting their physique and performing a brief, yet masterful, warm-up for their wrists. The fight does not take place in the arena, but on one of the Colosseum's superior corridors, where the plebs would get to their seats. It is quiet, the only spectator now is a little kitten watching the two intensely. The set director chose a choreography of angles and slow-motion close-ups, close and wide frames, providing what no ancient spectator could observe from anywhere inside the amphitheatre – the details of the fight. With a swift move, Bruce Lee rips off a wisp of hair from Chuck Norris's chest, the kitten meows and, with eyes wide open with curiosity, tries to anticipate the next move of the former. After a spectacular series of hits, each accompanied by the meowing sounds of both him and the kitten, and what sounds a little like a series of arrhythmic beats like flip-flops pacing on a beach, Bruce breaks Chuck's neck, puts his clothes back on and walks away. And we do the same thing.

Cat Năstăsoiu

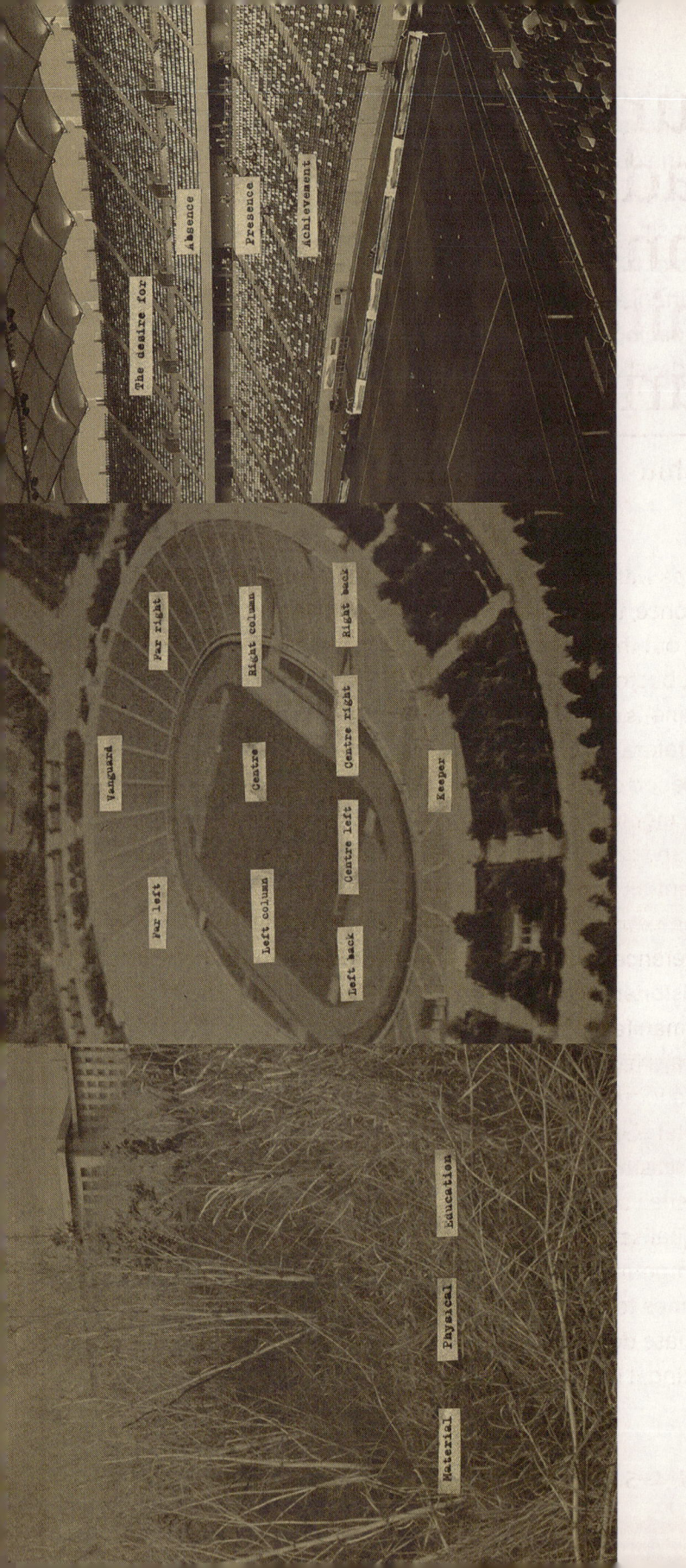

Irina Botea + Jon Dean
7 On the Bench, 11 On the Pitch, 2015
Photo collage, 24 × 72 cm

The Current State of the Stadium.
Technology, Architecture, Security, Spectacle

Bogdan Ghiu

Part 1

We were born in cities with stadiums. I don't think there is someone who has never gone, at least once, to a stadium. That is, to a football match. I don't think there's a settlement out there that doesn't have its stadium. I'm not referring here to a sports field, but to a *public arena*. For many, a stadium means football, and 'going to the game' is often a *rite of passage* in the father-son relationship. The stadium has therefore *always* functioned as an important political device. *Regardless* of time period or political regime, modern "mass design" – the constitution, redrawing, moulding of the masses, of society as mass – took place not only in factories and prisons, but also on stadiums, during football games.

    Drawing attention to this *continuity* is an important but contentious point in conversations about the 'new stadium'. 'Actualist' analysts are tempted to emphasise difference and historical ruptures produced by technological revolutions, while historians tend rather to point to intensifications and accelerations of already manifest processes. What can be said regardless is that the stadium has always represented an important social-*instrumental* asset.

    Presently, the football-spectacle stadium has become the privileged hyperobject, the 'total object', where the main vectors of current neoliberal financial semiocapitalism – spectacle, architecture, urbanism, security – intersect and can be analysed both separately and in synergy. In other words, we see the total digitalisation, delocalisation, and even derealisation of the collective sports competition as vented, channelled, subdued violence. Football increasingly comes to resemble a video game, a pure sign, an agonistic meta-spectacle of mass design. This implies a (transhuman) pacifying of humanity by transforming it into semio-financial flux.

At the same time, stadiums are turning into mega malls, situated on the outskirts of cities, conceived and designed to function as centres of urban animation, implantation, and, ultimately, development. They become, in other words, hyperintegrated (and, therefore, interrogating) macro-apparatuses, endowed with internal and external functions. We can even say that the 21st century stadium plays the vital role of socio-urbanistic operator – it becomes its own miniature city, while at the same time 'producing' the city, helping and stimulating it to development. In a nutshell, it displaces it, it moves it, helps it become something different. The stadium radiates both inwards and outwards. Its goal is to simultaneously concentrate and entertain (through dispossession), but also to project, reconfiguring space. It performs a pincer movement. This is why its form, its scheme, must be analysed according to the rhetorical trope known as *chiasmus*, as a permanent contradiction whose synthesis is not dialectical resolution but the maintaining of a divergent/convergent movement.

According to the projects of new stadiums, the so-called 'new stadium' – for, as we shall see, there is a single universal model – which is designed to function as a tool, as an apparatus for and operator of social remodelling, the sport itself almost becomes tangential. We no longer go to the stadium only for football, but to consume, to allow ourselves to be captive/ated. We go to the stadium to *live* within in. Both 'the old' but especially 'the new' stadium generates and inscribes as reflex the myth of total and merciless competition, which therefore helps propagate the structures of (neoclassical) capitalist economy.

The current stadium, more than ever, expresses its desire to become, in terms of structure and atmosphere, the city itself, capturing life in all its aspects. As one stadium manager said, the people have to arrive as early as possible and leave as late as possible. And when they leave they return to their real estate development projects generated and modelled by the stadium itself as recreational park. In the end, whether we are interested in sports – in the 'king of sports' – or not, we come to live in stadiums, in city-stadiums, living our lives *as if* in a stadium. The "carceral archipelago" (M. Foucault) or the "prison industrial complex" (Angela Davis) can still be defined nowadays as the modulation of a stadium continuum.

What does life in this continuum look like? To give a barebones answer, we could say it is the life of an *active consumer*, of people active only as consumers, of object-subjects of consumption, of a commodity among commodities, ensuring the cyclical and mirroring regeneration of capital and pure, literally *speculative*, profit.

New stadiums manage to both bring us together and keep us apart, isolated from one another. One of the techno-political stakes of the 'new stadium' is precisely the hindrance of coagulated crowds forming, of the mass constituting a collective subject – in the context of a singular focal point nonetheless. The new football stadiums – whose unified, standardised model, which they merely perpetuate materially, is the American Super Bowl stadium – despite bringing us together and trying to keep us within them as long as possible, are full of *screens*, of a hypertrophied, often highly personalised, informational offer that makes us dependent on our own devices, especially our smartphones. We therefore go to the stadium, but our gaze is permanently directed and mobilised on two fronts that communicate with one another: the sports spectacle itself and the small and large screens that crowd and structure the stadium. And this is because, due to so-called network technologies – which actually cover up, conceal, double the world by creating new *fields* – we are only information consumers and receivers in so far as we are also producers of information about ourselves (informer information), producing our own informational transformation, our own dissolution into information, into common denominators of the universal becoming-commodity: informatisation, informationalisation, commodification. The two fronts that permanently direct and mobilise our gaze on (in fact within) the new city-stadiums (or stadium-camps, prototypes for the future stadium-cities of the global spectacle economy) – that is, the terraces and the screen – have the implicit purpose of not allowing us to look around. They make it impossible to look at each other. Between spectacle and technology there is no room left for direct, immediate, unmediated, even fusional socialising, and our relationship with the sport comes to depend on an "all-you-can-eat" informational menu, a meal with pseudo-cognitive additives meant to transform us from supporters into consumers.

*

All of these tendencies that I have so far presented, so to say, in bulk, could easily be seen in the recent UEFA Championship in France. One essential note to this, which also sadly represents an important cultural difference between us and them, is that this immediate actuality was complemented, accompanied, even preceded by a critical one. In France, whole book stands and bookshop storefronts became dedicated to critical literature about the 'new stadium'. As homage to this critical spirit, the title of the present text is a reference to one of the relevant books on the topic: *Smart Stadium. Le stade numérique du spectacle sportif* (the author takes advantage of the French homonym *stade*, which can mean both *stadium* and *status*) by Marc Perelman,

Bogdan Ghiu

published by L'Échappée. The publishing house actually released a series of works on the social-political evolutions of sports.

I would like now to transition into the second part of this text. To continue the idea mentioned between parentheses above regarding the colonisation of the world with technologised architecture from the US, and which tendency this year's tournament made visible, we should mention, for instance, that Nantes, Rennes, and Nancy were among the candidate cities for hosting the event. They had to drop out however due to UEFA's obligatory task book, which, if in 1998, according to the mayor of Rennes, would have fitted inside a briefcase, now would require a whole closet. Why? Because not a single architectural decision must be entrusted to local architects. Everything must be planned out and made compliant to norms beforehand. In other words, the stadium has to be strictly *standardised*, to have one single form everywhere in order to fulfil its main function as strategic macro-apparatus of (imposed) globalisation.

Part 2: Potlatchitecture

The actual induced competition, as it is felt by the public and understood as emulation, consists not in having unique stadiums, but precisely in having 'arenas', as they call them now, that are as similar as possible: a kind of 'we also want to be like...' mentality, a need to catch up with (i.e. to be accepted into) the world. The sideline competition (administrative, financial, business, and, last but not least, architectural) is just like that on the field: qualifying into the global transnational elites' league, that of 'new stadium' owners. Regardless of how strong a team, a club, a city, or a country is - or was - if they don't have *a certain kind* of stadium, they cannot be chosen to organise standardised competitions (international finals between clubs or countries), and, therefore, do not exist. At the *edge* of, or *in the shadow* of, the visible competition - the football spectacle itself - a number of other competitions take place. Firstly that of being equipped with 'modern', cutting edge equipment (stadiums). These are as great a reason for pride (i.e. existence) as the acquisition (i.e. investment in) celebrity players.

The stadium therefore represents a device, a gadget only differentiated from a smartphone or a tablet by scale. It is not a surprise that one author (Marc Perelman) called it the *'Smart Stadium'*. Contemporary football has become a total competition, the game itself being only the tip of the iceberg. If it didn't generate parallel competitions structurally overlapping with the visible one, football could not maintain (through the media) this archetype of the *permanent competition*. In the race for standardised stadiums, a club president or even a mayor can become a celebrity, a hero every bit as irresistible as Ronaldo or Messi, who themselves, through a perverse twist, become mere surface effects of a competition that must be total: life itself, society at large.

What we see is not a rational economy (as rational as an economy can be, anyway) but a real *potlatch*: if you are not able to invest huge sums of money, that is, to show you can 'sumptuously' sacrifice yourself (as anthropologists put it, and especially Bataille in his *Accursed Share*) you are rejected, you are barred from entering the infra-competition or meta-race that frames, extends, and, in fact, makes the football spectacle possible. You are not qualified to share mega-profits as member of a total industrial elite.

As a general statement regarding the idea and phenomenon of the spectacle, which can only be generated by competitions: the competition is the spectacle. And the competition takes place, as I have said, on multiple levels, including that of architecture and technology. Architecture becomes, especially from the perspective of sports in general, particularly from that of European football, the great bringer of funds, a *spectacle-architecture*. And the competition, to return to our starting point, becomes paradoxical, if not outright perverse, given that it does not aim for particularisation and individualisation, but, on the contrary, for standardisation, levelling, upward homogenising. Around football, the spectacle of globalisation is on overt display.

This perverse spectacle of upwards levelling that generates its spectacle-architecture (among whose formats, or globally privileged hyperobjects, are also artworks and museums, especially those of contemporary art, and especially high-rises and airports) has its own winners, 'heroes', 'stars'. Have you ever heard of the American architectural practice Populous? No? As builder of the largest numbers of stadiums globally per year (it is a total competition, nobody is safe. Football or no football, everyone wants to 'score'!), it falls into what Pierre Bourdieu called *structural homology*. This exists for instance between Ronaldo and Messi (players), Real Madrid and Barcelona (club teams), Brazil, Argentina, Germany, Italy, Spain, etc. (national teams), and so on.

The France of the 2016 European Championship was invaded by the Unique Plan, the Unique Design of the architecture-business conceived not just by the above-mentioned practice, but also by other celebrity companies (from various fields – the competition is tight), always in accordance with the unique demands of the unique client: UEFA.

How does the Unique Stadium, the Global Stadium, the airport stadium coveted by all as an object of 'mimetic rivalry' – as René Girard said, because if there is an overarching theme for this discussion that is apparently only about

Bogdan Ghiu

stadiums, it is certainly the fact that we find ourselves in the field of basic anthropological mechanisms, that in the *total competition* which the football-spectacle has become (a football business, that is), these basic mechanisms are being mobilised, cultivated, amplified, totalised – which makes Arsenal's *Emirates Stadium*, for instance, look almost perfectly like Olympique Lyonnais's *Stade des Lumières*, thereby destroying the difference between London and Lyon? What are, in other words, "the aesthetics of the digitised stadium"? The description can be simpler or more detailed, but the principles are the same. Let us take a look at this description in a few steps, on multiple levels:

- "It is a bit like Lego. The structure is no longer made to be seen, but to support. There is something like surface enveloping the structure and a façade with a few motifs. Only with this enveloping surface is there some space for expression for the architect, but even this can be constrained for economic reasons. The architect's freedom will probably be reduced to the façade." (architect Loïc Coquin);

- "Nowadays the architect makes wallpaper. These stadiums built like Powerpoint presentations are entrepreneurial, not architectural works... There is no more creating." (Roger Taillabert architect of FC Paris Saint-Germain's Parc des Princes stadium);

- "Designing a stadium [generally] reduces the formal complexity of architecture (walls, reliefs, angles, proportions, etc.) simply to a form, if not to a simple form. The project of the stadium presents itself as a sort of watery white cloth, as a slightly flattened and elongated soap bubble seemingly waiting to gently spill over onto the neighbouring buildings. An architectural bubble that dilates, stretches, displays itself, unfolding its enormous mass, whose protrusions and filaments make their way into the surrounding urban tissue... an aesthetics of technological hygiene, of the immaculate machine free of all relief... a polished design." (M. Perelman, *Smart Stadium. Le stade numérique du spectacle sportif*, L'Échappée, Paris, 2016, pp. 66-68).

The contemporary unique stadium is first and foremost a *hyper-viewing* device whose main task is to allow the polyfocal viewing of the Total Spectacle of the Competition. Increasingly its core is represented by the 'Global Screen' (Gilles Lipovetsky, Jean Seroy, Polirom, 2008), but one that is *multiplied*, refracted. "After the camera and cinema, the stadium is now the one undergoing metamorphosis into a seeing device, into a quasi-medium in itself." (M. Perelman, op. cit., p. 85).

These oversized, almost closed-off arenas that are contemporary stadiums, with their covered stands, on increasingly steep slopes, fuller and fuller of increasingly comfortable lounges, become designs of ambient consumption. In terms of architecture, the pioneer of these forms is the recently deceased British-Iraqi architect Zaha Hadid, and the mind behind the bowl/nest stadium can only be Peter Sloterdijk, whose *Spheres* trilogy opens precisely with the *bubbles* of the contemporary world.

If Maracana, Wembley, or San Siro represented iconic particularities of the places they were located, offering an architectural idiom to the game, today they have to upgrade and update themselves, become nominal iterations of the supposedly multifunctional contemporary Arena, spaces of the unique competition-spectacle.

"There is a real simultaneity between the appearance of these truly original stadium forms and new technologies, with their compact, rounded aesthetics and dissimulated structures that come to conceal technology itself." (M. Perelman, op. cit., p. 68).

For it is exactly the unifying *technology* that commands the new standard architecture of the arena stadium. And this technology is, more than ever, *panoptical* (in Bentham's sense, which was then updated by Foucault): to see and be seen. What this does is inscribe, more than ever, football-as-a-factory into an information economy (and implicitly into an ecology of attention).

Part 3: The Improved Human and the Triumph of Truth

This total, *societal project* that is the new stadium – an already fulfilled project, a utopia in an advanced stage of construction – should, however, be approached especially from a *technological* point of view, as a meta-design ensuring the convergence of technologies aimed at immersing and digitalising the consumer-spectator. It becomes quite clear that we are faced with the apex of the society of the spectacle, prophesied by Guy Debord, that is, with a transcendence (by means of generalised digitalisation) of the dichotomies of producer-consumer, subject-object, actor-spectator, working time-leisure: we are entrenched more and more in a *society of signs* from which we are, at the same time, *separated*. The paradox is only apparent.

Let us take a step forward and begin, provocatively, by saying that even though the new stadium attracts and swallows (contains, channels in the most apparently non-exclusive way) us all, while we remain, in fact, outside. We are not allowed to enter the stadium without acquiescing – and believing we are in fact giving voice to 'our own' pre-formed desires (which raises questions about this voluntarily servile avatar we create for ourselves) – to transform and renounce ourselves and our own materiality and opacity (in the sense of consistency and depth), becoming reduced not just to *a sign among signs*, but also to a transparent medium, a standardised human-guised technology aligned with and integrated into the dominant (the winning) industrial-social complex. Like with the *church* in the past, the 'new stadium', with its inclusive ovoid shape, embodies the new 'ship', the 'ark' of a salvation with no utopia, everything existing 'here and now', of a humanity in predicament that is becoming increasingly hard to represent. Or, like in the *factory*, the new church-factory that is the stadium is the *industrial* producer of a new humanity, integrated and separated from itself, having finally achieved salvation. The emphasis on industry must be noted, given that it is somewhat novel. If until now atomisation – a socially individualised treatment – reigned supreme, the 'posthuman' mutation being already at an advanced stage (thought to be even irreversible, beyond any flexion or toppling point), the project is so far advanced it can exhibit itself openly, in *monumental* guise, unified and imposing: as a stadium, for instance. The 'new stadium' is itself a hyper-sign of triumph, a triumph arch, if you will, but not one commemorating past victory, but one that can brazenly and cynically affirm the success of its own project. A place of merciless *competition's* exacerbation and mythologisation as single social model, the 'new stadium' asserts and projects itself (in the architectural sense, but also as mental image) as *victor*, as the only project left standing, in a position to begin its process of domination and unconstrained proliferation. The game is over, the stadium (arena) has won, who is not with us is not even considered against us and is instead left out, irrelevant. As I was saying at the beginning of this paragraph, in order to enter the stadium you must renounce yourself and acquiesce undergoing metamorphosis, that is, becoming sublimated, abstracted and idealised: becoming simultaneously sign, medium, technological relay, a conductor of the unique flow (the light of Capital, travelling at absolute speed).

    Let us go more in depth. As Marc Perelman, this neo-Baudrillard analyst who influenced many of the views expressed in this piece, says in his aforementioned study, "mass narcissism" (p. 27), which pushes us towards "regressive narcissistic jubilations" (p. 29), makes us desire "to see everything here and now" (p. 33): the total image, or, more precisely, a kind of *hyper-vision* that cannot, however, be realised. We can only benefit from it at the price of being assimilated into it. What we desire more than anything: selfies with world champions, to be in the same image as them, to be images, like them. Or, rather, meta-images: a techno-scientific-financial infogram, a live feed of the stock market.

Stadiums are increasingly being filled with screens, our gaze moves along a controlled circuit in *three beats per measure*: from the playing field to the mega-screens crowding the stadium space to the micro-screens of our own devices that are bombarded with information.

Furthermore, we ourselves participate in our own transformation, our own dissolution. This synthesis, transformation of image, the passing from the mimetic visual, from the testimonial image of reality as such, to its 'completion', its live analysis through scientific-virtual (or scientometric) images, all of this happens before (and within) our very eyes. The images offered us – in which we are immersed, into which we accept to be transformed (along with reality itself), towards the realisation of the total confusion, indistinct, *immanence as image* (society as unique and total image) – are increasingly heterogeneous, hybrid, hyper-syntheses, which only (like the stadium itself) announce victory, asserting the fact that the graft (or the prosthesis) has been applied successfully. The body that has been operated on is no longer sick. The person no longer even feels it to be their own body, they feel it begin to fly away.

Between the screens within this egg of a new humanity that is the 'new stadium' lies the multifunctional and endlessly malleable *arena*. The human being is no longer, as the market ideology of 'communication' continues to claim, 'sender' or 'receiver'. Not even 'message'. No, the human being is increasingly becoming medium and relay: *a screen among screens*. And the synthesis – even fusion – this reabsorption into the new whole embodied by the Egg of the 'new stadium', the Nest of a new humanity, the dissolution of self into the glory of the unifying light, is the ultimate happiness, the ultimate anaesthesia (for the operation is not yet over). The sports spectacle continues to become the still, frozen image, the paradigm of the triumph of technology.

The supporter-human: the space between two gadgets in the midst of gadget society. Producing and becoming image.

To seal our challenge, we must ask directly: does the stadium still have anything to do with football? No: the 'new stadium' is a hyper-mall, a lab/incubator, a workshop/factory. As many of us as possible must go to the stadiums and stay there as long as possible, buy from the outlets and consume in the food courts that new stadiums have to come equipped with (like *train stations*), and during the competition itself come together and work towards our own hybridising, prostheticising, and dissolution through which the 'real' image gradually becomes the hypersynthetic image. Within it, the separation between material and ideal, or real and virtual, has been transcended through the *total spectacle*: a meta-competition of permanent, unique triumph. Is this for good?

Bogdan Ghiu

On the other hand – in a different register and from a different perspective – the hybridising between the real, mimetic image and the synthetic, virtual, measuring one, makes football become *moral*, a temple of unequivocal, *scientifically* proven truth. The work of the referee can no longer be fully trusted to imperfect humans. Determining the truth weaves *technology* and *law* together. And the included spectator (bound as sign-image) becomes the target and beneficiary of this universal and absolute surveillance spectacle. Transfixed and gleeful, they watch the process of judgment – of both game and life – unfold live: any mistake is immediately punished, no one can hide, everything is transparent and visible. They come to learn in the belly of the 'new stadium', which therefore becomes a *school*, a *re-education workshop*.

But this is, as I was saying, a different matter which still needs to be discussed.

Ion Grigorescu
Fotbal, 1976
Painting on photograph

In the We're Short a Guy exhibition Gabriele de Santis reconfigured Valentin Gallery's space in Paris into a locker room, a place of refuge and intimacy belonging (still) to the unknown, in which the superheroes of Space Jam and Captain Tsubasa meet art superstars — Boetti, Burri, de Dominicis, Fontana, Manzoni, Merz — represented on t-shirts belonging to AS Roma club — an item equally sacred, commercial and subversive. The mediums are dispersed, football and basketball coexist on the same sports field, a meeting mediated through Arte Povera, spatialism, poetry and sculpture. What will we remember of the present's immaterial back-and-forth in the future?

In the 2007 Derby della Capitalle, Francesco was celebrating his goal, which he had scored for AS Roma, when he redirected a sideline camera cart towards the supporters on the terrace. This way, he became a pitch-selfie pioneer through an iconic image which can be easily reconstructed from memory by any football cognoscente – Totti's headshot, the most loyal amongst the greats of contemporary football, hero of Stadio Olimpico, a sort of Colosseum of our days, sporting Rome's colours, the team in decline but still alive to replace the image of the empire. In the background, i tifosi from Curva Sud. Between the headshot and the supporters, Titto's hand and his smartphone, technology at work mediating the affective connection between him and the supporters. The moment of the shot: the euphoria of celebrating a goal.

Gabriele de Santis
Forever Young 5, 2015
Lambda print mounted on aluminum, 65 × 50 cm

Five Years a Slave

James Montague

The sun is setting in Doha as another day of work is coming to an end. As night encroaches, the grey buses filled with shattered migrant workers, their blue overalls and skin covered in sand and dirt, leave the building sites and head back to the camps that are hidden from view.

Doha is a city of skyscrapers and opulence. But if you happen to be a migrant worker who make up 90 per cent of the country's population, that side of the city is off limits to you. Everyone is governed by the kafala system, a form of sponsorship that puts the "ownership" of a person and their freedoms in the hands of their employers.

This has gone on in the Middle East for a long time, but only in recent years, thanks to the OPEC oil crisis in the '70s, did Gulf states like Saudi Arabia, the UAE and Qatar have the resources to rebuild their countries. And that required a stream of low paid construction workers, drivers, nannies and shop keepers from India, Pakistan, Bangladesh and beyond.

As the economies of these countries changed beyond all recognition, the treatment of the workers that built the malls and skyscrapers and stadiums didn't. They were third class citizens; underpaid, their passports seized, banned from even visiting the malls their built on their one day off. As Human Rights Watch and Amnesty International frequently told a largely apathetic Western audience, this was a form of "indentured slavery". Often workers were trapped in a cycle of debt that kept them from ever returning home. Some men I had met in Dubai were so desperate that they told stories of how colleagues would commit suicide by throwing themselves in front of traffic on the Sheikh Zayed Road. Their family would then receive some "blood money", which is enshrined in Emirati law. They felt they were worth more to their families dead than alive.

But then Qatar won the bid to host the 2022 World Cup finals. Suddenly, a microscope was placed over this tiny Persian Gulf state. In the years previous to that decision in 2010, Qatar had been something of a reform minded regime. It allowed a relatively free press, abolished censorship and talked about introducing democracy. Amongst the autocracies of the Gulf this was unheard of. But the world saw Qatar differently after the 2022 World Cup. It saw the kafala system and was appalled. No one knew how many workers died building the country's pre-World Cup infrastructure, because nobody bothered counting. The sight of men working in 50 degree heat was seared on to the public's consciousness. Suddenly, kafala was something that needed to be stopped.

And so Qatar has attempted to reform the system. A lucky few leaving the building sites at the end of the day will have a bed in the nearby Labor City, the brand new camp that will ultimately house a few thousand workers in much better conditions than those found elsewhere in Doha. In Labor City they will have a cinema and a cricket pitch, a barber's shop and a gym. Four men will live in each room, with air conditioning.

The roads are empty as you travel for an hour northwest of Doha, until a traffic jam suddenly halts you in what appears to be the middle of nowhere. Dozens of grey buses full of workers are backed up, surrounded by a swirl of dust. Up ahead, just visible on the horizon, is the single dirt track down which every bus wants to head, towards the labour camps of Al Shahaniya. It takes another 30 minutes of queuing just to get to the turning.

Our car, following a bus, bumps along the unlit track lined with a handful of garages dealing in scrap metal and reconditioned engine parts. A few enterprising men have set up grocery shops. The buses disappear, one by one, down separate unlit tracks, towards their assigned camps. Far away from Doha, far away from Labor City and far away from where the World Cup is being built, tens of thousands of men live in these camps that have spread into a township on the edge of Al Shahaniya, a tiny town in the centre of Qatar famous for its camel racing track. You can buy, or sell, a labour camp in Al Shahaniya easily. Real estate companies and online ads offer dozens of deals. One offers a camp that can hold 250 people, with five bathrooms and five kitchens, sleeping six men to a room. Yours for only 1,800 Qatari riyals a month about £370. Security guards prowl the entrance to each camp. We stop by the road that has the fewest security guards and wait in the shadows of an abandoned truck until a bus full of men turns down the track. We run next to it, hidden from the security guards on the other side of the vehicle. It's a further ten minutes down the track, past a few more shops set up to sell groceries and mobile phone credit to the workers, until we reach a track that turns right towards a camp. The smell of human sewage hits you first. Ahead, there are dozens of one-storey, breeze-block huts where the men live. Next to them is one toilet and a shower block, where the smell is coming from. One of the squat toilets is blocked, spilling its contents on the cracked, dirty white-tiled floor. On the other side of the yard is the kitchen, a block with two long sideboards carrying black heavy metal gas rings to cook on.

The walls and floors are covered in grease and dirt. "Come, let me show you", says Mohammed, a 36-year-old Indian who has been here for four years, working as a storekeeper. "Everything is bad here, look ..." He opens the door to his room. A filthy air-conditioning unit is struggling against the heat. There are ten men watching an Indian Premier League cricket match on an old TV that they have ingeniously hooked up to Indian TV. "Look, I've had this mattress for four years", he says, lifting a thin, threadbare, brown-stained mattress. "The air conditioning is not in good condition. There's no maintenance. The food we are cooking ourselves. The toilets and the kitchen are very bad." Down every narrow, bare-brick corridor, live dozens of men who have similar stories. The corridors go on, seemingly indefinitely; hundreds upon hundreds of people working for a complex network of contractors and subcontractors covering every kind of work and project in Qatar.

In one room, six Ghanaian men are sitting on the floor, a large Ghana flag hanging above them. The walls are covered in plastic sheeting. A tiny, filthy air-conditioning unit rattles in the corner. "We are building a tower. I can't remember the company, but the agent deceived us", says Simon, a 24-year-old stonemason. "Things in Qatar are not what we thought. We come over and we have no one over here so we just have to accept it like that and do the work. So we don't have any option." The six men are paid half the salary they were promised. "They said we are not qualified masons so they pay us less", he explains. Now he is only earning 1,000 riyals a month (just over £200). But he feels lucky in one respect: "The same agent is bringing people for 800 riyals now. "It is a buyers' market. The biggest surprise for the men is the hostility they have encountered. "There are people who talk to you like you are not a human being", Simon says. "In my country I don't get treated like this. I'm working for you, we live six to a room, we don't have anything to entertain ourselves. You come back after working you eat and you sleep. Early morning to work. Then work."

The men had each paid 7,000 Ghanaian cedi to an agent to get here (over £1,000). Once the money they spend on food and other expenses is taken out, they can only send 500 riyals back home every month at most. "You have kids' school fees", says Simon. "Mum and Dad, brothers to look after.

Five Years a Slave

How can you sustain that? It is not an option to leave. We are here already with a three-year contract. The lure of working in Qatar is strong. "We're here because we were told they have money all those buildings because of the World Cup", says Ismael, a 25-year-old labourer wearing a white, knitted Islamic kufi headdress. "We are putting all our efforts into Qatar hosting the World Cup. But the salary is so low." Each of the six men regrets coming but feel trapped. Even if they could break their contract, what would their families do back home? And how would they repay the agent? "I would rather stay in my own country and earn 600 cedi [around £115] a month. You cannot travel abroad to work and take this little money", says Ismail.

It was getting late and the men had to sleep, in preparation of their 4 a.m. alarm call. Ismail walked us out of the labyrinth of identical corridors and back to the yard with the filthy kitchen and broken toilets. "Look at the way things are", he said. "Tell people. We are like animals in here." We waited for another vehicle to pass. This time it was a lorry pulling a water tanker. As soon as it passed the security block, we ran, hidden from the security guards, and dived into the shadow of an abandoned lorry outside, back into our car, and back onto the road to Doha.

> Fragment from *The Billionaires Club: The Unstoppable Rise of Football's Super-Rich Owners*, Bloomsbury, 2017

James Montague

What It Means to Lose Your Head

The biopolitics and spheroidal kinetics of the cranium

Ștefan Tiron

– *'That na man play at the Fute-ball'* – *1424, King James I, proclamation before Parliament*
– *'OOOooo Noo'* – *Palermo, 22.05.03, h 24.00*

Prologue.

I never liked football. I never liked football matches, not between two, three, and certainly not between the same team. I never could stand seeing people getting all riled up and bickering over scores and points – the same thing each time.

And I seriously dislike that style of curating and art-making that capitalises on, and makes endless exhibitions on the back of championships, games, and players' charisma. Maybe I do have a weak spot for the apparel worn by fans and hooligans from Ghencea, Rahova, and Drumul Taberei, but that's a different beast. However, after I met Adriana Gheorghe through Ștefania Ferchedău from Ecumest I ended up at one of Florin Flueraș's rehearsals (not shows!) and quietly, in the darkness of the Round Room (the main performance space in the National Dance Centre's initial venue, in Bucharest), other regions of my body became contaminated. My brain began seriously rewiring itself.

When I was little I used to play with ball bearings in the junkyard behind Steaua Stadium in Ghencea. At one end of an army shooting range was a kind of junkyard mine full of semi-buried discarded technologies; basically everything the army was throwing away. Aside from the usual filterless gasmasks, I found mountains of yellow, slippery industrial lard, a kind of Vaseline for ball bearings. My dad, who would regularly take me there, told me how precious that artificial fat was and how many machines screeched for it.

CORNER #1

I never went to any games. Instead I would mess around in the empty stadium, among the green wooden benches with their rusty screws, because I liked the empty, Pompeii-like playing field that had just been swept clean of cigarette ash by teams of well-tanned military slaves, deployed from distant provinces.

I don't feel like getting into that kind of discussion that amplifies the playing field, giving it galactic meaning, like how in Mesoamerican – Mayan, to be more precise – those ball games where stars and constellations aligned according to scored goals. In the darkness, in the Round Room, I saw the choreographer slipping in his ball-kicking momentum. And from my perspective, the ball really seemed to take away his head in an instant. Yes, there, lying on the ground, he no longer had a head, instead of a head, on the black rubber field of the dim room was a football. After a pause, one of his shoulders hit the ball, which rolled away, and so his head returned.

The biopolitics of bodies left to their own devices ended with the regulation of the sport we nowadays call football. At one extreme there is the famous head of a certain Danish prince that was used as a ball after a victory on a battlefield – and at the other there is football as specialised body training, where the advice of nutritionists, gene therapies with the help of molecular biology, and the ball designer's smoke tunnel (the current geometry of a football is inspired by Buckminster Fuller's architecture, not the other way around) all compete. The body doesn't dance to the rhythm of the football, but to that of threats. Initially the game was so violent that rulers tried to ban it in order to protect the sons of the land from their own bloody customs. Games between villages after Lent, or on the streets of medieval English towns, would end in injury and death, pretty much everything was permitted for the ball – choking, biting, or bashing someone's head in. Reckless fun that was preferred to military bow training – the country's finest was being threatened by a custom that could not be co-opted into the service of the state.

It's allowed to be violent only if it makes you useful.
The Industrial Age – so-called *Muscular Christianity* – advocated for football in public schools as a maintenance tool for the country's male elite bodies. The child who does not go through the game is doomed to weak physique and promiscuity. Lack of character and of manliness is due to the lack of muscle on an undisciplined mind. Aggression needs to become calculated. If, in the Enlightenment, the football field is removed from church grounds, where it found itself for most of the Middle Ages and the Renaissance, the class physiology of industrial-age religious ideals seems to forget the laity of these new means of social training. 19th century football teams seem apostolic bands today and

the most radical refused to play for money, to play in championships, or to perform penalty kicks; in a sport for the missionaries of good manners, there's no place for unruliness. Shoot to kill.

Postlogue.

In high school my group of friends and I made up this game, a kind of primitive crypto-football, that had no real teams, many bruises and grazed knees and broken nails, no goals – we played with rocks of various sizes or with these tiny, uncontrollable balls that we didn't bother to bring back. We called it *fotpitzil* and we didn't play it on the main football field in the courtyard of the German High School in Bucharest, but somewhere between the paper recycling warehouse, the backyard fence of an old Baba Yaga's house with her famous club and a bucket of urine always ready, the school's wall, and the dumps. In practice, the dumps were really the field, because that's where the ball somehow ended up most of the time, there, in the mounds of half-incinerated trash, and we just had this irresistible urge to sully ourselves digging after it amidst semi-digested sandwiches, rotten apples, and burnt schoolbooks, basically everything 1st to 12th graders would puke out of their backpacks.

Post-postlogue.

I'd like to offer below a project proposal that combines a field recording with an acousmatic installation. Acousmatic – a Pythagorean term that was rediscovered by French theorist Jerome Peignot to describe the *musique concrète* school method of separating sound from its direct reference (source). Afterwards, P. Schaeffer claimed that such a separation between the visual origin of the sound and the sound itself was desirable.

Make a field recording of a football match in a vacant lot, an old courtyard, or an improvised playing field. The recording is then played back, on a speaker installation, in a spot in the city where such a place used to be, having been replaced by a parking lot, a new building, or any kind of urban redevelopment project.

I got the idea after listening to the recording by composer Domenico Sciajno (specialised in Max/MSP) for the *22-05-03 h24:00* project (a collective exploration of synchronicity) where, on May 22nd, multiple IXEM members pressed REC and captured the surrounding soundscape for two minutes. Everything was relayed acousmatically through an installation for three days, during the *Superfici Sonore* festival in Florence. Domenico recorded a neighbourhood football game in a small square for two minutes, with all the characteristic sonic details of the place.

What It Means to Lose Your Head

ONE

Florin Flueras

In the summer of 2006 I was in a residency in Azuga together with four other 'young artists', and each was working on their own performance. Florin Fieroiu was the 'coach' (in dance we use the term for someone with more experience who helps you during the process). Since we were in a sports hall, before we began any activity, I would play a bit of football with my coach and Ionuț, another artist from the project. After we transitioned from process to performance, we continued with the football thing. Even if we had the same kind of actions, taken from the football repertoire, what was going on had nothing to do with the game before. A choreographic attention took control of my body and of those watching this new kind of 'show'. Our behaviours and movements suddenly became significant on a more abstract level. There seemed to be two completely different kinds of attention for the two types of activities. In the months that followed, I began to see similarities between the two worlds.

Just like in performance art, and in art in general, in football you have fans of at least two types of aesthetic experiences. On the one hand there is 'beautiful football', a football based on cursivity of action and player virtuosity, how one 'draws a pass', on a certain composition and how the players are positioned on the pitch, a football of expression, where skill is fully expressed and appreciated. On the other hand there is also a more conceptual football, which values conception of play, strategy, game plan, the inspiration of the coach or of a 'visionary' player. This could be, as commentators would say, 'an ugly game, but one that works'. And then there could also be an aesthetic perspective, in which the emphasis is on the working process, on the team's dynamics, on how tight the game is. It's notable that the way one makes a game feel 'tight' can be very familar to a certain kind of contemporary performance: the game plan, schemes and diagrams, all are incorporated through dozens of rehearsals until they become habit.

ONE

CORNER #1

Just as there is a football imaginary, there is also an imaginary for the performance of those times, a sort of presence, attention and atmosphere that was specific to conceptual dance, which was still developing at the time. With subtle shifts in attitude or presence, one could navigate from 'the world of dance' to 'the football universe' and back. With minimal means, the two worlds could be conjured, overlapped, combined, and related in various ways. One could be perceived through the lens of the other. In choreographic terms, football is a kind of improvisation with strict constraints and with a certain 'repertoire of movements', like plays in football, that one could resort to in certain situations. Now we have to see what performance art, or art in general, means in football terms.

In 2014, I was at the Haus der Kulturen der Welt in Berlin for a project, when, one night, thousands of flag-bearing, face-painted people began gathering. They were there to see, on one of the few screens installed in the building, the semifinals of the World Cup: Germany – Brazil. It felt like being in a stadium, and everything was going perfectly for them: 1, 2, 3, 4-0 for Germany. It was an amazing result for such an encounter. But as the score increased, 5, 6, 7-0, a slightly odd atmosphere set in over the huge room of the HKW. There was something in the way things were happening that was stifling the normal reactions of joy, something about the oddness of the situation was blocking the expected response to a victory in the World Cup semifinals. It seems that, paradoxically, 3-0 would have been better than 7-0. 7-0 seemed to get dangerously close to suspending a certain normality necessary to the 'football spectacle'.

When it comes to extraordinary suspensions of normality, it seems billiards is where this can be pushed the farthest, at least in philosophy. After Hume had already laid the foundations, Meillassoux wrote about a game of billiards where the collisions between the balls cease to follow the laws of physics, because there is no necessity for them to exist in the form they currently have, for them to remain unchanged. It is merely a habit of thought to expect things to carry on the same way. As contingency is the only universal

ONE—ONE

law, the laws of physics can suddenly change. It's therefore possible that one day, during a game of billiards, as two balls collide, they'll start floating or disappear or merge together.

The laws of physics are determined in football, but, until those change, even small changes in behaviour can be hard to imagine. What if at one point during a 'high-stakes game' all the players, including the coaches and referees would start digging a hole in the middle of the field? Or what if the second period of a game were an attempt to repeat the first, with all the players and referees suddenly engaged in a game of re-enactment, of replaying the game from the start. Maybe the weirder of us would appreciate something like this, but, generally, such actions on the part of the team we support wouldn't be admired. After all, we expect the rules to be respected so that the game will be able 'to take place under normal conditions'.

Continuity, consistency, stability, these are all important values for the game to happen normally. And that's not a bad thing, sometimes that is exactly why we go to a live game or to see some blockbuster, because we know exactly what we're going to get. We don't always want to be destabilised. It's good for things to remain in the realm of comfortable surprises, like 4-0, or else the order, the foundation of conformity, begins to crumble, and we just want to 'enjoy the game'. 'The ball is round, anything can happen', but that's not quite true, and that's why we watch football, because it offers this appearance that anything can happen, but, in fact, nothing happens: one of two teams wins, or there is a draw, and that's about it.

It's like when you go to the theatre and you know that, invariably, you are going to see people acting out scripts, the same thing over and over again. Up until recently, in contemporary dance it was normal to come to a show and not know what to expect, there was this obsession of thwarting expectations. This was contemporary art's obsession too. Kosuth said that aesthetic experience takes place when things are pushed into areas that until that point were thought as being non-artistic, when they step outside the limits of what can be considered art. But things have changed in the meantime, the logic of limited surprise has taken over all art fields. As I was saying about football, this is not necessarily a bad thing, but that's all that there is– everything is football. But, who knows, maybe it's for the best, because in the end "It's all for the show".

Florin Flueras

"Instead of a library-mediatheque info point about gymnastics and sports, we have mediocre funeral statues, marble, bronze, pipes, meshes, small heads on large pedestals. Eminescus, clones..."
- Dan Perjovschi, Facebook, 2016

The Gymnasts' Alley in Deva (Romania) photographed by Laura Nicula, 2016

The Taming of the Body
The technologisation of the human in professional gymnastics

Vasile Mihalache

It might sound surprising, but it is not true that we are always born human. There are examples that we would prefer to think of as exceptional that can support this claim. A Jewish child born under the Third Reich would have not been considered human, and neither would his parents. The human, like many other things, is genetically but also culturally inherited.

There are also examples outside of the exceptional, from daily life, which flow slowly and do not frighten. If we look back in time or further into space we see that some did not have the fortune of being born human, and others are not human in all moments of their life. To be a capital-H Human being you need civil rights, freedom, security, the right to be informed, to private life, to equality – if equity seems too much even for the humanist. If we take a step back in time or space, you would not have been born human, if, say, you were born a girl into a traditional family in Fălticeni, România, that on June 4th 1982 already had two girls. Caught in the 'games of reproduction' you would soon realise that coming into this world is not just a biological thing, but one that is social and cultural, for which reason you will be 'guilty' of not being able to carry on the name of the family. Suddenly you will understand, even if retrospectively, that you were not born just to be human but also technology.

This falsely hypothetical situation is what opens Maria Olaru's autobiography *Prețul aurului. Sinceritate incomodă* (*The Price of Gold. Uncomfortable Sincerity,* Editura Vremea, București, 2016). A lot has been said about the book, many readers being especially interested in the 'shocking' details and the scenes describing beatings and other abuse that the gymnast went through. But these are just one part of the gamut of means through which the athlete, and especially the gymnast, was transformed into a cog in a machine that "worked impeccably: pump them full of sports and get results. Losses were, as they say, collateral". The main quality of the book is the description of the process through which the sportsperson is technologised, both at the level of the body and that of the human, about which we learn that it *should* be inalienable.

But what does this mean? Firstly, to achieve excellence, the unruly and weak body must be subdued, reduced or brought to acceptable standards. This happens as early as the selection process, when the coaches will be interested to know the genetic history of the father, who had maybe died in the meantime, but whose phantom height will still count even from his grave as a selection criterion. Then comes starvation, or "maintaining weight standards", in spite of the child's will, hence the smuggling in of chocolate and Furosemide (a drug that removed water from the body) or self-induced vomiting, in secret when in Romania or with relative freedom when abroad, where you "vomited in peace, relaxed, with the air of fulfilled duty". The body no longer belongs to the person that carries it from place to place, it is the property of the "Deva medal factory", of coaches, of people who know "what's best". "Back then we were minors. And, probably, unconstitutional", said Maria Olaru. Within this logic, punishment, beatings, interrogations, and written or even video recorded interrogations (less about clearing up the facts and more about scolding) were only natural. The body is an asset of the Club, the Olympic Centre, the State, and its "degradation" by those who merely dress it must be prevented. You are not always human when you are an athlete, all the more so when you are a 5, 10, or 16-year-old gymnast. Your fulfillment, even your existence as a human being, is deferred to a glorious future which, for most, will never come, because the "body-grinding mill" in Deva runs smoothly and only allows victories, medals, success, and "national glory" to be visible. Never failure, the loss of childhood, or physical trauma, which the body bears dignified until it finally collapses and gives up the fight out of its own biological will.

There is no human being in sight here, the body is left alone, it belongs to nobody and works for everybody, a technology-body that must be as efficient as possible at almost any cost. Ionela Loaieș will have frostbite on her hands after a training session in Păltiniș, and Maria's body will receive a titanium rod to stabilise her spine for the rest of her life. In fact, "we stupid peasant girls were not supposed to know what was going on with our bodies", writes Maria. Some will never know what had happened to their bodies after they start belonging to them again at retirement, as their histories will often be censored. Maria Olaru's medical record at the National Institute of Sports Medicine contains carelessly torn-out pages, perhaps by someone who wished to cover up information about her medication. The topic is not broached in the book, the only medication mentioned being the Furosemide smuggled in by the sportswomen (not administered at the advice of coaches or medics, it seems) and Andreea Răducan's famous Nurofen pill. Even though there were frequent rumours in the press about the use of "supplements" or even drugs meant to delay the gymnasts' first menstruation, the book says nothing about these. What we do find there, however, is a lack of medical care and information, as the girls where only taken to the hospital when they were crying in pain and were not informed about their condition by the physician themselves. Instead the diagnosis was delivered through the custodian of their bodies, the coach.

After a series of hospitalisations, Olaru is diagnosed with hepatitis B and is asked to deny being sick, as if it were her fault. The body becomes a subject of shame, a feeling enforced by one coach's suggestions that she had got it by sleeping with someone in the hospital. The technologised body is reverted to the biological (animal, if not human) when physical reproduction is brought up. This is a threat, because it hinders excellence and threatens the control upon the body. The gymnast's body must be controlled in its most intimate parts, biologically and sexually.

I now return to that technology that transpires in the corpus of memory, that which was supposed to be an extension of the human body, if we follow McLuhan, but which, in fact, transfigures the body and minimises the 'human', so that both human and body become extensions of technology. This is simply education as it is understood, in general but especially in the case of professional athletes. One of the most important mechanisms of this technology is humiliation, the easiest path toward dehumanisation. When the girls were found carrying sweets, the coaches ate them in front of them. When their bus stopped at Dealul Negru, the coaches went for a barbecue, while the gymnasts stayed behind in the car, where they learned "a lesson about moderation and character building". The repeated beatings and frequent reproaches are part of the same category, as are reading their letters, frisking, or that time when Mariana Bitang told Maria Olaru that her mother was too drunk to talk on the phone right before an exercise. The shame that overcomes you, the feeling, as Cătălin Tolontan writes in the book's preface, not only that you have "done wrong" but that you "are wrong", is the best way to control the body, the mind and the person. This technology and education is so effective that it is self-reproducing. In fact, it is the principle quality of technology of any kind to be able to produce objects serially, to reproduce,

Vasile Mihalache

to implement a model on a large scale. In the case of the gymnasts, who worked "in a herd", "peasants", like 'medal-breeding animals", education as technology produces a kind of Stockholm syndrome: a gymnast asks Bellu to slap her so she can focus.

Maria Olaru herself, although she manages to partially escape this mechanism through her book she also, to a certain extent, reproduces it; at one point she signs her leotard "OM" ("human being"), "so at least somebody sees I am a human being". At a fast-food restaurant, after giving money to a *puradel* (derogatory term for a Roma child), as she calls him, her wallet slips out of her pocket and she leaves without it. After she comes back, the employees tell her the beggar child has taken it, and so Maria decides to no longer show compassion to scoundrels. Because they are not fully Human and have no claim on our (real Human beings) compassion and love, right? Just like gymnasts aren't really human until they achieve excellence and bring glory to the nation.

Grădina Tranzit is an urban permaculture project conceived and maintained by tranzit.ro/ București since 2014 on strada Gazelei 44 together with Asociația în-Tranziție. In April 2016 you can find in Grădina Tranzit (sprouted, flowering, or ready to eat, resting, planted, or in passing): onions, garlic, rocket, orache spinach, tulips, daffodils, lemon balm, strawberries, lovage, turnips, beans, celandine, lavender, mock-orange, mint, raspberries, gooseberries, broccoli, lily-of-the-valleys, sage, a lemon tree, comfrey, roses, peas, nettles, a turtle from Dobrogea, an orange-and-white tomcat, bumblebees, blackbirds, snails, compost, poplars, sumac, a group of people, a contemporary art space, and more.

The Body as Technology for Spectacle in Contemporary Football

Alexadra Pirici

Visiting the FC Bayern museum in Munich inside the Allianz Arena one can follow quite an accurate evolution of the football phenomenon, of the economy around it and of the social relations which make it possible and which are being determined by it in return. FC Bayern Munich boasts a long tradition having been founded in 1900 by 11 members of a gymnastics' club football division. It's the most successful club in the history of German football as well, having an undisputable monopoly in the acquisition of young players, emerging talent from smaller clubs or rival players. And although Bayern is managed like a corporation, the club still owns 75% of its shares, thus abiding by the German Football League's "50+1" rule which states that, in order to compete in the Bundesliga, a club must have the majority of voting rights. This rule is meant to protect the clubs from investor's influence and from excessive spending - another rule to participate in the Bundesliga is for the club not to be in debt. In a discussion with the PR officer of the Bavarian club, one can sense a slight nostalgia and a shadow of doubt over the future of the club and of football in general. Working for one of the most wealthy and successful football clubs in the world, which still resonates with the idea of "tradition" and of football as public good, he told us with some regret that, most likely, in the following years we will witness a total chasm between "leisure" football, the sport in which the long-term support of its fans still matters, which will remain one for amateurs, and professional football, the one which, by the looks of NFL's plans, could even be played in empty stadiums, sold as VR experience, accessible from home and replicable online almost *ad infinitum*. Football players' income and the clubs' revenue tend to be increasingly generated by image rights and online streams, completely overtaking revenues from staging the actual live football event. The implicit contracts, which the players also sign with Electronic Arts, the producer of *FIFA* video game, upon signing a contract with a new club are also symptomatic of a prevalent image-based economy. The speed of circulation and the limitless capacity for distributing representation are becoming as important as, if not even more financially important, than the embodiment of the football match as live event. The motion capture processes that are facilitated by 'real' players for *FIFA*, enable the transformation of the game in an almost perfect simulator and, reversely, the spillover of the game's results in 'real' life. While being more of a speculation for the moment, it appears that some teams already take into account the results of their players' digital avatars manipulated online by thousands of gamers in the *FIFA* simulator and their performance online.

Another interesting and recent possibility, of monetising a players' image separated from their physical presence and their relationship with the team, is the online players' marketplace, *Football Index*, which also tracks and helps you monetise the players' coverage in the media. This would enable a player to become valuable in this system also through scandalous behaviour for example, not just for his playing skills.

In the same FC Bayern museum in the Allianz Arena you can see a kitschy reproduction of the football players' dinner the night before the game at the beginning of the '80s: pork leg roast and beer. A sign that they were eating together, in a common context in which the next day's performance was no more important than the social event and the relationships between players - the football club as something which brings people together, which creates a sense of participating in something beyond the individual (a participation circumscribed, of course, by a patriarchal system in which the community was exclusively male). Nothing farther, as sensation, from the image of today's professional football player - individual star – whose attributes are being separated from the physical body and are digitally quantified to be manipulated independently. The body of the football player thus transforms from something which belongs to the player, an instrument and a social technology which facilitates relationships and produces affective relations with other players, clubs and supporters, into a technology of spectacle in which the live football event and the embodiment of the game almost impede - though it still facilitates it - the circulation of his image and his endless monetisation.

The supporters' disappointment and their lack of live presence in the stadium, as a sign of protest, has influenced many times the outcome of the football game through the connection between physical presence and affective production experienced live in the stadium (without forgetting the legitimate critique of the stadium as simulator and apparatus of alleviating social tension, like the ancient Colosseum). New technologies for disembodiment and separation of the 'real', of the physical presence from its image in the hope of a representation's unhindered circulation, seem to dissolve, step by step, the relationship between the football event and audience, enabled by the stadium's physical space. It remains to be seen if this process, perfectly in sync with the fantasy of total flexibility promoted by neoliberal ideology and the possibility of infinite monetisation and financialisation of the real by discarding, separating its bodily materiality from representation, will advance unhindered or if it could also be subverted, appropriated and hijacked.

* With thanks to Andrei Dinu.

image: Lionel Messi in bespoke LED lights motion capture suit during video shootings for the *adizero f50 Messi* boots 'The New Speed of Light' ad campaign (2013), shot at 1000 frames per second to create a special visual display; photograph by ©Electronic Arts Inc. (EA)

Alexandra Pirici & Jonas Lund, *N Football,* 2018
A football match with FC Bayern male and female junior teams, with a changed set of rules, accompanied by software. Costume design: Andrei Dinu

Although the rules of football haven't radically changed over time, its context has. The game could always be understood as a social field on a micro scale, with its competitiveness, emotionality, and, recently, its involvement in globalisation and economic speculation. A working-class pastime played for pleasure evolved into a high-performance sport based on spending power and the monetisation of star players. FC Bayern, with its home in Munich at Allianz Arena, cultivates both an image of a homegrown Bavarian base as well as a global, tactical, and spectacular winner.

N Football is a football match with a changing set of rules played by FC Bayern junior male and female teams and connected to a real-time tracking system. Both teams are assigned fictional correspondences to various football clubs with different financial models. According to the new rules, the attackers may play against defenders or players may shift from competition to companionship. Considering the derivative economies produced, for example, by the FIFA video game, N Football attempts to make visible, within a live football event featuring future great players, what usually remains obscure: financial dynamics and a tendency toward monopoly or a business model increasingly difficult to regulate.

Football has an amazing, very positive influence on society in terms of social mobilisation or overcoming stereotypes or racist behaviour, among others. N Football stages a game as social practice in relation to its increased disembodiment, dislocation, circulation, and monetisation. The question remains: Can football, with its enormous influence, still be imagined as a public good that shapes society toward fairer ends? If so, how?

Gaming the Score

Alexandra Pirici and Jonas Lund in conversation with Harry Thorne and Moritz Hollinger of FC Bayern

Harry Thorne: The best place to start with such a complex and multi-layered project is, as always, at the beginning. Could you explain what it was that first appealed to you about working with football as a medium?

Alexandra Pirici: Football is such a huge sport with global impact at the moment. When we were invited to make work for Public Art Munich it became obvious that we would like to engage with football, not necessarily with FC Bayern as such, but with what FC Bayern represented as a platform. Our first site visit in Munich was to the Olympic Stadium, so very different in comparison to Allianz Arena, but also the former home of FC Bayern. We visited Allianz Arena afterwards, and the way we wanted to address football had more to do with this space, and with how football today is experienced as a global and professional sporting phenomenon. We were interested in the relations between football and economic, social, and political fields today. Of course, what we proposed was an experiment, but we did not want to stray too far from an actual football match, so we began to introduce small (but significant) shifts in how the game played out.

Jonas Lund: Our process became more about what *not to* do, instead of what *to do* because we were confined within the framework of a football match. We then went through several different ideas of what we could change, of what we could subvert, or not, but we always wanted to remain within the context of a football match.

HT: This is a good time to hear from Moritz. What were your thoughts at FC Bayern when you heard the proposition? (When you were first approached by PAM, Jonas, and Alexandra with this idea in mind...)

Moritz Hollinger: It was strange, because from the outset one doesn't know

EXTRA

what to expect. We are obviously first and foremost a football club, so when we get external proposals they primarily revolve around our first squad, or players from another squad. When they came with the idea of showing the commercial influence on sports, addressing the whole idea of FIFA, as well as the mediation of professional sports, it was more a question: so, you really want to do this with us? As a football club, what could we offer the project? After a while we understood what they wanted to do, and it then became clear how it could be implemented.

> HT: Alexandra, had you two expected that a vast franchise like FC Bayern, with such an important history, would be so open to the idea of making work like this?

AP: No, definitely not. I don't mean to project some sort of prejudice, but as you noted, it's a huge football club and so we assumed we didn't really have a chance. It was a wonderful surprise to discover that they were so open to think about and through football, because this is primarily what we were trying to do, to open up a space for reflection and discussion on the game. Our project was really a space of conversation on where football comes from, where it's going, and how our globalised financial environment changes the sport, while the sport also participates in changing society. We were interested in how this positive feedback loop functions, and for us it was really fascinating to find such a great partner to discuss this, not to mention how major it was that such a big football club was willing to take part.

> HT: You wanted to pick up on various areas of sport—as business, as culture, as social phenomenon—and perhaps we can talk through the modifications that you made to the traditional rulebook in order to do this. As an audience, the first thing we witnessed were two football teams paired off against each other. There were no additional guidelines just yet—no tweaks to the teams themselves. The first rule-changes saw the pitch physically halved and the introduction of collective crediting for goals. Could you talk about the latter: what drew you to emphasise the shared responsibility for goals—both scored and squandered?

AP: Football is a team sport, and within the team itself this is quite clear. The way the sporting event is mediated, however, and how it's represented creates different hierarchies and asymmetries of power between the players. Our collective crediting system was a response to the media's obsession of focusing on individual players, particularly on strikers. I think the most popular or well-known players are strikers or offensive players, so we wanted to emphasise the collective nature of achievements, and how the game is played as a team. We also wanted to emphasise that through our configuration of mixed gender teams and mixed groups.

MH: Yes, we already see this in ice hockey. When a goal is scored, all the players involved are credited.

HT: This is perhaps the perfect club to adopt as a case study when considering the recent growth of the "cult of celebrity". While there are undoubtedly talismans within the FC Bayern squad, it remains rational and squad-oriented. It also remains one of the major European teams that is capable of maintaining this philosophy while still triumphing over those who enlist superstars at costs of €200 million, and in doing so sacrifice the democratic notion of the 'team.' Moritz, do you feel that this idea of collective crediting might greater emphasise the importance of the collective unit over that which is assembled around a single multi-million euro luminary?

MH: I suppose it could foster an impact on the perception of the players, but when you look at a football match, and a goal is scored, there can be up to ten players involved in the process. In ice hockey, there are only five players without a goalie, so it's easier to credit everyone. But sure, the idea would attribute much more credit to all of the team members. On the other side, if you look at football matches or football teams right now, you indeed have the striker, and they tend to earn most of the money, but for fans of the game, they always acknowledge skilled mid-fielders, excellent passers, or very good crossers. The perception of good players is not always entirely focused on the strikers; they are good, although if you have a mediocre striker but a really talented midfielder, one will always appreciate the midfielder.

HT: Jonas, could you run us through the second layer that came in, which was the 50 percent split pitch. From where I was sitting, this seemed to speak to the similar strategies of corporate media companies, and their attempts to make the game more condensed, energetic and fiery; to prioritise the spectacle above all.

JL: There are a couple of different aspects to the 50 percent pitch restriction. One is this increased spectacularity, in the sense of accel-

Alexandra Pirici / Jonas Lund / Harry Thorne / Moritz Hollinger

erating the game, making it faster in order to respond to this idea that you require excitement to hook the audience. However the rule also addresses an imbalance with a team who is poorer, or performing poorly. For such a team, typically, the only way of winning a match is to play defensively, and then do some clever counter attack very quickly and get lucky. So the 50 percent pitch was a way to make this visible. I think that's how it played out in the game, the coaches also responded to it like this. Perhaps the ten minute time-slot for this rule was a bit long, because the game really increased in intensity and the players needed to be very fast.

HT: So, it was a counter-action to the top-heavy wealth of football clubs?

JL: It is ambiguous because it responded to both ideas. You suddenly had eleven attacking players, and eleven defending players, so these two specific strategies emerged. You can only play defensively, for instance, if you have no chance to score. Also, it is traditionally seen that defensive plays are more team-based, even though I am not sure if this is true because it is all in the team play.

AP: It also depends on what types of attack and what types of defense players can perform. What interested us was exactly the ambiguity of the proposal. On the one hand, it was introduced for the game to become more spectacular, while on the other hand, perhaps it was in fact less spectacular. During the game, when players used the whole pitch, sometimes the match was more spectacular than within the 50 percent restriction. But initially it was also about trying to even out the chances of getting close to the opponents' goal keeper.

HT: Were you making most decisions to re-choreograph the game? Or to redistribute power in real-time, or were they pre-programmed?

AP: Our setup was very DIY and experimental, so we tried to script as much as possible, but of course, there were some decisions that were made live. For instance, the final transfer of four players where we discussed with the coaches what players they would like to transfer, or which players they would like to purchase.

HT: The teams repeatedly

switching allegiances was particularly interesting, as it directly mirrors a contemporary trend in the Premier League. It has happened a few times in recent years: wealthy clubs have paid a lot of money for a player, failed to develop them in the right way (to put it diplomatically), and then sold them at a loss, only to purchase them once again for three times the original price.

AP: Initially the coaches wanted to transfer another player, as this was a decision we wanted to have prepared before the actual match, but then we decided to switch during the match (because of unexpected technical reasons), and right before the transfer, Sandro Porta, the player whom we decided to transfer to the other team, actually scored a goal for his team, so the team that had just received a goal from the opposing team via Sandro Porta got to purchase him immediately. I think the situation played out more poignantly, as it made even more visible the way in which purchasing power comes to make up for, or sometimes seems to make up for the long-term development of local players.

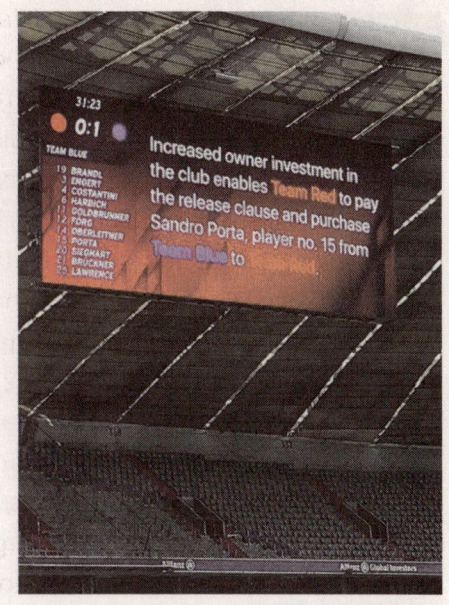

HT: Can we talk about the moment of silence for the 1966 World Cup. You have previously mentioned that you see this as the origin of football as a globally accessible—and therefore globally commodifiable—entity. Why was this important to bring in?

AP: We actually called it a moment of pause, not a moment of silence like when you commemorate a tragedy, but a pause where you stop and reflect. The black body-suit costumes that the players wore recall motion capture suits, similar to the motion capture technology used for the FIFA video game, but adapted so as to be visible in daylight, and on such a large pitch. These black suits signify a certain kind of abstraction, a particular possibility to extract someone's image and circulate it indefinitely, as well as the capacity to monetise that image indefinitely. I think the relationship of football to media and image— broadcasting rights, but also image rights when it comes to the players and where their biggest proportion of income comes from—was highly relevant to us. The 1966 World Cup is considered to be just such a key point in the globalisation of football because it had a massive TV broadcasting apparatus behind it. It was also the first time when the camera started to focus on the wives of the football players in the tribunes, introducing a shift in focus from the players on the pitch to their private lives, and this is again when the players and their images as brands became easier to monetise. There were a couple of shifts in that broadcasting strategy, and how the event was mediated, including the invention of the slow-motion machine, so the possibility to slow down and zoom in on something was enabled. This ability to zoom in on faces and on particular fragments allows for the extraction of those fragments from the overall context of the match, so it also pioneered a different way of looking at the game.

HT: Abstraction is a great way of putting it. The costumes, especially, helped create this effect. You mentioned this video game avatar—and your players were also able to switch back and forth, seemingly abiding by the laws of some omnipotent player who controls every single movement. That is really interesting, especially if we talk about the estrangement of the player—as a commodifiable individual—from their function as a footballer.

AP: Yes. I think that most of these changes are related to finance capital and investment in a club. We were also interested in visualising the dissolution of other types of allegiances that were active in the past. You can change teams because of financial spending power, so your allegiance to a particular club, to a place of birth, or to other types of connections, become increasingly less important for a professional footballer.

HT: An interesting way to look at that is the way sponsorship deals and affiliations with various corporations deny players the right to articulate a political stance. While the cult of the individual, the cult of celebrity, is more powerful than ever, these players have less of a voice than they have ever had in the history of the game. It's something easily recognisable in players' post-match interviews, when you hear the same script regurgitated in quite a robotic manner.

MH: That is a good point and I want to say something on this, since the whole issue is so heated. Football is a mass entertainment product—if you simply state your opinion or something negative as a player—there is a media frenzy as a result. For example, with our own player Sandro Wagner, he was a bit disappointed and quit the national team. After that all of the German press and media outlets talked about this decision for over a week. For the players, it's easier to keep your personal opinions to yourself and just perform the player everybody wants to see, otherwise you unleash media coverage where your girlfriend will be interviewed, and your parents as well. Journalists will camp-out in front of your house, and your parents' house, just to get comments. So, due to a few sentences, you drag everyone you know into the hysteria of the media. We really need to ask: Is it the players' fault, or is it the system and the entertainment product that they are involved with?

HT: In no way do I see this as a fault of the players. I feel the utmost sympathy for these players: Because of a talent they have, they are then funnelled through systems that are predetermined by both football clubs and mass media.

MH: Additionally, there was another case with Per Mertesacker. He gave an interview where he spoke about the pressure of being a player, and it was received quite negatively from a lot of players and the media. One has to be very careful what one says these days, given the whole media context we're in with sporting coverage multiple times a day, and daily consumption of it.

JL: Yes. The players' rather automated speech functions like a protection mechanism. You protect your position, you don't want to expose it. You become the professionalised version of the brand...

HT: Which is amazing when you recall the fact that this game is supposed to champion freedom of expression and creativity above all else. These are the moments that we will all remember till the end of our days, when a player does something extraordinary, and manages to express something beyond an accepted system. To then think that the system in which players are forced to

Alexandra Pirici / Jonas Lund / Harry Thorne / Moritz Hollinger

manoeuver is robbing them of this individual energy is a worrying thing to consider. Let's move on to the last of your in-game tweaks: the multiple transfer. Can you tell us why you decided to introduce this?

JL: It was a continuation of what happened in the first half, where there was increased owner investment in the red team that enabled them to purchase Sandro Porta because he had scored a goal. Then in the second half, it was not only an increased owner investment, but rather, a complete club takeover, which is very topical in the Bundesliga with the fifty plus one rule today, if you allow for a corporation or a person to purchase more than 50 percent of a club, to become a majority shareholder. In our fictitious scenario in the game, one entity takes over the club and injects so much capital that they are permitted to purchase multiple players resulting in a visible imbalance of power. So, it's no longer eleven versus eleven players, but in the end, it's fifteen against seven, making tangible this type of unfair financial play.

AP: We created a situation that departs from some of the conventions of a football game. However the point that we wanted to make was that the asymmetry of resources behind the pitch has implications on the pitch. Especially in terms of really big money and the types of investments that are made, in the sense that there is no limit as to how much you can spend. Following this tendency, the model of football that is easier to practice is one where the competition becomes one about money and not about anything else, about potentially buying an entire squad. This was the point of purchasing or transferring four or five players in the very end, and not just one, this capacity to virtually buy in bulk.

HT: Which played itself out beautifully when the team immediately scored three goals.

AP: We really wanted to visualise this asymmetry, because this difference in numbers or scale is still the best way to visualise imbalance or unfair premise.

MH: I'd like to add a sports perspective to this. The problem we have right now (in European football particularly) is that we have two systems. We have the "owner-owned" clubs and we have clubs running as enterprises. This structure produces a very unbalanced situation. Additionally, we have the European Union labour laws behind these systems, where basically one can spend as much money as possible when the club is owner-owned. Theoretically speaking, the owner can invest €300 million into their club and buy every player because it is the law within the EU to build up your company without limitation, and purchase the players since they can move freely. Compare this to the

US, where there is a closed sporting system with salary caps, and clubs are only permitted to spend a specific amount of money. This structure makes it more possible for smaller clubs to compete. In this case, the success of teams depends less on how much money is brought in, but depends on factors like: Is the team-owner solid? Is the trainer gifted? Are the funds available spent wisely? Currently the main problem in European football is that we have no clear rules governing the system, which is why many clubs are becoming so wealthy, and competition becomes unbalanced.

HT: I completely agree, and I believe that this imbalance (the manner in which capital is shaping the way the game is played) is detrimental for global football. This year, there have been more goals than we have come to expect from a typical UEFA Champions League, and I see that as a direct result of a small number of clubs receiving large influxes of cash, and desiring immediate success. In order to achieve this, they invest all of their money into attacking football, as opposed to looking to the long-term, and strengthening their entire squad from the ground up. I was wondering, Moritz: Do you envision a time in the near future when the fifty plus one rule will be retracted from the Bundesliga?

MH: I have to be really careful right now (laughs). Personally... actually, I cannot say. There would have to be huge changes in the system. A decision would have to be made about going with fifty plus one or not, otherwise it will become a rat race without limitations on spending power. We need a salary cap, which really concerns European policy makers to create certain laws governing sports, to truly see sport as a different social entity, and not subsuming it completely into an economic logic. In its current trajectory, the developments point towards some sort of super league. It's challenging at the moment because so many huge teams are becoming increasingly richer, while the football matches are losing their spectacularity since match outcomes become more predictable. We need to find a substantial solution, and it's one that concerns the governance of sport.

HT: There's a parallel here to be drawn from a recent article published by the BBC, which suggested that Russia 2018 may be the last example of a World Cup being hosted by a single country, because the costs have already risen to £8.8 billion. When you consider the fact that football, as an industry, continues to grow, you will see that this is not a sustainable model, which leads me to a closing question: Do you think this work is overly cynical, or do you see it as a positive project that reinvests in a communal activity?

Alexandra Pirici / Jonas Lund / Harry Thorne / Moritz Hollinger

AP: I do not think that our work is cynical. I don't think that revealing and making certain dynamics visible that usually stay off the pitch is being cynical. I've witnessed discussions about football matches where the game is of course discussed, but when someone brings in the question of money people are able to separate it from the game, which strikes me as strange: "Yes, the financial politics are problematic, but the game, I mean, they have all these great players." Making the connection between what happens on the pitch and what happens off the pitch is important because these factors determine what happens on the pitch, and subsequently what happens in the tribunes, and the relationship to supporters in both the local community and the global audience. Our project wasn't addressing football on totally national or local grounds, but was about opening questions and directions for thinking. In the end, although I am not sure how visible this was, we tried to switch off all of the LED lights on the uniforms (designating red and blue teams), cutting the markers of team allegiance, and we instructed players to choose with whom to play. In this instance, the game became about play itself, and not so much about a team. While of course, the existing allegiances stayed with their own teams kicked in, and that was something interesting to notice. So, no, I do not think that our proposal was cynical, what I hope is that it was an interesting point of departure for a broader discussion on the sport and its influence in society in relation to economics and politics.

HT: The idea that you are not really introducing anything 'new' to the discussion, but rather transposing these pre-existing (often negative) components into a more digestible language, gestures to what we've always been told: that football is, or can be, a universal language. There is something very valuable in that. I don't agree with my question, in that regard. I don't think the work is cynical at all. Rather, I see it as a re-investment in what can be taught through football and, with that in mind, a suggestion of how we might be able to alter the 'syllabus'.

The conversation took place on June 22nd 2018 at Allianz Arena after the N Football match had ended. The transcript has been initially published in *A City Curating Reader. Public Art Munich 2018* (Motto Books, Public Art Munich)
images: Alexandra Pirici & Jonas Lund, N Football (2018) - gameplay stills, costume design by Andrei Dinu (p.61, 68); collective crediting during the match (p. 65); announcement of a transfer during the match (p.67); translation of the gameplay by a sign language interpreter (p.69) ©Michael Fitzner, Paul Valentin, Public Art Munich

Gaming the Score

Dan Perjovschi
Untitled, drawing, 2015

OPERA CUP

Ion Dumitrescu

Sergiu Celibidache with Alfredo Di Stefano in Bologna

In the late '90s, as a Bucharest National Opera ballet dancer, I played football in the 'Opera Cup'. In those days, this para-event caught the attention of the institution's personnel more than any premiere. The starting teams represented various departments of the Opera. The most consistent ones were representing the Ballet, Orchestra, Choir, Firefighters, Technicians and Extras' departments: exclusively male teams. Occasionally some of the guys from the 'workshops' would join in; Stage Painting, Costumes, Props: under-numbered teams in terms of employees, that would never get past the elimination rounds anyway. For instance, the Painting department was so small, that its members often had to be 'transferred' to more solid teams: The Choir or Orchestra. Some inter-department exchanges were allowed. The 'Extras' were the most numerous – though not very loyal – while an 'accompanying pianist' could choose whether to play for the Orchestra or the Ballet team. Each department was involved with designing its own kit. Ballet, for instance, used to wear red t-shirts with the Manchester United logo woven on, bought by our 'captain' from the flea market and further customised.

On the entry wall of the Opera's personnel canteen, we had a printed display with the on-going results and fixtures, as the tournament map was constantly updated and talked about in-between rehearsals.

People from all sectors of the institution came to watch the games. Opera employees were also the spectators, sometimes accompanied by relatives and friends. Once, the cup final between 'Ballet' and 'Orchestra' was attended by the Ballet department's director - the legendary Ileana Iliescu.

We're speaking of a non-official initiative, strictly belonging to the collectives forming this theatre city-institution, a cultural structure built on a Soviet model.

The whole process echoed positions of the Opera's inner social classes, a stratification mirroring the hierarchies in 19th century librettos, where 'players' sung, danced, or worked next to or above the stage. In this panorama, we see on the stage - fictive - princes and peasants, kings and their subjects (or pharaohs and slaves), and around the stage, in the backstage or in the fly tower - real - toiled the invisible proletariat, working the machines; maintaining the spectacle and the convention for the eternal witness: the audience (the *meta* anonymous), the presidential box + the *loge* of emeritus artists.

Therefore, those who played football in the Opera Cup were mostly employees of the 'lower classes' of the institution; workers embodying two positions, fictional and real (the Ensemble, Choir, Extras) and those totally hidden to the public, the real-life proletariat (the technicians, props, firefighters, painting, and costume departments).

The 'kings', 'princes', and other 'aristocrats' never touched the ball, as that would have been too risky. Usually the games would take place between 3 and 5 pm and at 6:30 there would either be a show or evening rehearsals. The solo dancers could not afford to be tired or even worse, injured, while for the ballet ensemble (*le corps du ballet*), the football games could amount to a perfect warm-up to a *Czardas* number or a 'Polish' number in Act 1 of *Swan Lake*.

The analogy between the hierarchy of classical (Romantic) ballet plots and the stratification of its contemporary society were among the first critical observations I understood when I left the world of classical dance. Once you introduce the political into disciplinary art mythologies, when you watch *Giselle* with Marxist goggles, the classic convention becomes unbearable. An entire infrastructure (material and immaterial) becomes visible through the filter of class struggle. It seems that the institution itself becomes a bastion of conservatism camouflaged as perennial culture, an inexplicable colossal effort that involves hard body training and huge financial resources – all to keep alive the culture of a world from two centuries ago.

In the universe of football, the same spectacle takes places for the umpteenth time – another *El Clásico*. Only the actors are changing (as in Shakespeare plays). The activity of a ballet dancer stretches the same as that of a football player (or any professional athlete in general). Their bodies are revered mostly between 17 and 35. The decline will sometimes come abruptly: accidents or streaks of failures, while being progressively transferred to minor teams (companies). For football players, the exit is permanent unless they manage to stay in the club organisation. The carrier of a ballet dancer can pertain a slow ending, increasingly involving less technically demanding roles: "wise" characters: older kings or main characters' parents. Acting skills are the last assets of an experienced dancer. His/her mime virtuosity. But former star dancers, as football players, once their career is over, also tend to stay in the 'club'. Usually they become training coaches, choreographers, or department directors.

There is at least a double rapport with contemporary art. Football is a predictable show with the outcome always un-predictable. While contemporary art shows imply that one doesn't really knows what one is about to see and even less how it will end (or if it will ever end). On another level, in the world of classical librettos, one knows what show one is going to see (i.e. *Don Quixote*) and of course, how it will end.

It is of the essence both in the world of football and classical expression (theatres/museums) to know when the game/show will finish. Its fixed, precise duration is inscribed in the convention, and all spectators will expect just that. The moment when the audience leaves the convention must be clear, be it through a falling curtain or the whistle of a referee. Games are closed organisms that grow through self-combustion and which, for sustainability reasons, must remain pre-critical. Deconstruction means alienation, an area in which the foundations of high culture may not be probed into. Otherwise the whole edifice would come crashing down, the 'wings' of the stage would be mistaken for 'the proscenium', and as such, if the make-believe world would continue after the fall of the curtain, anxiety would grapple with the audience. Football was a counterintuitive presence in the world of classical ballet. In school we were forbidden to play football, as any accident could impend our incipient carriers. We were told repeatedly that football radically (de)forms our muscles, tendons, and even our bone structure. Especially for boys, the heavy rotated cliché was to juxtapose a ballet dancer to a football player, the first characterised by mythological grace and thinness, while the latter by robustness and 'thickness'. Football players were supposedly bow-legged and stocky, while the legs of ballet dancers had to exhibit Euclidian geometry. The bodies of ballet dancers had to 'draw' through space, while football professionals were allegedly rough and had no sense of aesthetics. Now I think Iniesta or Pogba glide with the same elegance of professional ballet dancers.

In spite of these recommendations, most of my colleagues loved football, some were obsessed by it. During middle school we would skip ballet class to go play football in the schoolyard or in the park. Usually against music students' teams, who were also afraid of getting hurt, though in different areas. The hands and delicate fingers of piano and violin players needed to be protected. And a ball shot in the face could ruin one's ability to play trumpet/horn/bassoon.

Ballet dancers were drawn to football in other ways too. At the end of the '90s and the beginning of the 2000s, a lot of dancers made ends meet out of 'events' outside the institutional score – so-called 'easy jobs': well-paid micro-shows inaugurating a new bank or introducing a new mobile phone network, fashionable initiatives of the new private companies that wanted to project a modern and in tune image. Dancers were performing in product presentations and featured in TV ads. In those days, professional trained dancers could only be the product of a few specialised dance schools, mainly located in Bucharest and Cluj, but also Iași and Constanța. In parallel, there was the Traditional (Popular) School of Arts, which trained dancers mostly for vaudevilles, the *Constantin Tănase Theatre* or various local folklore ensembles. All these schools and institutions were state-owned. Private schools were just emerging.

As salaries were precarious in those days, Opera ballet dancers would also seek to feature in entertainment shows as part-time jobs, outside the ballet environment.

That's how I also came to perform in the 1999-2000 football season, a mini-show for halftime during the Romanian Cup final game between Dinamo Bucharest and Universitatea Craiova. On the pitch, behind the goal, a small stage (compared to the size of the stadium) was installed, where for 15 minutes a series of musical and 'modern dance' bits were enacted. Or 'choreographic miniatures', as heard in the world of dance.

Performing on a stadium behind the goal, immersed in a deafening noise produced by fans completely indifferent to our performance. Clearly, not an optimal setup. The audience was busy in the stands, while in front of us lied the empty football pitch. Beyond the green perimeter, fans were occupied with pseudo-choreographic rituals of their own. The spectators were delivering another show.

The events took place on the now defunct *Lia Manoliu* stadium, and our performance was conceived or aimed rather at TV cameras. For most of us however, the real show (reward) was getting to watch the game at ground level, from behind the goal, seeing professional players engaged.

However, unlike us, football players didn't try ballet in their spare time.

image: Celibidache München Philharmoniker Beethoven, EMI Classics ©Private archive of the Celibidache family

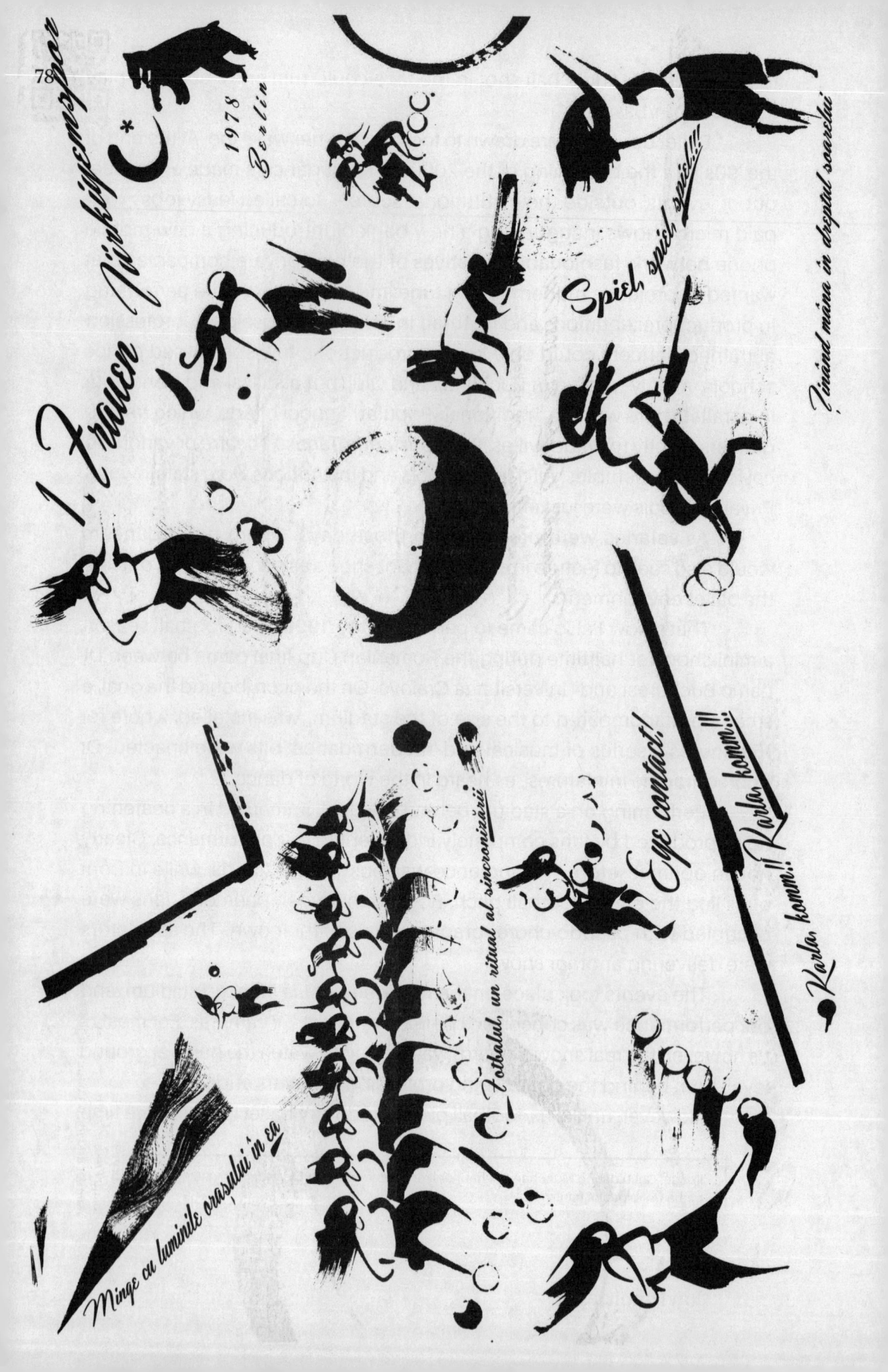

1. Frauen Türkischensport*
1978 Berlin

Spiel, spiel, spiel!!!

Ținând mâna în dreptul soarelui

Minge cu luminile orașului în ea

Fotbalul, un ritual al sincronizării

Eye contact!

• Karla, komm..!! Karla, komm...!!!

1. Frauen Türkiyemspor Berlin

Dedicat echipei de fotbal feminin

Mezughi: Dorsha 24.06.1989 TU
Guersoy: Alysse 07.03.1997
Wagner: Lena-Meltem 17.10.1995
Rab: Safiye 02.11.1978 C
Eloni: Vasfiye 26.02.1994
Krüger: Karla 28.02.1994
Salmen: Sinem 12.12.1995
Soylemez: Elif 21.11.1999
Kaminski: Jessica Maria 19.03.1988
Bernstein: Martha 27.05.1999
Kaplan: Denise 16.08.1980
Schauer: Anuska 17.10.1984
Kara: Ebru 25.04.1994
Kaya: Fatima 28.07.1994

Alex Bodea
Erste Frauen, 2016
Marker and ink on paper, digital collage

experiența ca sunet

Women's football, Petroșani, cca 1971, Aurel Dula archive

With Love, on Women's Football

> The first time I watched a football match I was 20 years old.

Irina Costache

My then boyfriend had taken me to a fancy bar to convince me to see the Final together. Germany was playing Brazil and it was a match that few men would have missed. I ordered an ice cream and watched the audience, bored; all kinds of men, but also a few lively women who were chugging beers and screaming wantonly. Neither the match nor the boyfriend convinced me.

From a boyfriend who was only interested in finals and weekend football, I moved on to a new boyfriend who was fully invested into football. Champions League matches, the English Premier League and all the Steaua matches were mandatory in our time together as a couple. In my spare time I started playing FIFA, hoping that we would soon do it together. My education in football was beginning to gain some consistency, and yet I did not find any enthusiasm for the game, and even less so passion or love. But I liked brave women, I read feminist literature and wanted to tear down any bastion of male domination (including the king of sports) - these were the topics I was passionate about. It didn't take long and I found my niche: women's football. At first, I just wanted to see a match, then a championship. Afterwards, I thought I'd do some sports and that wouldn't be bad for me to go to a training session. From here, I found myself writing a seminar paper on women's football, then a master's thesis and, a few years later, a book chapter. Between 2007 and 2010 I learned a lot about football and maybe even more about what it means to be a woman and to want to succeed in a man's field. I spent almost every autumn at the stadium at women's football matches across the country - I was the (only) supporter of the *Smart București* team. Foremost, I was a fan of some girls who didn't know how to give up. I became addicted to both football and the sisterhood. Even 10 years later, the girls from *Smart București* are still among the women I admire the most.

September 7th, 2009

I return to women footballers after a year and wonder how much I have learned in the meantime about the job I do. Do I understand anything of the stubbornness of these girls to sacrifice their bones and tendons on fields with potholes and stadiums without spectators? What do they ultimately have to gain, when playing women's football in Romania means fighting poverty and prejudice? Lili gave up, she told us at training today. She says it makes no sense because the team went down the drain and she no longer wants to hide from the coach the fact that they're smoking. Anyway, she says, this year there is no money at the club for organising matches. And, even if it were, she no longer wants to be called "lesbian" on the street. For Ely, passion is passion. You can't quit something you enjoy. She joined the masters at ANEFS (National University of Physical Education and Sport) this year, and next year she wants to write a thesis on women's football. "She'll be the first", says Ely. We change for training, although not everyone has football boots.

September 17th, 2009

The first visit to the new pitch. From now on, *Smart* will play at IMGB, on the Spiru Haret Stadium. Still, it's a real stadium, a stadium with 1000 seats and it has turf. Shorty left her hair longer and this season she wants high performance. But she is worried about something, and wants me to help. For a while, she seems to have problems with the referees - she's a defender and she gets tons of yellow cards. At the last friendly match they eliminated her because she swore at a referee. It slipped, and the ref took it seriously, she says. For several nights she dreams of getting a red card at the match and the team being left with one less player. Isn't there something I can do to help her? Bits of smiles thrown upon entering the pitch cross my mind. Sometimes from the girls, sometimes the referees. Some would say they'd look better sipping some juice in a bar.

I wonder how to help Shorty keep it together when even I surprise myself in the middle of the game running beside the coach yelling at them? We talk about the stakes of the game – isn't winning always the most important thing?

September 22th, 2009

It's the last training before the championship starts. Smart plays against 'Prison Galls', a team that trains on Jilava Prison's pitch. We warm up quickly and begin at once. Today we practice match tactics, and Butterfly, the girl in goal, defends shot after shot. We get caught up in the game, we change sides quite accurately, the passes flow and there are many goals. The girls seem confident, but the coach is dissatisfied: "You know, in this team there are 11 different personalities and they're all crazy in their special little way. It's hard to manage anything with these girls. First of all, they kick the ball without thinking, and secondly, they don't lead an athlete's life: they don't eat and don't rest

properly. Eh, some still smoke. I admire them only because they are stubborn."
Nea Marin was the first women's football coach in the country, meaning he is the oldest. In his lifetime, he trained teams of workers from socialist factories, which he had playing demonstrations during openings of classic derbies, such as Steaua-Dinamo and Sportul-Universitatea Craiova. Nea Marin admits he likes the girls - they play with their hearts. He also has some regrets; mainly that he has nothing to offer them, "as it happened in the old days - a job, a salary, equipment, a living through football". He feels that the future of football, but also of humanity is in the girls' feet: "The boys are hooligans interested in money, they have forgotten what true football is."

Today

After 10 years, my soul team is gone. I still have a passion for football, especially the one played by women, this time unconditioned by the hobbies of a boyfriend. The figures of the Romanian Football Federation stay true to Nea Marin's words. Today, women's football is the sport with the largest increase in the number of practitioners - from 400 players in 2010 to almost 10,000 in 2017. The internal championship has 3 divisions and 40 affiliated senior teams, while during our time with Nea Marin the federation could not manage to bring together a division. We do not have international performances yet, but neither are we as far behind the boys as we used to be – this close were the girls from the national team to qualify for Euro 2017 - but the presence of Olimpia Cluj in the Champions League is quite a performance.

image: CS Smart Sport București

Irina Costache

Young Hopes

Recorded by Florin Bobu

Zamfir Iulia-Adalmina: I am 17 and am in the 9th grade at the Gheorghe Asachi Technical Highschool in Iași. In the 2nd grade I was already playing football with my peers. In the 7th grade I ended up in a club more by chance. I was playing in the school's team and there was a tournament organised by Adrian Ambrosie, president of Navobi Iași. It's been four years since I have been playing for this team. Two years later came the invitations from the national youth team. It was a great achievement for me! I continue to work hard and hope to be invited again. My position is right-back, but I also like to find myself in front of the goal, to advance to the position of the midfielders or even the forwards. I like Messi's playstyle and character.

    I study in a class specialising in architecture, but I am thinking of applying to a sports faculty. I think I could become a coach, as I like teaching others what I know. I would even like to have my own team.

    I advise girls who wish to play football to focus on what they want to do and never give up. They say football is a boys' sport, but I don't believe that. Any sport can be practiced by anybody.

Hortensia Mi Kafchin
I know this guy you have no clue about, 2017
Xerox after drawing with crayon on paper, colored with felt tip pens, 24 × 32 cm

Anti-System Supporterism:

The fans of Rapid București and actions' of dissent

Pompiliu-Nicolae Constantin

Football, la bagatelle la plus sérieuse du monde (*Football, the World's Most Serious Trifle*) is the title of a book by ethnologist Christian Bromberger. The eponymous phrase really captures the resonance of this sport. From the interwar period, football captured the Romanian public's interest. From workers to intellectuals, all got involved in the phenomenon, as players or spectators. New teams were appearing at an accelerating rate and became increasingly well-defined identities in Romanian society.

Among them was Rapid București, founded in 1923 by workers at Atelierele Grivița (Grivița Workshops). Initially called CFR București in order to clearly identify with the institution of Căile Ferate Române (Romanian Railways), the football team established itself under the name Rapid, which it adopted in 1937. From a neighbourhood team, Rapid garnered national support once it entered the First League. In the interwar period they won their first trophies as well. The Giulești team earned their reputation as 'Cup specialists', having won the national cup in the years 1935, 1937, 1938, 1939, 1940, 1941, and 1942.

The arrival of the communist regime found a club with a well-established identity. Precisely because it became known as the team of the railway workers and labourers, Rapid was the perfect identity to symbolise communist sports. However, in time, with the arrival of the other major clubs, Steaua (1947) and Dinamo (1948), the supporters' attitude turned against the communist regime. Gradually, fans of Rapid built a rivalry with the

Bucharest-based clubs founded at the initiative of the new power. This kind of validates the idea propounded by French sociologist Pascal Duret, who noted that the spectacle of sports offers neither a perfectly pure scene nor a totally fair one. It is imperfect and sometimes unfair, as is the world.

This attitude of Rapid's fans, which manifested as episodic reactions towards the communist regime, also reflected their attitude towards the world and the newly shaped society. Whether we are speaking of individual opponents or groups expressing their discontent towards a government, each such event has its own particular context and must be analysed according to certain parameters: opportunity, rate of cohesion, importance of the moment, etc. A critical attitude towards the regime, manifested through songs, chants, or banners, developed in football stadiums from the sport's early days. Totalitarian regimes paid close attention to such moments, but, at the same time, showed an agreed-upon leniency, as access into the stadiums could not be perfectly controlled, nor could the behaviour of the supporters be fully constrained. On stadiums there was a sense of freedom.

Researching the phenomenon, I came across interesting examples of political dissent coming from supporters. There were instances of concrete disobedience, but also passive resistance, an important notion in this context, but also difficult to quantify. The homogeneity of the collective voice can be seen in multiple examples of disobedience, and its appearance can be spontaneous. To understand the dynamics of these cases it is important to make use of protest theory, developed by economist Timur Kuran, who says that in every society there is a spark, a nucleus that triggers the storm. I am referring here to unpredictable events that, in hindsight, appear to be inevitable. It is important to analyse the discourse of fans regarding the regime from this perspective.

Robert Edelman, Jim Riordan, Karol Nawrocki, Mariusz Kordek, and Alan McDougall are some of the historians who have researched the oppositional tactics practiced by football fans under communist regimes. Their criteria and observations can be applied to the case of Rapid București as well. Administratively, Rapid București was under the control of the regime, and the mission of the club's leadership was to administer their sport's divisions in the spirit of the received ideology. It is important to distinguish the club's administrative activity and that of its leaders from the attitude of its fans, which was often different and even antagonistic to the leadership's politics.

In the '50s, Rapid București was the most popular team in Romania, and the communist regime contributed to this by annihilating the main football clubs from the interwar period. For this reason, many fans of the former teams came to support Rapid. For instance, Gheorghe Scurtu, former fan of Carmen București, chose to support the CFR's team after the closing of the Mociornița family's club. "I followed the club where my favourite players went. Bazil Marian went to Rapid, so I started supporting the *white & burgundys* of Bucharest", said Scurtu, who, after the fall of communism, turned his house into a museum dedicated to the team.

Furthermore, the club's link to the CFR meant a solid number of fans out of institutional solidarity. Workers, artists, politicians all sat together in the stand at Rapid's games on home ground.

The popularity of the team's players and the expansion of the supporter phenomenon began being perceived as a threat to the communist regime. As a consequence, footballers were monitored by the *Securitate* (the former Secret Police), as its archives reveal.

The team's situation improved during the regime's liberal years, between 1965 and 1971. The Giulești footballers won the 1967 championship, which was received with spectacular enthusiasm. The fever pitch culminated in a moment that remained in the collective memory of football fandom: hundreds of Rapid fans went from Ploiești, the city where the important game had taken place, to Bucharest on foot. By 1967 Steaua had won six national tournaments, while Dinamo - five. With the occasion of this victory, the first anti-regime slogans started appearing, the most well-known being "Galeria lui Rapid nu e membră de partid!" ("Rapid's supporters are not party members!") and "Rapid, campioană, fără milă și pomană!" ("Rapid is the champion without anyone's charity!").

The most intense period of opposition coming from Rapid fans against Dinamo and Steaua, and, implicitly, against the regime, was in the '70s and

'80s. Because the club was facing multiple challenges and the influence of the rival teams was growing, Rapid's supporters assumed the role of 'peripherals'. This situation intensified due to the harsh everyday living conditions in communist Romania, the trust in one's neighbours diminishing dramatically. Exactly this was the reason why a new parallel system of relationships developed. Being a Rapid fan became a quality, at least for other Rapid fans. Accounts of the time confirm this. "If I needed a barber I went to one who supported Rapid. If I needed a suit, I looked for a skilled person, as long as they were a Rapid fan. It was hard to trust anyone else at the time", a supporter said. This can be seen in the *Securitate*'s archives as well. In the file of writer Fănuș Neagu, a well known supporter of Rapid, it is revealed that he helped his friends who supported the same team gain various privileges, and he also helped those from other cities obtain tickets to the team's matches.

"Cine-a băgat Rapidu-n B? Ceaușescu, PCR!" ("Who got Rapid into the second league? Ceaușescu and the Romanian Communist Party!") was the strongest slogan of the '70s. Communism and the *Securitate* were also seen by the fans as responsible for the death of one of the team's iconic players, Dan Coe. Nicknamed 'the Minister of Defence', both as a reference to the team's rivalry with Steaua and to emphasise his abilities as a defender, Dan Coe came from a family with Legionnaire sympathies. In 1981 he died in Germany. The official version said the former Rapid captain had died by suicide. The fans saw in this a plot by the *Securitate*, his former teammates believing the same. Dan Coe is considered a hero in Rapid culture and has become a symbol in the fans' post-1989 discourse.

Together with such great personalities, the small football magazines made by Radu Călin Cristea, who became a famous literary critic and journalist, and Rapid's anthem, written by Adrian Păunescu, also contributed to the team's identity. Păunescu also wrote a poem dedicated to the team in the '80s, *De ce țin cu Rapid (Why I Support Rapid)*, which became extremely popular among fans. In the same period, another anti-system chant targeted Valentin Ceaușescu's (son of dictator Nicolae Ceaușescu) influence on Steaua: "Noi vi-l dăm pe Damaschin, voi ni-l dați pe Valentin!" ("We'll give you Damaschin, you give us Valentin!"), chanted Rapid's fans at the game with Steaua in the 1983-1984 season.

A similar attitude can be seen in the Steaua-Rapid game of 1989. Though the game was not televised, a summary was broadcast on TVR after the fall of the regime during the show *Replay*. The context of the match is interesting. Rapid had been relegated to Division B (the Second League), but was going to play Steaua in the semifinals of the National Cup. The army's team had just played in the finals of the European Cup. Theoretically the difference between the two teams was great, but the game was balanced. The match took place on the Sportul Studențesc Stadium, and most of the crowd were Rapid supporters. The background noise of the game saw all the chants against Steaua and also against the referee. At each moment of discontent, Rapid's fans would yell ironically: "Asta este Steaua!" ("That's Steaua!"), implying that everyone knew they did not play fairly, while each of the referee's decisions would be followed by "Hoții! Hoții!" ("Thieves! Thieves!"), suggesting a link between the party and the team. This shows that tensions were high, and Rapid's fans had no qualms about demonstrating themselves freely, since such chants were frequent.

All of this supports the idea that Rapid's fans built their identity relative to their rivals. The aforementioned moments of dissent are concrete instances of disobedience towards the regime. This does not mean that the powers that be and the rival teams were seen as the sole culprits of the team's problems. The club's administration and their lack of sports value were also often mentioned by supporters. The obsession with persecution intensified starting from the '50s and became unbearable throughout the '80s. This feeling did not go away after 1989, when Rapid's fans established their anti-communist position more firmly, legitimating their rivalry with Dinamo and Steaua by still referencing the episodes mentioned above.

An additional step in this direction was the symbolic brothering between Rapid's fans and those from Timișoara. There was a profound link to the city that started the events that led to the fall of communism.

After December 1989, Rapid went through a process of reorganisation, the football team was separated from the other sports divisions and tried to build itself an independent existence on the western model. The one who speculated on Rapid's image capital was businessman George Copos, who saw in the team a means of gaining notoriety. The post-1993 period meant a reinvigoration for the Giulești team in terms of performance, with Copos as manager. Even so, Rapid always gave the feeling that it could do better. Obviously, the supporters wished for more trophies. But which supporter is ever fully satisfied?

Under George Copos's patronage, the team became champions twice, once in 1999 and once in 2003, which drew a wave of sympathy towards the businessman, to which contributed the fact that he managed to bring a coach like Mircea Lucescu to Giulești, as well as seasoned players. During these times the supporters would chant "George Copos, asta ești/ Berlusconi din Giulești!/ Cu Lucescu la echipă,/ Nici de Milan nu ni-i frică!" ("That's to you, George Copos, / A Berlusconi of Giulești! / With Lucescu in our team / Not even Milan scares us!"). But once the results faded and the economic crisis of 2008 struck, Copos became an enemy of the fans. A new oppositional niche appeared, aside from the already established ones against Dinamo and Steaua. Yet another wave of discontent came against the Professional Football League, the institution that organised the tournament, perceived as a totalitarian, biased management structure. The palette of enemies broadened, which the fans fought with for two decades and which gave birth to an interesting slogan: "Singuri împotriva tuturor" ("Alone against everyone").

Focused on so many external threats, the Rapid crowd neglected their own implosion. George Copos disappeared relatively quickly from the leadership of the club, in 2013, handing it over with debts of millions of euros to some obscure characters. In parallel a fragmentation of the fan core took place. The unity of the fans dissipated after internal conflicts, which led to a lowered ability for group mobilisation, especially after 2010. The team ended up on the brink of bankruptcy, and, for the first time since its founding, did not participate in the national championship in 2016-2017. The divergences between fans transpired from a lack of common vision in the face of this event. New teams appeared in the lower leagues who have tried to establish themselves as heirs to the bankrupt team.

images: Photographs from Octavian Pescaru's personal archive

Gheorghe Scurtu
Rapid Bucharest apartment museum

Watch the game, don't stare at me!

Interview with Powerpuff

How was your relationship built? When did you come out on the stadiums as an organised group?

> The story of our group started in 2007, at the match against Benfica, on February 22nd, when the DNL group was also formed. We met in the South terrace a few years before that and we were eight girls initially. Our desire to organise ourselves was encouraged and supported by the former BOYS members.

What does your name mean? How did you choose it? Did you think of any other options?

> No, we had no other options. We thought it would be the most appropriate name for us considering we have different personalities and one passion: Dinamo!

What symbolism have you used for your materials? What influenced you?

> Unlike other terraces, in South Dinamo everyone had the same scarf, white-red (classic, no tassels, no texts). The hoodies were black, identical, regardless of the group, only the T-shirts were different. We wrote the messages according to each event. All our actions (from messages and T-shirts, to banners and flags) took into account the style of the terrace. Sombre, like Black October.

CORNER #1

What do you think about other women in the stadium? What does your family/partner think about you and your activity in the stadium?

> But what do you think about men going to the theatre? Joking! Women have always been going to the stadium. We are neither the first nor the last. The reasons don't really matter and, anyway, it isn't any of our business. Yes, "women have no place in the stadiums", but there are exceptions. Our partners have always encouraged us to follow our passion. We had no family problems. Most of us were students or had already finished college when we decided to assemble the group, so there weren't too many restrictions.

The presence of women in stadiums very often takes a hypersexualised and objectified form (perceived only as accompanying men or as admirers of footballers).

> Our group was born and raised in the Free Speech Zone. As the boys encouraged and supported us to organise ourselves, we never had that problem. We were always their equals, we were respected and encouraged to come to the stadium and actively participate in all the actions of the SUD terrace (away games, meetings, fanzines, etc.).

How do you relate to the other supporters and other groups of ultras? How do they relate to you?

> We didn't interact very much with members of the other groups, and honestly, we didn't care about what others think of us, as long as we had support "back home".

How do you get along with other ultras/other groups of ultras girls? Was there any fighting? Are there people that make fun of you?

> There was no question of getting into fights with the other girls. We were already mature and experienced enough when we formed the group so we knew how to avoid falling into this kind of situation. Besides, that was a boys thing, we were just going to the stadium to support the team, PERIOD. The people who regularly go to the stadium never made fun of us. Those reactions might belong to TV supporters, 'sunflower-seed-nibblers' ... and they don't matter. Besides, it's just people who 'have it coming' that are being made fun of.

I noticed you had T-shirts with the message "watch the game, don't stare at me". Why this message ?

Watch the game, don't stare at me!

The message popped up after a joke. Maybe for the exact people who generalise and think all women end up on a stadium as a keychain.

Tell us about a trip.

There were many trips. Many in the country, many abroad (both with Dinamo and the national team). For the general public, perhaps the best known is the one from Nijmegen. We travelled separately, with the boys from the DOL and the DNL. We went by plane to Germany. There we rented a van, got a map and drove to Amsterdam. The match is famous; we can only tell you that we were seated close to the fence where all the 'action' took place. When we left, it was like war. All of us '300's were led to our buses by individuals armed to the teeth. Nothing new. This happens both here and abroad (only with Romanians, they treat their own people in a civilised manner). We found the van we rented with all the windows broken, so we spent several good hours at the station trying to explain to the Dutch, through hand gestures, what happened. We didn't have time to stay in Germany anymore. We arrived at 4 in the morning, we had a plane to catch in a few hours and we had to explain to the Germans (through hand gestures) what happened to the van and what their 'colleagues' from Holland wrote in the report. We got some two hours of sleep in that van with broken windows, in the cold weather and, like all respectable Romanians, on the benches in the airport.

How did you get along with the law enforcement? What is your perspective on the relationship between supporters and law enforcement?

Is anyone getting along with law enforcement?! They even make old people take off their shoes at the stadium's entrance. We, as girls, had no problems. Yes, they 'sprayed' us with tear gas many times, they pushed us around for no reason, but the boys saw to do us justice in their own way. Law enforcement women are just as bad; we even feel sorry for them in a way. Many tried to take our earrings or necklaces off so we wouldn't "throw them on the pitch". Should I mention seeing them using lip gloss after we threw them away?. No, cause it's sad and shameful.

Interview with Powerpuff

When did the group stop its official activity? Can you detail the reasons?

> Our group dissolved in 2010 - after the splitting of the SUD terrace. A press release was issued announcing that several groups, including our own, decided to move to the PCH. By the second half of the season, we were no longer an organisation. Some chose to stay in the SUD, some went to the North, others never came back or went to League IV matches, on the *maidan* (waste ground).

Do you still go to the stadium?

> We are still going to the stadium even now, we are all friends, we meet quite often and we make sure that every year we celebrate our 'birthday'. Those who decided to retire did it only because they became mothers in the meantime, but they will surely return to the stadium when the little ones manage to spell out loud: DI-NA-MO!

> Powerpuff is an ultras' girl group that was active in the South Dinamo Terrace between 2007 and 2010.

Watch the game, don't stare at me!

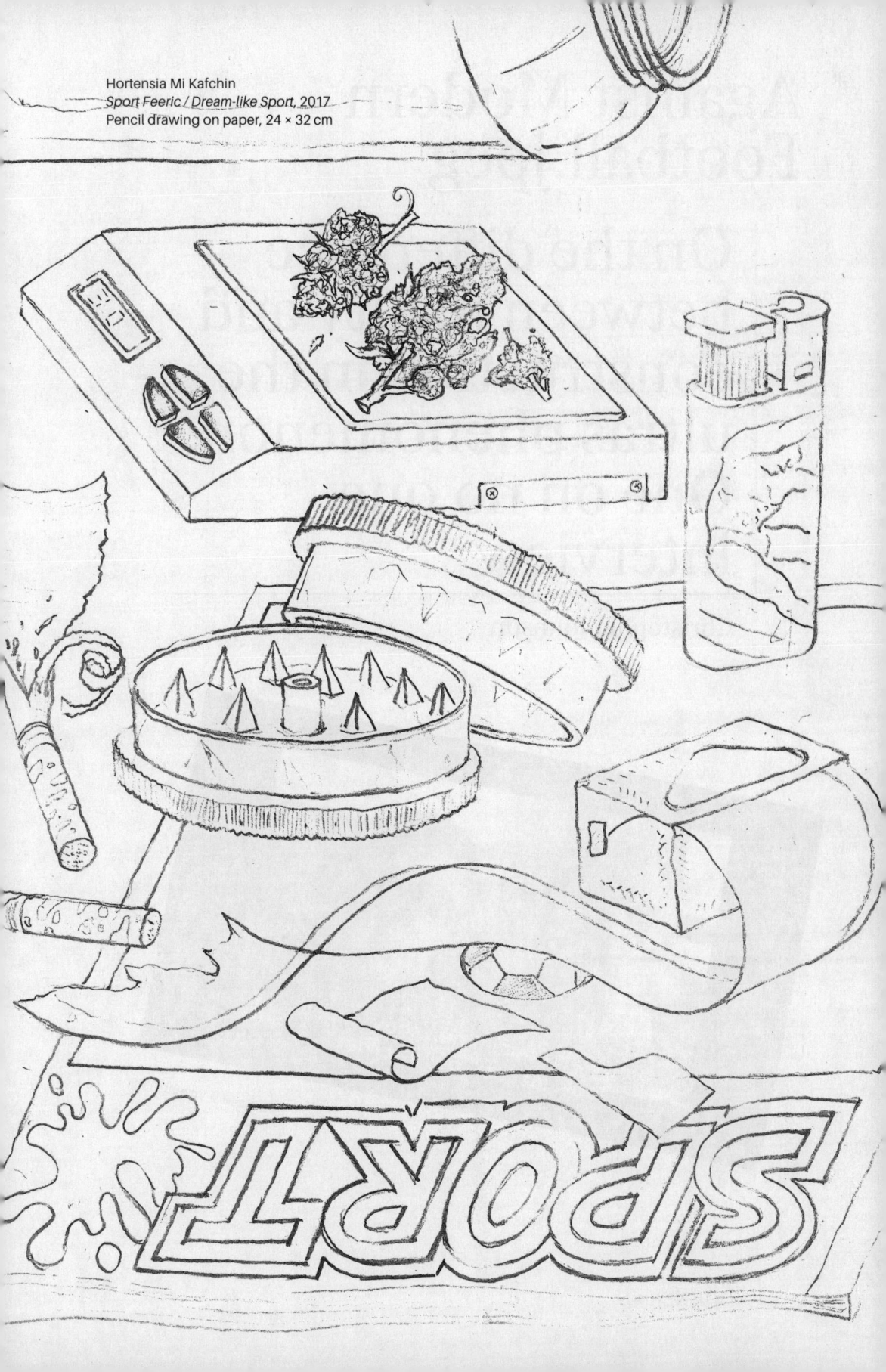

Hortensia Mi Kafchin
Sport Feeric / Dream-like Sport, 2017
Pencil drawing on paper, 24 × 32 cm

Against Modern Football.jpeg

On the difference between reality and construction in the ultras phenomenon. One on no one interview

Christopher Johnson

now is our time, they must look at us, on internet...

Alexandru Vitzentzatos

Pottret de grup in tren (2001), film still

- How do the imaginary and rhetoric form in the dynamics of supporter groups between the real and the virtual, between the terraces and the internet, between what happens and what is posted?

- Speaking of the beginnings of the ultras phenomenon and the '90s, what were the sources of inspiration and information flow? What role does migration in Italy play in this story? Is Super Tifo an exciting totem?

- What are the time periods in which you would split the history of the ultras phenomenon?

- Fence aesthetics. Where do the group names, banner fonts and logos come from? Do you see any patterns in the different time periods?

- Ultras use also colours other than the ones of the team they support. What are these and what is their significance?

- Are stickers the new propaganda literature?

- What is the origin of the obsession for the North and South cardinal points?

- More and more banners are being captured under conditions that do not take into account the unwritten rules of the phenomenon. What does "a capture is a capture" mean for you? What are the weirdest weapons you've heard of being used in 'interventions'?

- *White people in black clothes*. How do ultras dress? Do they have a certain dress code or uniform? What are the influences?

- How do they come up with the chants and their rhythms in the stands?

- In South America the supporters' chants are described by wavy hand movements, but in Europe the body choreography seems to be more rhythmic. Can we taxonomise and nuance these movements of the body geographically?

- Recontextualisations. Where do the texts from the messages and the choreographies etc. come from? Are they related to pop culture, hip-hop, commercials? Currently, the two subcultures that are also known for their form of social protest, the ultras movement and hip-hop, are treading nationalist, conspiratorial, mystical-religious waters. Where do you think they overlap?

- Who plays the role of the other in the rhetoric of the terraces?

- Any disturbing feelings when you go to matches in very large groups of men? *From father to son*, men who walk in large groups, is this a formula for homophobia and misogynism?

- Access to the stadium is regulated by certain rules, works like an airport gate and leads to a television studio. At the entrance you can often see various objects being left - lighters, coins, bottles, lipsticks - but no one seems to be concerned about the signs passing this filter, although they are subject to a technical process attended by representatives of the hosts, guests, law enforcement and the and the 4th official. Of the most repeated symbols in the terraces, besides the Celtic cross, the Confederate flag and the *tricolor* (national flag of Romania), there is one that I do not recognise. Could you tell me what is the meaning of the "pirate skull" for the ultras and what was its original significance?

- "United under the flag" or *united* without the flag?

Against Modern Football.jpeg

- *The team, the city, the homeland.* What effect do you think the "Support your local team" campaign had? How was this support interpreted and translated?

- While documenting for this interview, I noticed that in all the discussions with ultras the relationship with law enforcement comes up. I'm trying to project a mirror image between the supporter groups and security forces, wondering how they influenced each other. Chronologically, 'security' has been provided by the militiamen, military gendarmes, professional gendarmes after the Gendarmerie reform upon entry into the EU and, more recently, stewards, according to UEFA directives and Law 4. Could you provide me with a history of this 'other' the law enforcement?

- Although the signs and actions of the ultras groups have a clear direction, most of them claim to be apolitical. Is it a way of avoiding responsibility or a strategy?

- Are there direct links between supporter groups and nationalist organisations (Bessarabia Romanian Land) or fascist ones (New Right)? Or, rather, do these ideologies find their own way, authentically and autonomously, in the world of supporters?

A Plant for Processing the Irrational
Lines of flight, symptoms, signs

Ion Dumitrescu

Ancient Olympic Games initially functioned as a surrogate for war, an *Ersatz* for the on-going mutual bloody aggressions between Greek towns. The games were considered as emotional discharge channels for the irrepressible need for conflict between regions or citadels. The festivities operated as adrenaline generators for *free* citizens. Thus, very soon city-states recognised the political potential of sports.

Free Time

What to do after managing to 'survive', after one has paid one's dues to the society-state? The body engines still need fuel, and the fuel is of a primal kind: 'danger', 'prestige', 'loyalty' and the imperative of 'belonging' coupled with an urge to manifest oneself.

A conventional space must be designated for unleashing the primitive drives. The power drive is sometimes directed towards sports, an area with strict rules; where it never gets lethal, but where one can still 'win'. A chosen place where one can humiliate and avenge, where tribes can howl in unison. An arrangement for primary affective drives – echoing the ancestral struggle for survival – to be diverted and not repressed. We are following Georges Bataille, *la part maudite*, 'the accursed share', which must be fed regularly. In any vision of the future, the irrational must be accounted for without rational prejudice.

Ultras (die-hard fans) have always planned fights before or after football games. They still do it. The ritual, place and time are agreed by those involved, and fans of both teams start to organise days before the event. Specific pacts and codes rule this world. "Hooligans don't fight with just anybody, it is done mostly with their peers." (*The Firm*, Alan Clarke, 1989). One supporter I know – a former Rapid *ultra*-fan - who now travels with international fan groups (currently with Olympiacos FC for a game in the Champions League), was telling me how they arranged a skirmish with the Juventus *ultra*-fans but ended up on the wrong terrace, with "families, people in suits drinking wine": "I mean, you can't fight «citizens»!" In the end, they found those whom they were supposed to fight with. And they fought.

The Romanian Football Disintegration and its Effects on Local Social Dynamics

The local football institutional landscape is uncovering. We see supporters who don't find their team anymore, and teams nobody watches are featured in the first division. Fans still sit in the stands and act just as passionately. But lately it has become increasingly difficult to justify the original cohesion. Even harder to conduct its former power towards a concrete processing. Choreographies, anthems, slogans, the collective strength, all sound empty when the object of the covenant disappears. When clubs go into bankruptcy, are dismantled or relegated into oblivion; broken into multiple entities of reduced consistency, bizarre pseudo-clubs, blurred spectres of the past. Perhaps that's why my friend is looking for international fan fraternities, looking for the same experience somewhere else, sadly, away from his true passion: Rapid București. Because Rapid is nowhere, being everywhere.

Gradually, during the last 10-15 years, the game itself has ceased to be the culminating point for the Romanian supporter. The fragmentation, dissolving, splitting of clubs, spills into their respective communities, in neighbourhoods. By extension, supporter groups also break apart. It is a fragmentation that runs deep, on multiple layers, in parallel with the failures, bankruptcies, and the break of traditional clubs with tens of thousands of fans: Rapid, Steaua, Universitatea Craiova, and, on a smaller scale, Oțelul Galați and Farul Constanța.

A Domino of Undoing

People can't find their 'stadium' anymore, their 'homes' are losing ground. *Ultra*-fan leaders have to consolidate their positions and test the loyalty of their 'brigades' even more. The constant conflict with management contributes to a toxic ambiance, where money and political interests become priorities. When the football field slips from underneath your feet, fans remain suspended in the air. Even when the game doesn't matter anymore, the football machine pushes on, still chewing up subjectivities, this time in absence of a goal, of a *telos*. When football traditions and their social bonds break, 'the gangs' are back and have nothing to lose. The irrational is unleashed, cut off from its channels of processing, the mechanisms that can safely dispose of it. A processing plant working also to alleviate economic frustrations, something the nation-state cannot supply. Football competitions always had this cathartic function, metamorphosing the irrational *au ralenti*.

The communal assemblage inherent to a fanclub culture is crumbling down. The series of shocks that impacted upon Romanian football have weakened the social dimension related to football teams. Football matches have lost their function within communities, no more domesticating primary drives.

It seems only the violent dimension is left. Fans continue to get their primal fix, expressing the raw affect. When that doesn't work, they either leave with international teams or it leaks out into society. Repressed tensions reverberate further in neighbourhoods, families and micro social circles. A diffuse disappointment leaks into all aspects of life. Discharge outbursts then find different ways to surface and are perceived stridently in social environments.

Neither the national team nor the clubs; Romanian football is not delivering either on the international level nor on the national one. Local football is fading out and this event is dragging down an entire societal network, a social fabric woven in decades. While the starting point was the British model, where cricket and football clubs (e.g. Manchester City) emerged in the 19th century as a diversion and long-term solution to the rivalry of gangs.

Pre-critical Identity

The 'tree of life' featured in *Avatar* (2009), whose collapse dooms also the community around it. When our identity-torso is fractured, when the structure growing within (in symbiosis) falls, an entire *modus vivendi* follows with it.

The *beyond* becoming temporarily visible in the mechanics of collective rituals, in the self-replicable *event* that assures coherence to a reality; when ceremonies, sacraments, rites or any other trans-generational formalities are enacted in a non-redundant loop. Not an absolute truth, but a functional one. The *meta*-'tree', the foundation that supports a perimeter of meaning.

What keeps *homo sapiens* tribes together? Just because we are of the same species and contingently born in the same time and space? Just because, apparently, we speak the same language? Nothing seems to suffice. Without an exterior *meta* binding we can't really connect. The *neighbourhood* can perform this function, as it solidifies above each individual. And the football team joins in and strengthens the neighbourhood, city, even the nation. (In post-war Germany, only after winning the World Cup in 1954, national demonstrations were again allowed.)

Various essential sediments of an identity are necessary to the state-nation apparatus (the rational and emotional traits of belonging). The collective euphoria, the synchronised masses projecting an abstract body that goes beyond the individual, one that harvests an immense energy.

A transfinite force, manifesting when millions of minds vibrate for a second in unison, when the whole becomes greater than the sum of its parts.

The energy generated by a social group acts upon itself as any mass-drug, a production of meaning and ecstasy that can be channelled in many ways. But sports' production of euphoria had a benign function. Although a pre-critical type of self-manipulation, it worked! Neighbourhoods got together and enjoyed games! For a long while, it *made* sense.

The Inner Match, the Last Match

Today, fans of the same team fight amongst themselves. A seasoned *ultra* of CSA Steaua București (a division of former Steaua B) was telling me, disengaged as if destined to be involved in fan fights forever, that "in the Fourth League you have fifteen thousand spectators attending. And most of them, after (but also during) the game, brawl not with the opposing team's supporters, usually counting less than 200, but among themselves". They are the spectacle.

My friend was telling me that, recently, his wife made him choose between the family and the football fan life; without hesitation, he chose football. He knows, like everyone else, that Romanian football is on the brink, perhaps already dead, but he wants to continue. He made me be believe that there is really no choice, it's too late for him to quit. After 17 years of fan-club commitment, involving arrests, trials, fights, hospitals, and adventures, there is no turning back. The subject is constructed around the team and the codes of its supporters, which are all deeply embedded.

One shouldn't miss or glorify football fan-clubs in their static forms. The core 'values' of the *ultras* were most of the time conservative if not all-out reactionary. Mono-identities it seems, very quickly find ways to solidify. Racism and homophobia have some seats in the terraces.

The Rapid *ultra*-fan continued without pathos, recalling how in the past he would beat up gays "for fun". "We'd do that sometimes; 8 years ago, I was on TV for beating homosexuals. The entire terrace knew me."

Ultras everywhere are not ready for multiple realities, let alone multiple identities. The ability of a subject to live outside of a mono-identity culture demands a lengthy, personal effort, a self-alteration disposition.

Ion Dumitrescu

DON'T RUN. HOOLIGANS ON E

Matei Sâmihăian

The history of rave culture between 1987-1995 is closely related to stadium culture and to supporters' organised groups. The text that follows speaks of two cases that highlight this phenomenon: the '87-'90 English warehouse party scene and the mid-'90s Rotterdam gabber scene.

The Promised Land

After the tragedy at the European Cup Final between Liverpool and Juventus that occurred on May 29th 1985, at the Heysel stadium in Brussels, Margaret Thatcher initiated a war on hooliganism and suggested that UEFA expel the English teams from European competitions. The Nyon forum approved their elimination from the circuit on an indefinite term, a ban that came to expire in 1990. Shortly afterwards, the clubs created a common front against state and league politics, and they started the process of forming a new league with a professional structure. In 1992, the Premier League emerges as a money-making machine.

Living shared experiences through fighting with other organisations; chanting the same anthems, inebriation, the initiation rites, the cult of violence and sacrifice and the simulated tribal experiences inside these gangs which championed the colours of their football clubs.

Even on an organisational level, the groups had cult-like structures, with a general who mobilised or kept the others in check, and with an arsenal of distinctive signs: tattoos with the names of players or with the symbols of the organisation they belonged to. Under the two crossed hammers of the Inter City Firm, a group of hooligans associated with West Ham United and one of the first associations with an organised structure in the history of England, stands the following motto: "Don't run."

Between 1987 and 1988, everything was about to change: the members of the most hostile organisations danced together and exchanged drugs. The wave of amphetamines and house music crashed into the supporters' heads, and now the wonder-drug seemed to magically sort conflicts out. Everyone was convinced they were in for a chemically sustained eternal bliss - an orgy of testosterone and adrenaline, sustained by the sounds of the Roland TB-303 and E. The irony made that this explosion of machismo merged with music imported from US East Coast gay clubs... But, by the early '90s, the communion had gone stale. The initiators of the local scene were now trying to stand out against the neon kids who were popping pills like Tic-Tacs. They were returning to the early '80s casual fashion, when hooligans shoplifted designer clothes from the Italian cities they travelled to along with the team. The glam clubs' new sound is luscious and chill. Diva voices are being mixed over beats, while people were snorting coke. Paradise Garage for straight people, chicks in mini dresses and boys wearing shirts and dress shoes. Against this backdrop, supporters started to get the idea there's money to be flipped. The aforementioned Inter City Firm monopolises parties on the ships passing in the night on the Thames. Under the centrifugal movement of the parties and entering an underground economy, the illegal opening of warehouses and derelict buildings on the outskirts, the ICF becomes a mob organisation that controls the drug dealing around events and offers protection to party organisers. Street-fight-hardened boys were now bouncers, charging entrance and selling pills.

The raves were organised by the most influential groups of supporters, who had control over a certain area, or by small promoters, with the hooligans' support and protection. The supporter organisations had infiltrated the entire club scene, a phenomenon that was spreading throughout the whole of England. Even small city pirate radio stations were being supported by local organisations. In April 1989, at the *Labyrinth* warehouse party, in the London district of Silvertown, the dancefloor was under assault by punks waving machetes, who attacked the ravers of colour. Promoter Joe Wieczorek claims that the event had been targeted by the ICF because they hadn't accepted their protection, which implied hiring 10 guys for 185 quid each.

One year later in *Madchester*, "World in Motion", the song by New Order and the national anthem of England for the World Cup in Italy, was being launched. Initially, its title was supposed to be "E is for England", but the federation refused the obvious association with the pills. It seems the original lyrics went like this: "E is for England, England starts with E/ We'll all be smiling when we're in Italy." Although the FA forced the British band to change the lyrics, the song had all the acid house clichés, from the 303 sounds to the piano riff inserted in the middle. Right before this, I could even see Gazza juggling and lip syncing.

"World in Motion" marked a genre, that had already begun to get fragmented into micro-genres, going mainstream. The song's release also coincided with a drastic decrease in violent acts in English stadiums. Supporters preferred to bond with other peers on E when going to the match. "Love's got the world in motion", as the song went. At the same time, its release was also the swansong for acid house. People were ready for rougher things, stronger drugs, and the hooligans were going back to alcohol intoxication and street fights.

Rotterdam Hooligan

In 1992, Rotterdam is where one of the most radical forms of hardcore music emerges - gabber. In Dutch, the word means 'friend', 'mate', and it was associated by the dockers with the sound boys make when they are chilling. If you went to club Parkzikt in '92, you would find a tribe that was sporting the same style – multicoloured or customised Aussie sweatshirts, AIR Max sneakers and shaved heads. Gabber also emerged as a form of distancing from the mild house beats that were trending in Amsterdam. A minimalistic hardcore, focused on the rhythm and on pushing the BPM to the extreme, this musical subgenre was a moment of liberation for the ecocity of Feyenoord, a breath that propelled the gabbers among the rave generation's most interesting subcultures.

DJ Paul Elstak recounts how hooligans from the organisations in Rotterdam would go out to gabber parties on Saturday, stay up on pills and coke till the next day, and then head straight for the Feyenoord game match. For that matter, Elstak's first release in 1992 was titled *Amsterdam Waar Lech Dat Dan?* (*Amsterdam, where is that?*). The ever-growing hostility between the two clubs, and between the cities, with diametrically opposed values and politics, makes the brutal music released by the producers in Rotterdam sound like war songs, gabber culture becomes assimilated by hooligans, while hooliganism becomes part of raves. If in England it was about two different cultures overlapping, in Rotterdam it was an organic fusion, a melding going as far as assimilation/cannibalisation of two cultures that glorify aesthetic and physical violence. Hardcore music, hardcore fans. This is what the local scene looked like in Rotterdam, until the whole movement got hijacked by far-right groups, which makes gabber producers respond with the slogan "United Gabbers against Racism & Fascism", printed on releases.

DON'T RUN. HOOLIGANS ON E

Not unlike England, the local scene here also came to be controlled by groups of hooligans that were dealing drugs and organising illegal parties. Rotterdam Terror Cops (RTC) became the representative DJ brigade that supported the values of gabber culture – "Rotterdam Hooligan", included on hardcore compilations, would become a new gabber hymn for the local hooligans – while Paul Elstak was disowned for turning to happy hardcore. However, he managed to bounce back onto the Rotterdam scene in 2015, as a warm up act for supporters before the Europa League match between Feyenoord and A.S. Roma. Meanwhile, he had released the song "You're a Hardcore Hooligan". If, back in the mid '90s, a show like this would have been impossible to imagine by the real *gabbers*, in 2015, Paul Elstak was shaking the terraces with a happy hardcore song, and fans were singing together the chorus of the hit "Luv You More".

The two examples are not unique for that era, but further movements have been influenced by these strains of rave culture. Italy and Austria were soon embracing the gabber aesthetic and associating the music with ultras gangs. In Scotland, following the same pattern of differentiation, happy hardcore was trending. In Germany, Eurodance and trance had been embraced by the middle-class and by supporters, and, a few years later, were going to be exported – in some cases, bastardised – successfully on the terraces of Eastern Europe.

Matei Sâmihăian

Casual Terrace Style

Side notes and remarks regarding the affective link between fashion and violence in the culture of football supporters

Cosima Opârtan

Anne Connel, Manchester, 1887.

"Life in some parts of Manchester is just as dangerous and insecure as in the middle of a land of savages" - the end of Judge Wills' speech after the arrest and conviction for murder of one of the members of the Angel Meadow scuttler gang, from a Manchester slum. The Scuttlers represented the lower strata of Victorian society and were organised into youth gangs, associated with property crimes and, more rarely, crimes against individuals. They took their name according to the area of the city they came from: Ancoats, Bengal Tigers, Greengate, Angel Meadow, etc. and they were distinguished at first sight from the rest of society by precise dress codes.

Thus, a regular scuttler wore shoes or sabots with a sharp metal tip, flared trousers, a plaid silk scarf and, perhaps most importantly, a custom bronze buckle strap, which was often used as a prop in the brawls between the gangs. The hair was cut short around the head above the ears, and the fringe hugged the forehead, covering the left eye. Above all, a cap was also worn on the left side of the head. In an 1898 interview with The Guardian, a member of the Ancoats gang said that it is enough to appear with these signifiers in Salford - a former industrial city, now incorporated in Greater Manchester - to cause a scandal. Therefore, in Victorian England there was already a close connection between fashion and violence, which, over time, fuelled critical movements, such as Mods, Punks, Skinheads and Teddy Boys, etc., oposing the ruling class and the political system.

In 1890, in their desperate attempts to stop the phenomenon, without actually analysing the real causes of these violent events, and because the prisons were already overcrowded with members of the Manchester gangs, the authorities unsuccessfully proposed the introduction of punishment by whipping, following the Liverpool model. The solution, however, came from Anne Connel, who 15 years prior had established, with the help of her father, the parish priest Arthur Connel, a men's cricket club in the parish church of

St. Mark's, in West Gorton, Manchester, out of concern for lowering the rate of violent acts committed by gang members in the area. As an alternative to the cricket game, which could only be played during summer, St. Mark's was transformed into a football club in 1880, and from 1884 was active under the name Gorton Association Football Club. With the establishment of the second football league in 1892, the club changed its name to Ardwick and, at the end of the first season of the new league, it became Manchester City for good.

From now on the fight moves from the streets to stadiums, between supporters of rival teams, Manchester being considered by Andrew Davies (*The Gangs of Manchester: The Story of the Scuttlers, Britain's First Youth Cult*, 2009) the city that gave birth to hooliganism.

Fragment from "Dialogue between Fashion and Death" - Operetti Morali, Giacomo Leopardi 1824

Fashion: Oh come! By the love you cherish for the seven cardinal sins, stop a moment and look at me!

Death: I am looking at you.

Fashion: And do you mean to say you don't know me?

Death. You should know that my sight is bad, and that I can't use spectacles, since the English now make none that suit me; and if they did, I have no nose to stick them on.

Fashion: Why, I am Fashion, your own sister.

Death:. My sister!

Fashion: Aye; don't you remember that we are both the children of Frailty?

Death: What have I to do with remembering—I, who am the sworn enemy of memory?

Fashion: But I remember the circumstance well; and I also know that both of us are alike employed continually in the destruction and change of all things here below, although you take one way of doing so, and I another.

Death: Unless you are talking to yourself, or with some person you have there inside you, I beg you will raise your voice a little and articulate your words better, for if you go on muttering to me between your teeth like that with that voice like a spider's, I'll never hear you, since, as you know, my hearing is as bad as my sight.

Fashion: Well, although it is not good manners to speak plainly, and though in France nobody speaks so as to be heard, yet, since we are sisters and need not stand on ceremony with each other, I'll speak as you wish. I say, then, that the tendency and operation common to us both is to be continually renewing the world. But whereas you have from the beginning aimed your efforts directly against the bodily constitutions and the lives of men, I am content to limit my operations to such things as their beards, their hair, their clothing, their furniture, their dwellings, and the like. Nevertheless, it is a fact that I have not failed at times to play men certain tricks not altogether unworthy to be compared to your own work; as, for example, boring men's ears, or lips, or noses, and lacerating them with the trinkets which I place therein; or scorching their bodies with hot irons, which I persuade them to apply to their persons by way of improving their beauty. Then again, I sometimes squeeze the heads of their children with ligatures and other appliances, rendering it obligatory that all the inhabitants of a country should have heads of the same shape, as I have ere now accomplished in America and Asia. I also cripple mankind with shoes too small for their feet, and stifle their respiration, and make their eyes nearly start out of their heads with tightly laced corsets, and many more follies of this kind. In short, I contrive to persuade the more ambitious of mortals daily to endure countless inconveniences, sometimes torture and mutilation, aye, and even death itself, for the love they bear toward me. I say nothing of the headaches, and colds, and catarrhs, and fevers of all sorts, quotidian, tertian, and quartan, which men contract through their worship of me, inasmuch as they are willing to shiver with cold or stifle with heat at my command, adopting the most preposterous kinds of clothing to please me, and perpetrating a thousand follies in my name, regardless of the consequences to themselves.

Death: By my faith, I begin to believe that you are my sister after all. Nay, it is as sure as Death, and you have no need to produce the birth certificate of the parish priest in order to prove it. But standing still exhausts me, so if you've no objection, I wish you would run on alongside of me; but see you don't break down, for I run at a great pace. As we run, you can tell me what it is you want of me; and even if you would rather not keep me company, still, in consideration of your relationship to me, I promise you that when I die I'll leave you all my effects and residuary estate, and much good may it do you.

"The docile bodies" vs. Fashion

"The best clothing inspires fear" - Cintra Wilson, writer, performer and cultural critic. The notion of *casual terrace*, relaxed, informal style for the stand appears in football culture in the late '70s, when FC Liverpool supporters were travelling to Europe to participate in matches in the European Cup. Noticing the supporters of the opposing teams dressed elegantly during matches, in street wear, the British supporters immediately followed this style and used it as a way of social camouflage, ditching the club's insignia and thus becoming invisible to British law enforcement. No one would have suspected these well-groomed and fashion-conscious spectators to be capable of violent acts. Moreover, the competition between the football fans was being carried out from now on also on a strictly aesthetic level (outdressing the rivals).

"Some of Coventry City's top boys were sporting Fila, who had been in business, but had gone out of fashion in London at least a month before. Instead of launching ourselves at them, we were lambasting them for sartorial tardiness. As it dawned on them they had been outdone in the style stakes, you could see the will for the contest wane. They'd been beaten and they knew it "(Robert Elms, *The Way We Wore*, 2005).

The connection between fashion and the culture associated with football is a two way street. The fashion world lends functional accessories exclusively dedicated to sport, and the players and the fans of the teams consume luxury fashion, relying on the latest trends to prove their superiority over the opponents, either on the field or in the terrace. On some level, this dual exchange is definitely contaminated by affects and affective dispositions that infiltrate and bleed into both directions. On the one hand, high fashion contaminates the terrace, ignoring the environment in which it infiltrates, while on the other hand, the supporters' violence becomes an aesthetic that is subsequently appropriated and sold back by the fashion industry. Moreover, from this loop of class resistance stems a penetrating disgust towards the passivity of the bourgeoisie, which supporters, hooligans, casuals, lads, ultras

Cosima Opârtan

apparently imitate. Violence as a last form of subversion, as opposed to what Foucault called "docile bodies", that is, bodies in uniform. The supporters are bodies that do not respect their uniform.

Another version of the birth of the fashion-centered hooliganism cult is the "Perry Boys", a gang of Manchester United supporters who appeared in Manchester/Salford around 1979. The name reflects their particular fondness for Fred Perry polo shirts. Part of this group lays the foundation for what will later define *Madchester*, namely the local clubbing scene and everything that will be associated with British rave culture, from '80s-specific electronic music, to drugs and fashion. And this connection is speculated impeccably, with a nostalgic look at the moment of lost innocence, by Mark Leckey in the short film *Fiorucci Made Me Hardcore* (1999): "In subtext, an examination of the ritual behaviour of heterosexuals on the verge of maturity" (Ruth White, *An Investigation of the Role of Photobooks in Representing British Working Class Life Since 1975 Through Research and Practice*, 2012).

The phenomenon is neither geographically nor temporally restricted, with casual culture spreading in different forms and under different names, contaminating and developing other subcultures. "Manchester, then, had its 'Perry Boys' and Merseyside had its 'Scallies' – and London, as can be seen below, eventually had its 'Chavs'. These were ostensibly, to the insiders at least, 'glamorous hooligans' but they were frequently involved in soccer gang violence and vandalism as a result of their fashion style, fierce territoriality, and obsessive soccer fandom" (Steve Redhead, *Soccer Casuals: A Slight Return of Youth Culture*, 2012).

Various clothing brands contribute to the support and recognition of this terrace culture. An important detail is to make the garments easily recognisable by means of symbols characteristic of the respective brand and the guarantee of the legitimacy as a supporter, once the agreed symbols or the logo-sign were displayed. During their trip occasioned by the European Championship in Sweden in 1992, English supporters raided a store selling Stone Island jackets. From then on, the course and evolution of the Stone Island logo on the casual scene can be traced throughout time, from its first appearance in the press. It is just one of the examples where a relatively obscure fashion brand quickly becomes massively present in the terraces, exposed to an audience that it did not have access to, afterwards to get propelled outside this culture by the media exposure of sports violence in the media.

Media works in this sense as a kind of lubricant between the two worlds, the violent stand and the exclusive high fashion. Media is often disputed for the role it played from the start of the Thatcher crusade against the "enemy within", the terrace supporter, and until it is accused of influencing the decision to convict *casual* Hibs supporters in Edinburgh (Richard Giulianotti, Norman Bonney, Mike Hepworth, *Football, Violence and Social Identity*, 1994).

The Burberry case

From the year 2000, the British fashion label Burberry, the inventor of waterproof material, registered a decline in sales and hired an American executive director, who implemented a series of marketing strategies designed at increasing the company's sales' figures. Among them, introducing an accessories' line (hats, underwear, scarves, etc.) at affordable prices and the exposure of Burberry's specific tartan pattern on most of their products, in order to increase the brand's visibility. Very quickly, however, Burberry becomes the victim of its own success, when its popularity among members of football terraces increases (caught in the media during violent acts bearing the marks of this brand) and in the social group *chavs*, defined by its "allegiance to the lower classes of society, and who ostensibly present themselves in original or fake brand clothes" (conf. Wikipedia).

The influx of news on this topic, the overexposure on blogs dedicated to the topic of "Chavs & Burberry", the appearance of memes, TV shows, etc. drove the brand's popularity into a downward spiral, losing any trace of respect and credibility from their former audience and becoming a tabloid subject (Burberry vs. The Chavs, BBC Money Programme, 2005).

Burberry marks and brand logos were then used as elements of identification by law enforcement or by owners of pubs and clubs for customer selection, being associated with the violent behaviour of those who wear them. Burberry is the most popular and most widely publicised brand case associated with violent culture. In Romania, the Burberry tartan scarf generates a similar wave of comments and memes when associated with the suicide attempt of Romania's former Prime Minister, Adrian Năstase. Moreover, scarfs are important elements in the process of identifying supporters of various clubs, while at the same time being used by those involved in scandals in the terraces to mask their face.

Power dressing

With the emergence of sophisticated surveillance systems and methods of preventing possible violent acts through facial recognition, risk groups, such as supporters, had to adapt their dress style, switching from purely aesthetic to strictly functional choices. "Any visual surveillance system will ultimately shape the dress & manner of fashion that discipline will impose on the bodies" (Dr.

Cosima Opârtan

The casual supporter makes room in his wardrobe for scarfs (which no longer bears the club's logo), sunglasses, hooded sweatshirts, all of which constitute a kind of a *scramble suit* (Philip K. Dick, *A Scanner Darkly*, 1977) intended to confuse the authorities.

"Clothing concerns all of the human person, all the body, all the relationships of Man to body as well as the relationships of the body to society [...] Sartre treats this question from a philosophical point of view when he shows that clothing allows Man to 'assume his freedom', to constitute himself as he chooses, even if what he has chosen to be represents what others have chosen for him: society made Genet into a thief, and so Genet chooses to be a thief. Clothing is very close to this phenomenon; it seems that it has interested writers and philosophers because of its links with personality, of its capacity to change one's being for another; personality makes fashion; it makes clothing; but inversely, clothing makes personality. There certainly is a dialectic between these two elements" (Roland Barthes, *The Language of Fashion*, 1969/2006). And if the personality is reproduced through clothing, this entire aesthetic construct made up of brands and *styling* denotes power; power that at one time manifests itself within its own social class in the abstract, by sporting expensive clothes for which there is no care or respect during the inevitable violent episodes, and at the same time, power obtained through physical and symbolic violence onto those outside the ultras' community.

"The stadium becomes a place with a high degree of homosociality for thousands of men. This is where they discuss last week's events, share impressions, etc. In any case, at least in Europe, the predominant model for watching a football match at the stadium is not that of a family unit, but rather that of the predominantly male communities" (Dinu Guțu, *The last Men. An ethnography of a Football Terrace*, 2015).

The casual terrace style, inextricably linked to the culture of violence and power, along with everything it represents at a symbolic level, is imported from the stadium into street fashion by social groups that have no connection with football culture. Street fashion becomes today, under certain conditions, audaciusly ultramasculine, containing its latent violence woven into the fibre of the fabric, merged with marketing violence; famous bloodstained logos leave invisible traces.

images: Gosha Rubchinskiy SS17: ©Umberto Fratini, Indigital.tv / Portrait of William 'Bill' Brooks (Scuttler): ©Greater Manchester Police Museum and Archives

Casual Terrace Style

FOOTBALL SCARVES GO WELL WITH
CROSS STITCH EMBROIDERY
AS MASCULINITY CODES MELT AWAY.
www.prosper-center.squarespace.com

Prosper Center
Ad, 2015

"We are the best amongst Romanians!/ We are Oltenians/ And always we will sing/ Go Craiova!" is a slogan created by the supporters of Craiova, taken and adapted by other terraces in the country, which sort of blurred its xenophobic nuances. Chanted for a short while in Târgu Mureș, in Romanian, by a mixed terrace composed of Romanians and Hungarians alike, the lyrics dotted every spectacular moment of the game and every victory, especially those against central clubs, with longer history and bigger prestige and financial power.

The supporters would attend the games in large numbers, even though the authenticity of the team, composed of international football "mercenaries", and not local players, and the legitimacy of the club, built on the ruins of a former sports base of the Army, were disputed. This issue was at the root of the formation of many groups activating in parallel, but, foremost, created the premises for euphoric collective dissolutions, from identitarian and ethnic points of view. The team's performance culminated with the participation in European competitions and coincided with the involvement of the board in corruption lawsuits, bank accounts freezing and insolvency.

The results were increasingly weaker, the public backed down, and being a supporter became almost a job, the official supporters being awarded with jobs in public administration. Financial support from public funds stopped, which built another hypothesis, one of relegation and a possible dissolution. The translation of the slogan in Hungarian is a symbolic rehabilitation of local pride moments. The colours of the supporter flag are similar to the ones of Târgu Mureș city, as well as Székely flags.

Monotremu
We Are the Best Amongst Romanians, 2016, Scarf

Supporters – The Heart of the Game

Ben Shave

Supporter ownership of football clubs is not something strange, or new, or confined to the margins of European football. It is embedded in its history and the current fabric of the game. Almost all football clubs began their life as associations of people wanting to participate in football and organise collectively. In many countries, member ownership of clubs was the norm until very recently.

Supporters do not make money from their clubs: they invest in them. They are not employed by their clubs: they support the employment of others. They do not change clubs when things go poorly on or off the pitch: they remain. Supporters do not view football clubs as sources of profit, or as markets, or as sources of customers: rather they are the umbilical link between a club and its local communities. Clubs represent them and their locale as much as supporters represent the club.

Today, supporter ownership touches all levels of the game, from the largest clubs, such as Barcelona and Real Madrid in Spain or Bayern Munich and Schalke 04 in Germany, to the smallest – Ancona in the 5th tier (Serie D) of Italian football or FC United in the 6th tier of English football. It is evident in the Premier League in England at Swansea City, in the Bundesliga and in the Swedish Allsvenskan.

Supporters Direct Europe has expanded from a standing start in 2007 to its current operation in over 20 countries across Europe; and demand to assist supporters in developing ownership and involvement in running clubs continues to grow. Why? Because despite the wealth that flows through the upper reaches of the game, many football clubs in Europe are in financial turmoil, the game suffers from the effects of poor governance at club and national levels, and because the potential to deliver social and economic benefits from the game is not being realised. Increasing numbers of supporters are seeking assistance in becoming involved in decision making: forming democratic organisations often known as supporters' trusts, representing supporters' interests, and building strong community links.

At the same time supporter ownership, and the idea of supporter involvement in decision-making in football, has never been under more pressure. The dominance of commercial/corporate models of governance has seen supporter ownership and involvement under threat in several countries; even where it is firmly embedded and regulated there are pressures to relax such rules; and even where clubs are successfully run as supporter owned entities, they have to operate in an environment where they compete against clubs reliant on 'benefactor' owners, willing to load them with debt in order to 'chase the dream' – a phrase that strikes fear into the hearts of Leeds United supporters, and many like them across Europe.

We believe sport will be improved through the increased involvement of supporters in governance and decision-making - and that this will also deliver wider social and economic benefits. We believe that the mutual or co-operative business structure and accompanying financial model is the most appropriate for sport as it balances cultural, sporting and economic dimensions. Our campaigns such as Supporter Ownership Week in the UK, as well as our long-term work to help supporters in France, Ireland, Italy, and elsewhere establish national organisations with the aiming of launching positive, constructive dialogue with the authorities in their countries; show that supporters are, as the motto of the Swansea City Supporters' Trust goes, "here for a long time, not just a good time."

To find out more about our work, please visit www.supporters-direct.coop. We're on Twitter @SDEurope07, and you can also like us on Facebook – search Supporters Direct Europe.

image: FC United of Manchester supporters ©Mark van Spall

Minor Football

> Stella Rossa, ASD Quartograd, Lokomotiv Flegrea Bagnoli, Atletico Brigante di Benevento, Afro Napoli United, RFC Lions di Caserta, Spartak Lecce, Brutium Cosenza, Ardita Due Mari Taranto, Atletico San Lorenzo, Liberi Nantes, Spartak Lidense, Spartak Apuane, Gagarin Teramo, AC Pozzo, San Precario Padova, Frazione Calcistica Dal Pozzo, Ardita San Paolo, C.S. Lebowski... What do these names say?

Mihnea Anțilă

The names above belong to some minor clubs from the Italian lower leagues. Minor clubs because, indeed, they are in a minority compared to the big world of football: they are minor football. In what way minor? I take here into consideration the meaning used in Deleuzian jargon. Therefore, "minor" is not a quantitive expression, but a relationship between forces, a power relationship. But the concept of "minor", in the Deleuzian sense, is not disconnected completely from the common meaning of the term "minor". The same is the case for minor football.

ALTERNATIVA CALCIO POPOLARE

Some of the aforementioned clubs represent minorities in the common usage of the term. The most illustrative example is that of Liberi Nantes, whose team is made up exclusively of refugees. Leave aside this particular case, it must be mentioned that all clubs which represent the *calcio popolare* (popular football) phenomenon, as that is the subject we refer to, adopt causes that are representative for minorities accounting for different facets of the social spectrum: racial, sexual minorities, etc. *Calcio popolare* is a generic term ascribed to certain relatively recently founded clubs that have in common a series of values, as well as a certain type of organisation. From an organisational point of view, *calcio popolare* clubs represent a model of direct democracy in which everyone, both fans and players participate and are directly involved in the life of the club and of the projects that are developed around it, the responsibility being collective. As for values, these are diverse, yet the invariable elements are named: anti-racism, anti-sexism, anti-fascism and an active involvement in the life of the local community.

Yet perhaps it is precisely this feature, of being an intersectional node of different political causes, that constitutes the stake of minor football. Multiplicity and heterogeneity seem to be the constitutive coordinates of these clubs, turning into genuine lines of flight. In Deleuzian terms, lines of flights are events, intensive thresholds that mark a transition from one phase to another – just like water changes its state [of aggregation] at 0 or 100 degrees Celsius –, being accompanied by processes of deterritorialisation that imply an increase in the heterogeneity of an ensemble, thus opening to it new perspectives. Therefore, the minority of these clubs does not consist in the desire to be recognised as minorities with rights equal to the majority, which is what traditional minority groups aim for, but in their craving to offer islands that are local, alternative to the ideology that dominates the world of football today. Because, to be frank, football today is a mirror of neoliberal ideology – a totalising, ideologised and ideologising machinery, rigidly stratified, football being seen exclusively as a commodified element. By contrast, *calcio popolare* proposes to us a process of strategical rethinking of the commodifying vision. Stadiums of modern football, these 'mall-cathedrals' in which bodies are seen exclusively as consumers, passive consumers, parts of an underlying libidinal economy, face the alternative of open assemblages, horizontally and democratically organised, in which bodies fulfill active functions, forming a collective organism, including the fans, which is nevertheless heterogenous and diverse. Therefore, from the suburbs of Naples, through the decadent and proletarian Roman [neighbourhood of] San Lorenzo, and all the way to historical Florence, standardised, molar, and globalising football is challenged by a molecular assemblage. In other words, there is an alternative to what is already standardised, typified and encoded, an alternative of opening, of an area of indetermination that allows the possibility of imagining other coordinates.

FOOTBALL AND DIRECT DEMOCRACY

Although *calcio popolare* has its predecessor in England – the United of Manchester club was founded in 2005 by some of the fans of Manchester United, displeased by the new corporate direction instilled by the arrival of the American owner Malcolm Glazer –, this phenomenon is conceptually aligned to the tradition (likewise minor) of Italian operaismo and autonomism. Unlike the intentions that motivated the founding of United of Manchester, respectively a return to certain original values, motivations seem to be different in the case of the *calcio popolare* phenomenon. In Italy there is no schism pertaining to a moment of origin, but what is put forward is rather a founding based on wholly new inflexion and check points. *Calcio popolare* does not enter a 'game of clones' or 'game of truth', like its English counterpart, because that could only determine a restoration of identitary politics.

The most important characteristic of clubs that make up *calcio popolare* is that they impose a reconfiguration of power. Thus, power is split equally between supporters (1 person = 1 vote), as they contribute actively to all the decision-taking within the club. Hence, there is a significant difference from clubs organised by the socios model (like Barcelona or Benfica), where a kind of representative democracy is being put into practice. In our case, we mean a model of transversal organisation, a type of direct democracy. This way, power is no longer appointed from the bottom-up, hierarchically organised, but we are exposed to a rhizomatic model, a fact meant to prevent the alienation of the 'common' supporter, thus empowering them. Power no longer has a radial shape, but rather a fractal one. The effect of this reconfiguration consists in the recovery of a direct connection, even in terms of affects, between the supporter and the team they support.

Because, it must be said, football was born and made possible by those who shared a common background, such as students, workers, inhabitants of the same neighbourhood, etc. However, today, the emotional connection and the common purpose of the relationship between modern clubs and their supporters can only be translated in the terms of a logic of the quantitative: "Let's have one more goal than the opponent !" - "Let's score as high as possible in the championship to obtain increasingly consistent earnings!" - "They better be good at the match, since I spent so much money on the ticket!" etc.

I do not have the intention of idealising the image of a 'romantic' football and connect it with the *calcio popolare* phenomenon, neither do I think this is what we should aim for nor do I think its representatives should choose to idealise a 'romantic' past. The clubs that are part of this phenomenon are all too immersed in the reality of current football, otherwise they would not have signed for the Italian championship, and could have fairly simply set up a parallel league, all of their own, resulting in ghettoisation and isolation. *Calcio popolare* clubs propose and desire to be genuine hotbeds of resistance, situated in a perspective of contemporary reality. Therefore, it is praiseworthy that those involved in these clubs are completely aware that resistance and the alternative cannot be performed somewhere 'outside' history, but must consider material and social conditions that are peculiar to the present age. There is no place here for nostalgia! Another interesting aspect is that these

Mihnea Anțilă

clubs also focus on developing the juvenile section, and this represents a major step ahead, since children are being permeated at an early age with the values *calcio popolare* sanctions. This phenomenon is not just a present bulwark of resistance, but also prepares the next generations at a grassroots level.

Adopting such a path is not at all easy. Primarily because there are no predecessors, the oldest club is at most 10 years old, so there are no paradigms to follow. However, this could also represent an advantage, since the future is open and not predefined. But the path taken by these clubs is one that is extremely difficult. Being in a state of minority implies confronting problems of all kinds: logistic, material, organisational, etc. So we must take into account the fact that the success of these teams was attained through enormous work, with limited resources and through a division of work that implies collective effort and responsibility. For this reason, the attitude we should have regarding the future of *calcio popolare* may be deduced from an extract of *Spinoza for Our Time: Politics and Postmodernity*, the 2013 book by Italian sociologist and philosopher Antonio Negri, that itself brings up Spinoza: "You will recall the passage from the *Tractatus theologico-politicus* where Spinoza shows that the way in which Moses built a constitution for the mutinous Jewish people who had left Egypt could not have been grounded in fear, but that it had to rest on hope, in other words, on a strong act of the imagination."[1]

---

1) Antonio Negri, *Spinoza for Our Time: Politics and Postmodernity*, translated by William McCuaig, Columbia University Press, New York, p. 47.

HOW TO MAKE YOUR OWN FOOTBALL TEAM – A GUIDE*/**

A newly established team begins its activity
- in the fifth league in the case of men's football
- in the third league in the case of women's football

In order for a football team to be enrolled in a tournament, a 'sports structure' (structură sportivă) is needed. These can be
- Sports club as non-profit private-law legal entity
- Sports club organised as a joint stock company
- County association
- Sports association ***

To found a 'sports structure' you must submit the following documents to the Trade Register (Registrul Comerțului)
- status
- headquarters
- bank account

The documents must be submitted in the original with a copy certified by a notary of the Ministry of Sports (Ministerul Tineretului și Sportului) in order to receive your Sports Identity Certificate (Certificat de Identitate Sportivă). The registration number obtained from the MTS must be submitted, together with all aforementioned documents in the original plus certified true copy to the Municipal Football Association Bucharest (Asociația Municipală de Fotbal București) in order to obtain the affiliation. Founding a sports club takes around 6 months, during which time a court must issue a decision in writing. The sports association can be done in a day. The affiliation process takes a week at most, if all documents are in order.

The staff of a football team must comprise at least
- one president
- one legal representative
- one qualified coach
- one security manager
- medical staff

The player roster
The players must be transferred if they are already registered with a different team (see the transfer forms on the AMFB's website) or will be registered at the sports club, for which they need their ID in the original, plus copies, a registration request (see the form on the AMFB's website), a health check at a sports clinic, and two photos.

A team is made up of
- 11 players + maximum 7 substitutes, a maximum of 2 extra-community players on the field at the same time. The minimum age for an adult player is 14.

The players' status can be
- amateur – are not paid
- professional – have professional player contracts

Logistic expenses
- a stadium can be rented for 250-1000 lei per match;
- Referee tax – 250 lei per match;
- Referee observer tax – 50 lei per game.

* In officially recognised tournaments.
** The deadline for the following season is August 20th.
*** A sports association (asociație sportivă) is a sports structure that has a sports identity certificate but lacks legal personality. It can only be registered into county-level competitions (organised by county association).
A sports club on the other hand has legal personality. The initial assets needed for founding an association are around 800 lei.

Information for this text was provided by Asociația Municipală de Fotbal București – AMFB. For other areas, please contact Asociația Județeană de Fotbal

Football Dispatches about the End of the World, Immigrants, and History in Images

Ovidiu Țichindeleanu

Football, the sport of the people, has turned in the past three decades into the most expensive platform of the capitalist culture industry, and it all has to do with the full-on corporate transformation of the global and continental governing bodies of football and with the technology of cable and satellite television. So why are ever-increasing numbers of people attentively watching football, on green screens with moving dots that capture and unify billions of vestibulo-ocular reflexes from the most diverse cultures on Earth?

The answer that no sports journalist will ever give is the following: this happens because the people watching at the most white-washing peaks of modernity are feeling increasingly drained, weak and gloomy. Yes, the increasingly sunken eyes of the crowds lost in TV screens need flashy lights moving against neon backgrounds, they need to attach on the fixed gaze of TV anchors, set against plastic orange skin, they need all this in order to keep on seeing beauty in this world. Beyond any simple televised football game, behind the increasingly thin screens, almost all produced inevitably by the three-starred corporation, we are stalked by the shadow of our sombre, everyday complicity to the greatest crime: the banal and disgraceful end of our world. The more desperately greater and flashier the greatest show on Earth is, the stronger becomes our attachment to a way of life that is based on the destruction of the Earth.

That is my gloomy answer. However, XM, a comrade originally from Puerto Rico, gave me a different, optimistic answer: she watches football because the times when she sees Messi live, usually in the middle of the day in the US, are also, in the midst of the avalanche of mediocrity that is the North-American media, the few moments where she feels he has access to history in the making, enjoying at the same time some respite in the middle of a workday.

In the spectrum between these two opposite affects, traversed by the perception of historical conscience, what chronicle is being written and incorporated into football itself? Let us observe three historical moments from the year 2015.

Fidel and Maradona: working against the end of the world

The year of grace 2015 came with good news: Fidel was telling the world in January that the rumours about his death were greatly exaggerated. And the bearer of the message was none other than Maradona. The footballer signalled thus his return on Telesur, the pan-American TV station founded more than a decade ago in Caracas by Hugo Chavez, showing a photo (taken from a discreet distance) of the letter received personally from the former Cuban leader. Given the whole aura of mystery – despite Maradona's big mouth – the letter seemed to have descended onto earth from a kind of heaven for the great retirees. Two months later, comrade Fidel himself would make the very matter-of-fact, analytic content of his letter public. In his correspondence with Maradona, Fidel was expressing his concerns with and exposing the oil export figures to date, in barrels, of the main countries involved in the global extractivist economy (Saudi Arabia, USA, Russia, China, Canada, Iran, and the United Arab Emirates), whose activity "poses a serious threat for the future of humankind." Fidel did not forget to mention Chavez's gesture, who had reminded the North Americans that there is another America out there, and ended his message with the following words, addressed personally to Maradona: "as you can see, I try to be impartial, and you can be sure it troubles me." As we can see, the power to situate ourselves at a crossroads in history where we still have the option to do something is being tested to the limit.

Adebayor and the endless duty of the migrant

At the end of spring, in May, a series of unexpected letters by Emmanuel Adebayor were published, in which the Togolese footballer – a few months before the outbreak of the refugee crisis in Europe – brought to light the complex situation at the other end of modern migration, of being situated in a wave that has already traversed historical bifurcations. Namely, he wrote from the standpoint of the end of the career of a successful migrant worker from an industry where the wage really feels like capital. However, the success of the migrant becomes an implicit obligation, an endless duty towards the extended family 'back home'. Adebayor listed a litany of incidents coming out of this obligation that left him drained of cash, feelings, and unconditional attachments. He ended with the following reflection: "A lot of people are saying that I never went to school, but they forget that it is because we could not afford it.

I never blamed my parents for that... Today I am able to speak more than three languages and I can send my daughter to school. I am proud of that. People can accuse me of not going to school, but in the end it is all about who you become and what you teach to the others. It is also about what life teaches you and what you learn from it. Many times I wanted to give up. Just ask my sister Iyabo Adebayor how many times I have called and was ready to commit suicide? I kept these stories for years... But if I die, no one would know my story, no one would learn from it...Some people say I should keep these stories private, but someone has to sacrifice himself; someone has to talk about it." A few years prior, when commenting on Tottenham's fans' abusive chants, Adebayor reflected stoically that, despite the civilised façade, racism is just a part of everyday life in England. Together, the limitless duty of the migrant towards his or her "home", and the everyday racism of the adopted Western "home", delimitate the tightest common space where the pilgrims of modernity are concentrated. The people 'back home' deny the historical consciousness of immigration and therefore their own peripheral condition, whereas those from the country of capital, always find new ways to express and direct Western racism. The experience of a Togolese migrant, with a lot of experience in Europe, offers many lessons, both for the middle-class Eastern-European migrants, who do everything they can to deny their condition, putting on layer after layer of white skin, and accruing as many symbolic and real debts. There's lessons to be learned also for the racists who occupy most of the public and intellectual sphere in Romania, voices in the modern chorus of a monolithic history, sailing to the end of a flat Earth.

Messi relative to the image

Summer ended with an unexpected contribution from the football world to the question about the relationship between image and history in contemporaneity. The question is all the more interesting given that in this case, history is being written with the feet and is expressed through images, by way of a literature written on the body. Also, the relationship of the character in question to speech, to discourse is... minimal. To return to comrade XM's opinion, in an age where most simple people of the world are denied the right to write their own history, what is the relationship with the image of a person who is able to 'write history'? Well, until last year, Lionel Messi's relationship to the image was simple but promising: the person who writes history could not be satisfied with his existence as a moving image on the screens around the world; so, relatively recently, in the second half of his career, he began inscribing his body with his own meanings. First, he got the portrait of his mother on his shoulder blade; then, his left leg, the maker of history, began being inscribed. On his calf, a drawing with baby hands and the name of his first child inside a heart appeared; then his shin got embellished with a kind of emblem or coat of arms: a sword flanked by roses, angel wings, the number 10, and a football. Thus far, the semantic field of the images only comprised of immediately obvious meanings and surprisingly generic symbols. What was promising was perhaps the paradigmatic contrast between the courage of tattooing two realistic images taken from life (the mother's face, the child's hands) on the skin and the predictable gesture of creating a dynastic emblem – as Benjamin would have said, allegory as favoured semantic form in the age of the commodity. But then, starting with his 2015 tattoo, also done by Robert Lopez (who specialises in portraits), Messi's choices, perspectives and the histories into which he writes himself, began to take a different shape. On his right arm, diagonally from his left leg, starting from the top are: on his triceps, Jesus with the crown of thorns; underneath, the rose-window of the Sagrada Familia; a vividly coloured lotus flower; on his forearm, on the most visible spot, a mechanical clock. That is: the sacrifice of the other as a principle of life; his gratitude towards the place that gave the most meaning to his life (Barcelona); the conviction that talent and beauty can come from anywhere, including from mud (the lotus); and the humble awareness that time passes for everybody.

Here are three *stanzas* from the world of football that speak in three distinct ways about contemporary history: those at the end of a self-made journey seeking the remaining open options in a seemingly inescapable and doomed situation; those at the end of a road that they found themselves walking on, simply putting their hopes into a message in a bottle for a stranded world; and those who still walk the road of their own making, who are taking care to write their own history, while remaining aware of their own limits.

Ovidiu Țichindeleanu

F.C. Refugees

Warren St. John, *Outcasts United: An American Town, a Refugee Team, and One Woman's Quest to Make a Difference,* Spiegel & Grau, New York, 2009

Florin Poenaru

The book tells the story of a football team – The Fugees – from an amateur league of the American Bible Belt. What is so remarkable about it? First of all, this is European football and the members of the team are kids with ages between 13 and 17 years. They have nothing in common, other than being refugees from countries such as Liberia, Kosovo, Sudan, Congo, Afghanistan, Iraq, or other war-torn countries. They ended up in Clarkston, on the outskirts of Atlanta, as a consequence of their families – in most cases, precarious and broken by conflicts – receiving refugee status in the United States. The book, by way of this one-of-a-kind football team, explores a multitude of overlapping social worlds, with all their contradictions and tensions. Although lacking academic or theoretical ambitions, the book offers one of the most convincing depictions of the uprooting caused by the refugee status, as well as of the unifying qualities of playing football.

The coach of this team is Luma Mufleh, a 31 year old Jordanian woman who decided to stay in the US after graduating from college. Here she attempted a series of businesses that turned out to be unsuccessful, but her inclination for social activities persisted. Having a passion for football, which she played during college, she takes it upon herself to coach a girls' team in Atlanta. One day, while running errands, she happens to arrive in Clarkston, which, in spite of being next to the city's airport, and thus, a periphery of Atlanta, it maintains its city status. Here, Luma is surprised to find a world completely different from the orthodox American south: women wearing burkas, African men, oriental shops, kids who barely speak English and communicate in Swahili. Quickly it turns out that the city is far from ordinary.

In the '80s, state officials decided the city of Clarkston meets all the necessary conditions to take in the refugees that the United States has pledged to relocate from the refugee camps from different conflict zones. The high-rises, the proximity to Atlanta, the highway – all of these made the city eligible for the US Government program. Of course, such a decision couldn't have left the social tissue of the place unchanged, the old inhabitants (white, religious, conservative) being disturbed by the newcomers, so that many chose to leave, while the ones that stayed developed hostile relationships with the refugees. The story of this urban transformation is in itself an important resource of sociological perspectives, yet the book does not focus on these matters that much, as, through the main characters – the kids forming the football team –, we are transported into the world they were now living in, but also into the worlds they were lucky to escape from.

The USA has a program through which, after very rigorous selection, some of the refugees from refugee camps are being brought into the country and encouraged to start a new life there. A sort of green card lottery for refugees. And indeed, for most of them this truly is a salvation, on par with the difference between life and death. But it's not as simple as it seems. The American Federal Administration does not give away, but only lends money for families to cover the travel expenses and the additional costs necessary to relocate. This amount works like an initial loan that the refugees will have to pay back from their future earnings. The administration provides support to the refugees for only three months, after which they are left on their own. Of course, many of the refugees, especially Africans, come from rural areas or lack professional training that would qualify them for better paid jobs. Many do not speak English, others are in a foreign country for the very first time. Furthermore, due to the nature of the conflicts, most of the refugee families are just women with children, their men having already been killed in the clashes or are still engaged in them. Hence, women have to work either two jobs at a time or, in any case, work very long hours in order to survive and pay their debts. The children, who have their own problems from being uprooted from their native environments and thrown into schools with rigors that they do not comprehend, sometimes not even comprehending the language and have to take care of themselves most of the day, especially after school.

Here is when Luma takes the stage again. Seeing a few boys kicking a well-worn ball, Luma decides to announce an enrollment in order to form a team. The team is organised into three age groups: under 13, under 15, and under 17. The large number of children attending the trials, but also the distance between Atlanta and Clarkston, persuade Luma to fully commit, voluntarily, to this activity. The first thing the coach does is to enforce regulations. These are strict and seemingly bizarre. The players are not allowed to skip training or be late, or else they won't get selected in the team. They also aren't allowed to have long hair or swear, and all of them have to promise they will not leave any girl pregnant. The training is exhausting and difficult, and the very strict rules alienate some of the young boys and lead to conflicts. The ones who manage to continue are fully dedicated to the team and to the coach. Also, the ones who stay don't join gangs and tend to steer clear of drugs and other temptations. The football team becomes a social support network, just as Luma becomes a member of the community and a helping hand for the kids and their parents.

The idealist image from the beginning runs immediately against material limitations. First of all, the team doesn't have any funds, while the coach's incessant attempts to receive financial support obtain modest results. At first, the poor refugee kids were playing ball with only one boot on their feet, hitting a rag. Luma will manage to provide them with sports boots, T-shirts, and footballs through donations. Initially, they trained and played on the local high school's sports field, but tensions arose with the local community, especially with the old dwellers, so they moved to a barren field. *This is like in Africa*, as one of the kids puts it upon seeing the place. Despite this, the training sessions stay just as intense, and the discipline is unbreakable. Their commitment starts to bear fruit and the team starts winning in the amateur league championship in which it is enrolled.

The pages which describe the first contact between the refugee team and the local teams, formed by children coming from the local white, well-off, middle-class families, prove to be truly memorable. The contrast could not be higher, just like the social gap separating the two worlds. However, the scores The Fugees will administer to their rivals once Luma's coaching starts to pay off turn out to be just as high.

It goes without saying that football enables social integration, espe-

F.C. Refugees

cially for those who are most marginalised and precarious, and that it offers the prospect of a community for those who are part of the team. All these are obvious in this case as well. But what really stands out here is exactly the way football represents something familiar for the refugees even before they met one another: most of them used to play football in the camps just to kill time. Their skill, their technique, which will make them stand out from the American children, was initially shaped there. This way, football appears as the only form of identity which can be transported. It's the only thing refugees can take with them from the refugee camp, the only thing that is truly their own. Football appears as a form of embodied identity that is simultaneously personal and universal.

Aside from the piercing social observations that it enables, but also the dramatic life stories it tells, the book is a homage to the power and trans-territorial quality of football. The only drawback for which the book may be criticised is that it tells us nothing about the girls from the community. They are missing altogether and it's a shame, since Luma started with coaching a girl's team. Despite its emancipating nature, football still remains, nevertheless, a masculine story.

Florin Poenaru

HAUNTED SWIMMING

Anamaria Pravicencu

I am an aspiring swimmer. I aspire to correctness. I like right angles, parallel lines, orthogonal geometry, descriptive geography, logical calculations, and efficiency. I naturally tend towards order and discipline. I count lengths, kicks, breaths, and respect a self-imposed stroke-alternating routine. I draw up plans, make checklists, number items, and check each of them off in order. For me swimmers fall into the following categories: divers, synchronised swimmers, record breakers, marathon runners, scuba divers, amateurs, dilettantes, professionals, holiday floaters, and Sunday swimmers. The first reception circle includes the other participants: you exist if you don't drown. The second comprises pool owners, record collectors, patrons, coaches, various Maecenas, professors, critics, and bureaucrats. The third circle, the audience, is articulated by the media (recordings and video broadcasts of competitions, online tutorials). The prerequisites include water and equipment. The domain's conditioning is ensured by social security, the market, value, prices, copyright, and status. The mediation within and beyond the circles is done based on reputation, relationship, history, theory, and critical studies. The means of expression fall into fixed formal categories: official, traditional, experimental, alternative, underground, and trendsetting. The subjective under layer occasionally and symbolically transpires as illness, deviancy, alienation, depression, innovation, style, grace, or subtlety. Outside the system we find miracle makers and keepers of secrets.

My sports education was not exactly neglected by my parents, but ended during childhood, even though my grandparents were committed swimmers, forced away from the water at around the age of 30 due to the political conditions of the country at the time. My mother's dual relationship to swimming became clear to me only later, when I began understanding her inner struggle between blind admiration and exhausting practice. My father quit swimming much earlier, convinced of his lack of talent, and dedicated himself to pedagogy.

During school, water was simply there. I was encouraged to dive, I received the basic technical notions, but I was never truly initiated into the harsh poetry of endurance swimming. I let myself get carried away, I went to a prestigious school, I was a hard-working pupil, and I became increasingly curious about other swimmers, water conditions, history, new techniques, and, above all, the miraculous mark of sustained practice. The Olympic swimming pool seemed a stone's throw away, but at the same time, I would curiously find myself increasingly attracted to the ocean.

Solitary swimming in running waters kept me away from pools and their social codes. Step by step they became inaccessible, while the ocean began to terrify me. I asked a lot from swimming, and, paradoxically, my own demands pushed me out of the water. Later I dedicated my work to young swimmers, building new and well-equipped swimming pools, and creating a public for new techniques and expressions. I began to believe there is life outside the water while the sound of the ocean was thundering in my ears.

Crawl is the technique that offers the greatest underwater visibility, mainly to the sides. One recent crawl technique, developed for triathlon athletes, involves a strong axis rotation of the torso at each arm stroke, keeping the elbows locked in 'windmill' position, and a slow kick of the legs. This technique keeps the body lower than in the classic crawl, the swimmer's face being approximately 20 centimetres underwater, perpendicular to the surface during lateral movement. This way the swimmer's view can traverse the width of the pool, depending on their position in the pool. If with most techniques the swimmer sees mostly the bottom of the pool, with this alternative crawl they can also see the number, technique, and speed of those in the neighbouring lanes, but also the beauty of bodies in underwater motion. The legs seem longer, the thighs stronger, the hips suppler, the shoulders more defined, the skin smoother. If from the edge of the pool the swimmers seem imitations of other swimmers, underwater each is singular and spectacular. The purpose of swimming is survival in water through forward motion. The swimmer is almost completely immersed. Contact with the air (with the real) is made only when breathing or treading water. Movement in the air is useless; it does not propel forward, and energy is lost when one body part traverses the air with strong muscle contraction (see the arms during a front or back crawl). Only when it is immersed does the body regain its perfect logic of posture and will. The visible amelioration of the body, even if only in the eyes of the other swimmers, proves the incompatibility between the two worlds and the firmness of the barrier separating them. While swimming can only borrow from styles of movement in air (see the butterfly), the air world enjoys a greater affirmation of swimming bodies and minds, of a heightened gaze, a refinement of one's relation to the air. The benefits of prolonged active experiences in waters of diverse conditions and consistencies are integrated into the air world's frame of interpretation, with varying degrees of manifestation: ability to connect notions transversally, freedom of ideas, creativity, inventiveness, vision, quality conversation.

I prefer the notion of technique to that of style. Henri Michaux believed you need to look so deep inside yourself that style – an air world notion – can no longer follow you. Immersion is encouraged and glorified by countless religions, thousands of languages and millions of transcripts, productions, and applications throughout history. Although having mostly depended on clean-water pools, swimmers have benefitted from exceptional liberties (perhaps comparable to the court jester's) but also some of the cruellest punishments for heresy, crime, scientific or moral libertinage, incompatibility with the times, unmarketability, fashion inconsistency, dependence on social circles(the public), star system.

As notions related to fame, status, education, health, and dress codes are easy to name, what remains still in the air is the question of the swimmer's solitude and underwater silence. We know that the speed of sound in water is approximately 4.3 times as high as in air. The variations are due to viscosity, with factors like salinity and temperature. There is a speed of sound in fresh water and another one in seawater. Depending on the state of the water, some frequencies are favoured. The silence in water becomes the effect of a 'lessening' inversely proportional to the speed of sound. It is as if, paradoxically, the conditions of respite came together on the side of a highway.

A Few Years Ago Exactly or the First Winter

Octav Avramescu

\\We talk about trust. Sports and political theory. Ski or sky, nebulous orthography or being in the civil registry. Appearances of courage, rebellion, contempt, and the avant-garde; they are not collective, but they develop a subjectivity with critical agency upon daily life. On his skis the skier skis. sNownows. Only sports. Real experience typified for the prosthetic shallowness of life. Affect or dialectics? The first ice skates discovered were made from horse bone. Hermeneutics or cognitive marketing? A city decided to rename itself after its sport, more precisely after a move from said sport: Christiania is now called Oslo.

//Swerve negotiation of a negationist class. Commodities are immediate infrareality and cannot be alienated for the consumer in the snow. If such a thing must be discussed, this can be done during the suiting up phase, when perfected devices for the removal and/or presurgical control of the direct experience of cold and the centripetal force on a ramp are applied normally. There is an 'afterwards' – free from mediation, specialisation, domination, or hierarchy – that can be packaged, used by bureaucrats to syphon natural resources extracted from the white gold. The skiing context successfully avoids the conflict between individual and world, it's to be eaten like a good apple. Corporally-accredited complete retroprimitive holiday, with daily minutes parabolically interrogating two old enemies: free time and team building. Alienating a part of the resource to bring it onto the slope, where it is instantly absorbed affectively into the subjectivity of the noble savage. Rousseau is the ultimate brand in skiing. Perpetuating inequitable relationships of productions in capitalist society, which have brought skiing to the wallets of the proletariat through the phenomenon of the season – summer – seaside, winter – skiing, which overlap fatalistically and ridiculously.

\\"So far, philosophers and artists have only interpreted situations", they declared, paraphrasing Marx and taking a swipe at Sartre: "The point now is to transform them, to create human situations. Since the individual is defined by his situation, he wants the pow(d)er to create situations worthy of his desires."

//The natural separation of the human subject from the world vs. demand of the impossible development of a consciousness capable of overcoming an alienation which was really the natural attribute of consciousness. You need tact. Can you tell what is purely nature and what is a social construct? In order to not live a historical adventure, of historical life? The holidays fulfil your dreams.

\\The perpetuation of alienated relations of production beyond the need for survival. Overequipped prehistory. What acceleration to use for skiing? Capitalist relations of production have always been justified on the grounds that they facilitate the minimum basic needs, and if work performed in order to survive has been the stick of capitalist relations, the possibility of achieving freedom from this necessity has been its carrot. The desire to belong in the world.

// Oh, what fun it is to suck / In a one-horse open sleigh

\\The members of this club invite themselves. The first side of the geometric space that is this free-time-consuming alley opens for a fee; it takes the form of rent. Ideally, a space where no extraordinary events can be organised. Once we are inside and have reached a thermodynamic balance with the (co-created, regardless of the concrete means – the snow you see is frozen time) natural conditions, the lack of commodities becomes obvious, as does the ubiquity of choice for inscribing pre-discursive desire on the snow, without the need for shortcuts or too much collective efficacy. Fully equipped time becomes space, and that's good. The constant struggle for satisfaction (also co-created) has partially gone beyond sports alienation, the identification with equipment in the race for perfection. It stops in its tracks when the use (and the hearing) begins, the individual emancipation of a person regardless of their degree of shelved reification and employment, alone in the complete simulacrum of victory over appropriated nature. The amortisation of equipment is realised through the amortisation of shocks, a form of spectacular prestige when seen from outside, but who looks in on this strange logic? Affective trap in understanding the phenomenon, disco ballerinas, '80s synths, Donna Summer's vestal virgins, they don't qualify due to ambient temperature and photosynthetical bombardment. Through which the concentration balance is mechanised. The kinships of kin are remarkable through their complementarity, it seems we will not go beyond these worlds anytime soon, and there is a *sine qua non* that in describing skiing we synchronise with the disco-syntagm, however anti-slope, nocturnal, flattened or erotic. Another point of rupture here, next to the open *liberté-égalité-fraternité*: on these arenas

A Few Years Ago Exactly or the First Winter

there is a complete potential of satisfying needs, whose representations they are. What differs is the fragmentation of the drive continuum. Everything is vibration. Disillusionment corresponds to a series of diverging illusions. Overstimulation and nothing left behind, nothing to take home?

//About obsolescence: desires are lifted once again high up onto the peak of the exploited mountain, which satisfies them as actuator of the ski-lift wheels. The wait as attraction/repelling point at the top is incorporated. Lifted to be let go of. And there really is nothing to be taken from the top – the momentum, the perspective are just instantiations of magnetic attraction/repelling. On Earth as it is on top – a new finality to the last forgotten finality with accelerated speed. *Așa'Isus*. Cyclical time triumphs there, infinitesimal, the linear time of means of cable transport production, a horizontal line that vanishes at the vertical. The past is too short.

\\Same as for the DJs, the equipment is yours, but not the beat. I propose a translation. So, progress is expelled, externalised between up and down, immaterial and asocial accumulation of the need to change something. But, as in literature, some characters die on the page. This is not about a style of skiing somehow similar to tragedy or to certain Romanian naturalist-feminist tendencies that associate the end of the page to the end of the character toward a certain lesson. It's no classical drama either. The representative regime is also incorporated. We are talking about the user, dependence and safety for one who discovers they have (pharmaco-)superpowers that cannot however be transferred outside the body for vigilante purposes. As the Anglophone concrete poets remarked, there is 'now' in 'snow'. And S. Above and below, more S's, in the matrix. Ow! Frost on the other hand seems more

Octav Avramescu

of a decoration thing. Old Man Frost. We're all out of ice. Powder, a material to cut-up, to overlay or subtract, to turn up or down, pass through loops.

//Snowboarding is expected to deny the spectacle that brought it into being and to reclaim its subjectivity as something else than the alternative to the union of two mythologising dreams. Silent as reading \\ Externalising touch means dreaming // Reciprocal colonisation with the locals \\ Internal immigration // Weaving tinsel for the mountain \\ The nature of describing skiing

//Sport! The skier is a critic of the snow: mythical antecedents do not burden them as they attempt to associate something like a meaning to a form. The slope is the science of snow for (but not from) skiers; the network of trails on which they glide is language, they are language. Only the first to understand that they can execute a turn has read, has spoken a myth. All the others who just follow participate in the interpretation. A search where nothing is to be found, only to make links within the finite boundaries of a circle of nonsense. However, seen from the standpoint of myth, the practice of skiing, today or yesterday, is a delirium that can still be controlled. Conversely, it is not the slope that makes meaning, extravagant extrapolations are up for grabs. Structurally, meaning is created not by repetition, but by difference.

\\Postăvarul, Vatra Dornei, ...impossible optical constraints. Nothing to reflect on, just guided transformations. Total, coherent, in a single direction.

//I had pornography and he had religion.

\\Everything cultivated belongs to culture.

A Few Years Ago Exactly or the First Winter

Cătălin Mihalache
Simona Halep, #1 Worldwide
Sculpture, 2017
acrylic paint on reinforced concrete

Raluca Popa
Reclining Round, 2017
Crayons on "statistics" inscribed paper

Ethnicity and Community vs. Nationalism and Fantasy
Thoughts about the ethnic clubs in Romania

Claudiu Revnic

An article on the Romanian sports channel DigiSport website announced that a name emblematic for interwar Romanian football was being chucked out of the life-support section of football nostalgia. Carmen București, the football pet project of the wealthy family of factory owners Mociornița was being reinstated nearly 70 years after being dissolved during the communist era. Having been closed down in 1947 as a result of political pressures the team was re-submitted into club football via League V in June 2017. The article, with a slight lingering over the paradise lost, attracted a diverse array of online comments, many of which referred to other names of the footballing past such as Venus or Juventus București, themselves victims of the nationalisation of football teams and premises that took part in that era. One comment stood out, with its user dreaming of seeing Maccabi București brought back to life. This comment was welcomed by a 'friendly' inquisitorial remark over the user's ethnic origin: „Are you a Jew?"

      Probably the most under-appreciated name on this list, Maccabi made history in the interwar period as well in the short period of diffuse capitalist football of the early post-WW2 years, around 3-4 years before it was closed down. The first Jewish football team in Bucharest, Maccabi started as an amateur club and gradually grew into a strong squad, that gave the national team a goal-keeper and several memorable matches. Beyond its status as a symbol of the Jewish community, Maccabi represents a context that is rarely explored and is generally relegated to mere footnotes in the grand history of national football: the context of ethnic football clubs. This context commences as a thorn in the side of the post-1918 national and ethnic uniformisation project and ends with an exercise in administrative power conducted by the communist authorities. In Romania, these ethnic clubs not only played a key part in the development of football in the country, but also contributed organically to the consolidation of local communities and inter-ethnic dialogue.

A professional league, my kingdom for a professional league!

After the formation of Greater Romania, through the unification of the various Romanian speaking territories in 1918, the authorities of the newly formed state channelled their efforts towards the consolidation of state identity. A sport such as football became a prime interest in this respect. In his 2014 study, *Playing for and against the nation: football in interwar Romania*, on the role the consolidation of a professional football league played in the national agenda, the anthropologist Florin Faje describes how these ethnic teams, mostly local amateur clubs, actually made up the nucleus of footballing activity prior to 1919. The most competitive teams in Romania were the sports clubs in the Transylvania and Banat regions, that belonged to the local Hungarian, Jewish or German communities. They would compete in a series of friendly matches that would come together in a sort of regional league.

In 1926, the region of Bucovina had its fair share of friendly matches between teams like Polonia, Hakoah and Jahn, all stemming from the town of Cernăuți, nowadays Czernowitz in Ukraine, representing the Polish, Jewish and German communities of that region. Many of the Romanian clubs were set up later through the intervention of academic institutions and state ministries, with the ethnic teams soon becoming the only private alternatives. One such example is the city of Iași, where the university team, Concordia, and the military one, Victoria, were managed by the state while the Jewish community supported a local private club called Hakoah. Of Hakoah, a newspaper article of the time wrote that it was the only team in the city that "played for pleasure and not to fulfil orders."

In 1921, the Federation of Sports Societies in Romania (FSSR), set up in 1912, enrolled in the plan to consolidate national sports, and as far as football was concerned that entailed creating a unified nation-wide league. FSSR had, within its administrative reach, 110 teams, however, there were some other 160 clubs that opted not to join the organisation, choosing to keep already existing more or less informal regional networks, of recurring matches and championships.

The attitude of state authorities when it comes to ethnic teams, particularly the Hungarian ones, transpires from the 1937 statement of Viorel Virgil Tilea, a former director of the Romanian Football Federation: "It's unacceptable to have a state within a state." There was even talk of an abusive minority, and those that asked for the teams be forced to join the FSSR's league or be disbanded were not few at all. After the efforts to envelop the ethnic teams had failed, some voices like that of professor Silviu Dragomir of Cluj University, suggested that these clubs be allowed to continue their activity and that the FSSR's efforts be geared towards creating new national clubs, with their own state-financed infrastructure, where dialogue between teams would take place only in Romanian. Thus, the idea of a national sports identity would shape up more clearly and some desired this, in addition to sealing off the ethnic teams. The football club Universitatea Cluj is set up in 1919, and the following year, through a petition, the Hungarian Athletic Club of Cluj University/Kolozsvári Egyetemi Atletikai Club is set up. The title history of this club stopped being part of the University's identity after the Unification.

iniorii asociației „Macabi" înaintea matchului de Foot-Bal de Dumînecă 17 August cu echipa C. F. R. în București.

Not even the agents were spared the nationalist scrutiny football was being subjected to. As their trade was in mere infancy in Romania, the agents were being labelled as traitors and mercenaries that sold off players to the "eternal enemy" that was Hungary. Towards the end of the 1920s, as described in Faje's article, the Hungarian championship had become quite competitive, more financially rewarding and more stable than any of the leagues in Romania. Hungary had become a popular destination for the best players in Transylvania, which at the time fostered the most competitive football in Romania.

Claudiu Revnic

In spite of the nationalist push and the efforts of the authorities, there was a good sense of communication between the Romanian and Hungarian players. Faje mentions a Hungarian coach for the Romanian Athletics Club as well as common training sessions between the Hungarian and the Romanian football players. Fair-play and friendship between players emanated from within and outside the football field. In spite of the polarisation on ethnic grounds and the nationalist re-contextualisation of sports, their respect for football managed to forge bonds between them.

The first ethnic teams in the south made their way within the same climate, particularly those in Bucharest and Constanța: places with the widest ethnic diversity in the region. There were Greek teams (Elpis Constanța), Jewish (Maccabi București), Armenian (EFA, in Constanța and București), Albanian (Flaga Constanța), Bulgarian (Slavia Constanța) and Turkish (Kiazim Constanța). Of all of these, Maccabi is probably the most interesting, not only due to its remarkable footballing achievements but also because its story speaks clearly about the impact ethnic amateur teams had on various communities at that time.

Maccabi: A forgotten history

The Bucharest team was part of an international Jewish sports movement that encompassed all of Central and Eastern Europe at that time. The first sports team by the name of Maccabi was set up in Istanbul in 1895, according to data published by *maccabi.org*. Various Jewish sports clubs had existed prior to that in Eastern Europe, dating as far back as the middle of the 19th Century. The founding of these teams was a reaction to the intense antisemitism and nationalism of the 'Century of Nations', with the movement growing larger in the 20th century and then expanding to contain numerous sports, from track and field to volleyball. Maccabi teams from all over Europe would take part in a competition called the Maccabiad, which is still held today. Although Maccabi was meant as socialising platform and a way of channelling the energy of young Jews, it had become, in some cases, a way in which young people from the community would explore the world outside.

Aurel Vainer, Chairman of the Federation of Jewish Communities in Romania, had played for Maccabi București Juniors team, in 1945, a few years before the team was disbanded. Vainer remembers what the Jewish sports clubs meant for the young people in the community: "In general, these ethnic clubs would take the kids out of their traditional world and into a more modern one, also helping them develop their physical abilities along the way. It was something! Just think that at that time it was very hard to get real football equipment.

Until we had that, we played in work boots and with footballs made from rags." The former Maccabist remembers also Aurora, another Jewish sports organisation, that he played basketball for. These were good occasions to get out of the community and interact with others: "I always remember how well I got along with the Armenian kids. They had a very good basketball team, EFA." Aurora also gave a few, very valuable, players to the national handball squad: "There were many young Jews that got into national teams for various sports. They were spread across various clubs, without grouping themselves on ethnic grounds anymore." In Romania there were numerous teams bearing the title of Maccabi, whether it was Maccabi București, Dorohoi or Constanța. Such teams existed in the towns and villages with a more numerous Jewish population: "I was born in Ștefănești, Botoșani country, in the year 1930. When we left there in '41, I was 9 years old. I know for a fact that there was a Maccabi in Ștefănești. My older brother got to play football for them", adds the FJCR chairman. What is even more compelling is that Maccabi Ștefănești has stayed in the memory of the locals more than the team in Bucharest did: "This Maccabi Ștefănești became so embedded in the memory of its people that today they have set up an association called Maccabi there, although there is no Jew in sight!", says Vainer. This comes from the fact that ethnic teams are inextricably linked to the environment within which they develop. These teams become the representatives of a community and of all of its people.

The neighbourhood of Dudești was that supporting community for Maccabi București. Many Jewish people lived there, with grocery shops and workshops on streets called Avram Goldfaden, Filip Westfried or Maximilian Popper; streets that have either disappeared or that now bear a different name. Maccabi had become emblematic also for the Roma community in the area. Talented football players like Jack Moisescu inspired them to get involved in sports. Aurel Vainer remembers: "There were a lot of Roma that would come to Maccabi stadium. Close to Dudești, there was a neighbourhood named Raion, where many Roma lived. Some would come to play for Maccabi or just for casual matches on the field. I remember this young man we used to call Macali, I cannot recall his real name. He was a formidable player, with incredible dribbling abilities, that would emulate the more famous Moisescu." Moisescu was the legendary top scorer of Maccabi in the post-war period.

Maccabi had a few notable achievements in football. In 1930, it became probably the first ethnic football team that gave the national team a player, in the form of goal keeper Sami Zauber, who defended the goal of the Romanian national side at the World Cup in Uruguay. Moreover, Zauber also

Claudiu Revnic

became the first agent in Bucharest. Maccabi played most of the interwar period in the second division. It was later to be dismantled, in 1940, together with the other Jewish teams, through an order given by the then far-right minister of sports. This was followed by years in which the Jewish community would be decimated through the massacres, pogroms and massive deportations orchestrated by Marshal Ion Antonescu.

Maccabi resurfaced in 1944, now under the name of 'The Hammer', or 'Ciocanul' in Romanian, this being the translation of the Hebrew word. It sees the best years in that period, in a confusing Bucharest, with one foot in capitalism and the other in communism. Hungary born Jewish coach Bela Gutman, who had played for the Hungarian national football team, was then building, at Maccabi, a strong team that could easily go head to head with any of the big names of Romanian football like Venus, Rapid or Carmen. In '48, Ciocanul București is disbanded once again, but in a rather bitter move, through a fusion with Unirea Tricolorul, a side with a strongly nationalistic support base, to create what we call today Dinamo București. The history of Maccabi stops at this point, being kept alive by the few supporters still living.

Lost and found

Maccabi's story is important not only for the historiography of ethnic communities in Romania, but also to illustrate how important the amateur clubs were for a community. These were real spaces where people met, socialised and interacted with other groups. Nationalist tendencies and the efforts to create national football, nurtured what Eric Hobsbawm called an imaginary community-when a team of 11 players stands for a community of millions that will never meet each other.

Political scientist M.E. Duerr wrote in his 2017 study, *Models of ethnic and civic nationalism in club football/soccer*, that nationalism is fuelled by fantasies, triumphant narratives and by the distance between players and supporters. The tangibility of amateur and ethnic clubs reduces this distance and conveys a real and human face to the sport.

Interesting case studies in this respect are the ethnic football clubs of Germany and the UK, which have enabled the formation of closer ties between communities and have transformed the ethnic identities of their clubs in a symbol of cohesion and continuity.

The story of Berlin based Turkish club Türkiyemspor is a wholly eloquent way to illustrate this statement. The team was founded in 1978 and was part of a wave of Turkish sports clubs set up by immigrants. The clubs were also born out of the Turkish community's desire to practice sports in an environment that was safe from the racism encountered in the '70s and '80s. Initially born as socialising platforms, the Turkish clubs had become a bridge between the immigrants and German society. Currently, the composition of the team is much more diverse: "The club has transformed itself. We went from being a Turkish club to a Berlin club" pointed out in 2013, its then chairman, Murat Dogan. He did not focus on the Turkish identity of the club as much as on the idea of a community club and the strong connection that Türkiyemspor has with the neighbourhood it calls home, Kreuzberg." Since the club was founded, we've represented the neighbourhood. The neighbourhood represents the club. The club and the neighbourhood belong together, they can't be separated" is how Dogan explained this interdependence for an article in the online politics journal opendemocracy.org.

The ethnic clubs evolve together with the community that contains them. In the UK, teams like Highfield Rangers, that represents the Afro-Caribbean community in an area of Sheffield, has also had many players of Indian or Pakistani origin as well as white players, as illustrated in the article written by sociologist Daniel Burdsey, *Forgotten Fields? Centralizing the experiences of ethnic men's football clubs in England* in 2009 for the journal *Soccer & Society*. A local football league, League Bangla, recorded than in 2007 that only 67 per cent of their players had origins in Bangladesh or India, Pakistan, and Sri Lanka, the rest pertaining to various ethnic groups, of which 12 per cent were white.

We have a similar such example in Romania, with Greek club Elpis Constanța that registered its best ever performance in the national league in 1934, when it ranked third at the end of the season, with a very ethnically diverse first eleven.

The experiences of clubs such as Highfield Rangers sau Türkiyemspor are indicators of what could have the ethnic teams have brought to Romania should they have been kept running. Maybe this is a far-fetched and daring exercise of the imagination. What is certain is that these teams are not only part of Romania's sport history, but also part of the history of communities and belonging to communities. Their story shows that the concepts of multi-ethnicity and multiculturalism are not foreign to this country and are not implanted or adapted by force and how much nationalism has dictated, and still does, many sermons of football nostalgia in Romania.

> image: "The Juniors of the «Macabi» association before the Foot-Bal match on Sunday August 17 with the C.F.R. team in Bucharest in 1930" - image from *The Jewish Illustrated*, year I, no. 1, 1930; courtesy of The Archive of the Centre for Jewish History in Romania

Claudiu Revnic

Sergiu Sas
Looking for Brâncuși, 2015, film still
With Vasile Leac & Sergiu Sas
Video Production: Mihai Sălăjan

PERFORMERS & PERFORMANCE

Florin Oprea

In the beginning there was... the regional championship

I started football, like any kid in Oltenia, on the edge of a field. The football field of my native town, Băilești. Dad, who worked as a notary, used to be, for a long time, the goalkeeper of the local team, Gloria (later Progresul). At some point, he quit and became the coach of the team, and I was co-opted, as junior, into the big team. I was centre-forward. In a regional championship away game, much tougher than today's second and third leagues, the keeper was unable to arrive on time and, because I was tall, dad decided that I should take his place between the posts. And there is where I stayed.

In the '60s, Romania's established teams had what we call today *scouters* — talent finders. Ion Voinescu, the former keeper of the legendary CCA and of the national team, arrived one day in Băilești and, upon noticing me, he introduced me to the national junior lots. Then the offers came in: Progresul București and Universitatea Craiova. My father, being a down-to-earth man, feared letting me move to the capital at the tender age of 18. That is how I arrived at the training camp of Universitatea, after a train journey to Băile Herculane.

Youth, The Pride Of The Country

A national league cannot go up in value without winning a youth championship. During my time there was a competition for youth-reserves. The young footballers played alongside players from the big team who either got suspended, returned after recovering from injury or could not get in the final 16 batch for the senior match. Just think that at Craiova, for example, young players like Cîrțu, Negrilă or Balaci played on the same team with Țarălungă, Bălan, Niculescu, Ivan, Deliu, Bîtlan and against Dinu, Lucescu and Liță Dumitru. A symbiosis which enabled great performances was being created. The youngsters hardened next to the big names. That is how, in the '73-'74 season, Balaci and Negrilă were promoted to seniors of Universitatea. That is how, in 1976, coach Constantin Teașcă got to change "the Champion of a great love" generation with "Craiova Maxima". That is also how we took up the torch from Vasilescu, Papuc, Decebal Neagu, Sfîrlogea and Deliu.

Playing in the First Eleven at Universitatea

What huge names there were in 1967 on that team! Keepers Vasilescu and Papuc, captain Deliu, Titi Bitlan, Marin Marcel, Cîrciumărescu, Mincă, a Germano of Craiova, Martinovici, the first Oltenian selected for the National, Deselnicu and, of course, the great Nelu Oblemenco. I was under tests for the youth reserve team for one year, where I also won a national title, under the guidance of Constantin Oțet. In the last fixture of the '67-'68 season tour, I entered the field in the 60th minute of the match with Rapid. In the first game of the retour (second part) of the championship I was playing in the first eleven — nil-nil in the away game in Petroșani. Without exaggerating, I put in tremmendous efforts in order to debut in the senior team: double training, both with seniors and youth. It wasn't like today, when two or three journalists write about you and you get famous overnight. Playing Division A was not for everyone. Recommendations were not enough, you had to prove in training and in matches you are worthy of playing. And a goalkeeper's life is not exactly easy. You need sharp reflexes, quick response time, courage, the capacity to coordinate and communicate with your own teammates. You have to work relentlessly.

Around Europe in 90 Minutes

I took pride in playing in the T-shirt of Universitatea in the Balkans Cup. Then followed the Inter-Cities Fairs Cup — later known as the UEFA Cup — and the European Champions Cup. Starting with the '72-'73 season, when we eliminated AC Fiorentina, and up until 1988, Craiova did not miss the European cups. Our coaches realised that international matches increase competitive experience. This is how we came to play friendly matches with teams from Bulgaria, Turkey, England, East Germany, Italy, France, Brazil, Syria, Iran and USSR. I recall the grand tournament at Dushanbe, in today's Tadjikistan, during which we played against the famous ȚSKA Moscow in the finals, or the '75 tournament in Brazil.

A Team Like a Figure of Speech

In the '72-'73 season, Dinamo took advantage of two of our defeats through diverse schemes, winning the goal average title in the last fixture. Adrian

Păunescu caused a stir by publishing an article, illustrated with two pictures of Dinamo, in black and white, and Universitatea Craiova, in colour, and launched the idea that we were the moral champions. He called us "the Champion of a great love", due to the special relationship between the supporters and our team. Universitatea Craiova always had special supporters: ambitious Oltenians - university professors, students, and working men from the former main industrial platform of Craiova - all of them sons of peasants from the villages of Oltenia. For a regular championship match, which usually started at 17:00, about 5,000-10,000 people were gathering in the stadium early in the morning, with backgammon, chess, sunflower seeds, Cico [soft drink] or packed lunch from home. The youth played at around 15:00 and the stands were numbering around 30,000 supporters. Well, by the time we were warming up, around 16:45, there were 50,000! The show was remarkable: the whole stadium chanted, sang and waved flags, "Ajax" was written on some of them, because the team coached by Ștefan Covaci was very popular. And how could you not give your best for these people? How could you not win? The supporters truly loved us. What effusion of sympathy around the country! We, those who were fighting with the department teams from the capital, with the Army, the Militia, the *Securitate* [former Secret Police]! And we'd also beat them! The public truly was the 12th player of "the Champion of a great love"! They loved us, but we also loved them. Even today, supporters who have seen me playing are still stopping me on the street to chat about football.

The Longest Day

June 19th 1974, the last fixture. Us, leading the match in an away game in Ploiești. [FC] Petrolul [Ploiești], already relegated, yet "stimulated" by Dinamo. Dinamo, home match with Dobrin's Argeșul. Nervous tension. The second consecutive season ending with a decisive match. Coach: Cernăianu, formerly for 10 years at Petrolul, where he also won a championship. Sandu Boc [Alexandru Boc], who debuted at Petrolul. Constantin Dinulescu's exceptional refereeing. As a remember moment, these were Universitatea's players: Oprea — Negrilă, Bădin, Boc, Berneanu — Strîmbeanu, Deselnicu, Ivan — Niță (Bălan), Oblemenco (Balaci), Țarălungă. Sportul newspaper graded me with an 8, debutant Negrilă took 9, while Boc scored 10! Further on? Let me tell you what second coach Oțet had written in his diary: "Goalkeeper Oprea has a miraculous moment and God does justice. Craiova is champion!!!". As if I closed off the goal.

Yet all colleagues played fiercely, since we also had to resist psychologically. Dinamo were scoring like there was no tomorrow: 7-0, close to overtaking us on goal difference if we lost. Not to mention that their match began 15 minutes later. At halftime, as I was heading towards the cabins, I stumbled upon the referees' brigade. The centre, who showed a rare fairness in that match, asked a linesman about the score in Bucharest. The answer: "4-0 to Dinamo. If it goes on like this, the match here will be nil-nil". And so it was! After the game, conflicting moods: wonder and extreme joy, tears and laughter, chants and inner thoughts.

A White-Blue Love

I achieved performance in woollen sports equipment, admittedly fine wool, manufactured at the "Tricolorul" Factory in the capital. It was white and blue, at first with striped T-shirts. Later they became blue with a wide white vertical stripe, like those of Ajax. For a long time I wore the classic goalkeeper equipment, black, but without spongey elbow pads and, for a while, without gloves. During winter I'd sometimes wear woollen gloves with front sides taken off from table tennis rackets for grip. I bought my first pair of goalkeeper gloves from Sweden, in 1974, on the return match with Åtvidabergs FF, in the European Champions Cup. At international matches we looked with envy at the opponents' Puma or Adidas T-shirts. Boots? Repaired dozens of times by ol' Jan, the stadium cobbler. The first foreign boots, for me, were Bulgarian ones. Towards the end of my career at Craiova I finally got hold of Puma boots.

The pennants and the football programmes were done by the County Council of Physical Education and Sports, the institution of the university, and the actors from the National Theatre and the Polygraphic Company. They would also draw us caricatures and dedicate epigrams to us, but one could feel sympathy in the authors' pens. Universitatea Craiova was an authentic state of mind in those days. We truly were personalities of the city. VIPs, like they say today. With flared jeans and long hair, the hippie or flower power look, like our Western opponents would wear. We, the actors from the National [Theatre] and the university professors, were the city's "cream of the crop". After each victory, supporters would come and sing to us from under the balconies, and we offered them candies. With university colleagues we were not fussy at all, because, when it came to professors and subject matters, we were all equals. We were aware of the fact that, after retiring, we will go into production and live off of the pension from our work. In football you're on top only while you play.

That '70s Show

1970s football was more valuable than the one today. Selection was extremely thorough. Every Division A team had at least three valuable players as key figures: Dinu, Lucescu and Nunwailler at Dinamo, Bölöni, Ispir and Ciorceri at

ASA, Adamache, Pescaru, Nagy and Gherghely at Steagul Roșu Brașov, Dumitru, Puiu Ionescu, Niky Dumitriu, Codreanu, Năsturescu at Rapid, Iordănescu, Tătaru, Suciu and Sătmăreanu at Steaua. Europe was dominated back then by teams from England and Germany, while on a global level Brazil was leading. Our contemporaries were Beckenbauer, Cruyff, Pelé, Gerd Müller, George Best and Sandro Mazzola.

Returning to Craiova, a phenomenon was happening here. At each match in Bănie [Craiova] there would be 50,000 Oltenians in the stands. Then there was the charm of Bucharest meetings, in Republicii or 23rd August stadiums, where we were watched by as many as 100,000 spectators. Only one match per fixture was televised at the time, usually derbies. The press was quite subjective towards us, the provincials. There were the daily newspapers Sportul, the Fotbal magazine and the local newspaper Înainte. But on air we were champions, thanks to the one and only Sebastian Domozină! The anchor of the stadium was Costică Popescu. On the TV, we were "being commentated" by names like Cristian Țopescu or Mircea M. Ionescu. The world was crazy about football because it really was spectacularly played. Imagine what a direct duel between Oblemenco and Dinu meant or between Deselnicu and Dumitrache! Or when Lucică Strîmbeanu and Iordănescu or Sandu Boc and Dobrin clashed in the middle. It was an honour to know that your match was on air and that, on top of that, you were being watched by tens of thousands of spectators.

Outside The Field

The '70s had a certain charm. We were among the protagonists of Romanian social life in those years, for our sports performances and, more infrequently, for some minor, harmless fashionable niceties. Elvis Presley dominated the music charts, but in the discotheques there were also The Beatles, Dire Straits, The Rolling Stones, Smokie, Julio Iglesias, Led Zeppelin, Pink Floyd, ABBA, Boney M and Gianni Morandi. In Romania, there were the emerging or already famous: Gil Dobrică, Aurelian Andreescu, Olimpia Panciu, Dan Spătaru, Phoenix, Roșu și Negru and Mondial. At Craiova we had Gelu Moraru, Nikos Temistocle, Gabriel Cotabiță, Mugurel Vrabete of Holograph (n.r. — former members of the band Redivivus), Paul Negoiță and Ciri Mayer. It was the age of rock music, thus long hair was trendy, especially among public people in the artsy world, but also in the sports world. In the world of cinema, Sergiu Nicolaescu started his series with the commissars Moldovan and Miclovan, Amza Pellea was a notable representative of Oltenia, Florin Piersic was in full creative swing. We were profoundly amused by Dem Rădulescu and fascinated by the art of Toma Caragiu. Stars like Telly Savalas, Marlon Brando, Alain

Florin Oprea

Delon, Roger Moore, Robert Redford, Claudia Cardinale and Anthony Quinn were shining in international cinema. Even my colleague Sandu Boc played in a beautiful film, *Nu filmăm să ne-amuzăm* [We do not film to amuse ourselves], alongside Toma Caragiu, Gheorghe Dinică, Jean Constantin, Gina Patrichi and Aimée Iacobescu. Sandu was a worldy personality, engaged at one point with the beautiful Salomea, the niece of the Shah of Iran. Another famous Romanian, Ilie Năstase, was a world-class playboy.

Football on System

We were a students' team. We fought against the political influences of the era, with the totalitarian, communist ideology. Their exponents were the Militia, the Securitate and the obtuse thinking of certain influential people, who put pressure or gave way to pressure when it came to achieving athletic performances. All Romanians experienced privations. Such as, for example, the impossibility of having access to the international music of those times. Not to mention colour TVs, coffee and cigarettes or foreign cars. It is true that we, sportsmen, earned more than the average person. On top of that, we would benefit from other perks: knowing someone at the grocery store, a good auto repairman, a good tailor, a barber who would take us without appointment, a good doctor. Sometimes we got easier access, although paid, to theatre tickets. But we could not compare to those from Dinamo. They could pass the border with foreign currency on them, they could smuggle objects brought 'from the outside'. On a sports level, we also wished for quality equipment. But perhaps also the lack of it fuelled our ambition to beat those who had it! While the great crisis under Ceaușescu had not begun yet, we had a fairly good living in Romania. We were, indeed, among the privileged, but not because we knew insiders or held political functions, but because we managed to achieve high performance through seriousness. Sports performance attracted appreciation and goodwill for us. It is said that, in the '70s, Romanians identified freedom of expression with the writers in exile, Radio Free Europe, the Flacăra movement and the results of "the Champion of a great love!"

But compared to today's football players, as Nelu Oblemenco would put it, all our lives we played football „for badges". We held amateur status, yet we achieved high performance! At some point, in the stadium's car park there were only three cars: I had an old Skoda 1000 MB, while Nicu Ivan and Boc each had a Renault 16. We could have afforded a Dacia 1300 only near the end of our career, or after retirement. Maybe all of us who practiced a sports discipline at a national level deserved a special pension or benefits. Now, in our retirement years, those of us who are still around have started to be chased by illnesses and bone pains. Back when we played football we had no recovery practices. We rarely went for a sauna at the communal baths. Only later did we have a recovery pool at the stadium. But that's life! We are left with the pride of having played football at Craiova, having won the championship and keep on being "the Champion of a great love". We, the generation of 1974!

UNIVERSITATEA CRAIOVA
ROMANIA

The young generations must learn the truth about "the Champion of a great love". About who we were and who we are. That is also what I am trying, between the lines, to tell my niece Ioana Daria, eminent pupil in the third grade and pianist at "Marin Sorescu" Art School. We must admit a fact: the authorities forgot about us, although they sometimes used our achievements for their election campaigns. As for the white-blue record, to which we also had a contribution, I read in the press that it is being disputed in the courts. This record, which normally belongs to the city, should be enriched, not subject to trial. And in Craiova, neither football nor Universitatea team should be politicised, precisely because we were opposing the dictatorial regime in Romania at some point. But we did it with an expression of values that was transported through sports performance.

> Florin Oprea interviewed by the Collective Museum Universitatea Craiova
> images: Craiova away game in Bucharest with; Euro Football '78 Panini

Florin Oprea

Now It's for Money

Landscapes of privatised children's football in Bucharest

Andrei Mihail

If Hagi, Balaci and Dobrin were at junior level now, having come from the same families, they would have no chance of reaching the heights they did. Viorel Kraus, son of the former Rapid and Sportul Studențesc player, is now the president and coach of the VK Football Sports Club. The NGO he runs is unique among the football schools in Bucharest. With the goal of using football as a social assistance tool for those who come from poor families, V.K. is the only private club in Bucharest that does not inhibit a child's access via fees taken from parents. In Bucharest, football, once a factor of integration and social mobility for children from poor families, is becoming more and more accessible only to those whose parents are in a decent financial situation. "In the past, the children were much embittered and they saw football as a rescue, an exit from the monotony of everyday life, a hope for a better future. They had "the eye of the tiger", as in Rocky, says Cristian Popescu, former goalkeeper at the Progresul București and founder of the Voievod Sports Association of Bucharest.

Schools now cost money and the places where one can simply play football with their friends without paying are not many left. The spaces near the apartment buildings have been transformed by the city hall into parks that are not suitable for the game, the school grounds have been privatised or fenced off, while the football clubs for juniors belonging to Bucharest's traditional clubs, such as Progresul or Sportul Studențesc have disappeared together with the teams or they are going stale under team owners forced by law to support at least three groups of children and juniors.

Football is a commodity: children in the age of competition

According to *scoaladefotbal.ro*, there are 53 private football schools for children in Bucharest, distributed somewhat evenly throughout the neighbourhoods inhabited by the new middle class. In Sector 5 district, the poorest of the city, there are only two schools but one of them actually belongs to Sector 4. The fees that parents have to cover vary between 100 and 300 lei per month, to which costs for equipment, the ground, referees, transport or training camps are added. Football should be harnessed for the survival and profit of most schools. One of these schools states very clearly in the manifesto published on the same website: "The main reason why football is so popular is the simplicity of the game. It requires a ball and a minimum of two players. The goals can be improvised with backpacks or clothes, and the pitch can be any banal car park. The CS Cadet Football School aims to change this landscape and provides children with everything that is necessary for the smooth running of sports activities".

The change of scenery in children's football has brought along strong competition, forcing schools to motivate their high prices to parents by offering perks such as private security of the sports ground, home transport, medical assistance or even "cutting edge lawns" and "playing surface from treaded soil or sand (not concrete), thus ensuring maximum protection for the ligaments", "zero scratches or injuries", "FIFA certified natural rubber particles, CANCER FREE!"

Voievod București opened in 2010. Like all the other clubs, it survives on monthly fees from the parents, but it also accepts children whose parents can't afford the contribution. Popescu says that it is very difficult to keep them in school without the Ministry of Education or the Romanian Football Federation, through the Municipal Football Association of Bucharest, taking an interest in subsidising these cases. This context forces private clubs to enroll as many children as possible whose parents are willing to pay the fees. "Most clubs are only interested in profit, as quickly as possible. This is true about any club, regardless of size." Gabriela Popescu, Viorel Kraus's colleague from V.K. Football, added: "The phenomenon consists in considering the child as a kind of, ugly as it may sound, commodity. You pay, you play. You don't pay, you can leave."

The highly attractive market made room for certain owners who, without having too much experience in football, have found a niche where minimal investment can produce motivating profits, as long as the parents are convinced enough to empty their pockets. Thus, the children are sought after from an early age in Bucharest's kindergartens with the selection process starting sometimes as early as age four. The little ones get into the logic of high performance sports which develops their individualism and competitiveness. Coaches, in order to attract parents to their schools, market the championship results of their teams, push the children to ever higher physical performance and use training techniques imported from professional football. The children play in competitions, they are taken to training camps and they are prepped so that parents can see how their money translates into results on the pitch. Cristian Popescu says that the coaches' practices rob children of the joy of truly knowing football, considering that up to the age of 12-13 years old they should not undergo rigorous physical training and restrictive sports goals, but simply be shown how to play football, to use the ball and to learn the basic elements of physical movement. Football, once played for leisure or at school, is being taken away from these children who, from a very young age, are pushed to function in the logic of individual success which cancels out the collective character of a team sport.

In this landscape, poor children are dispossessed of both football as game and also football as sport. The 'free' plots of land in the vicinity of houses have been transformed or privatised. The schools conceded their sports grounds to investors, which equipped them for renting, outside sports education hours. Vacant lots, once used as makeshift pitches, were also renovated or closed. Besides this, Popescu believes that today children from poor families no longer have access to football because of the monthly fee, which they cannot afford. Football is a commodity. Whoever can't afford it can't have access to it.

The wonderful and forgotten old world. The apocalypse after Andronescu

The infrastructure that enabled high performance in football until the 2000s adds to this landscape of exclusion, spiraling into perpetual decay. School Sports Clubs are one of the few remnants of the old system. In Bucharest there are just seven left and only four of them have football fields. The SSCs are still subsidised by the Ministry of National Education and Scientific Research, although the amounts received are diminishing. Parents today are forced to bear the cost of sports equipment as well as the referees' fees. In the past, this problem didn't exist, with the SCC providing the young players with accommodation in their own boarding schools and everything else needed for practising sports. The decay of sports infrastructure made parents send their children to private clubs, which offered attractive conditions. SCCs have remained the only solution for families with very low incomes. Tiberiu Mălăelea, football coach at the School Sports Club No. 1 Pajura in Bucharest, considers that the overall situation has undergone a dramatic evolution in recent years. Until the mid-2000s, when private children's football began to develop, those who used to play here formed much more heterogeneous groups in terms of parents' income. Now, the situation risks producing sports "ghettos" which, despite reaching a high performance level, are having a harder time surviving on the sports *market*.

As is the case with other sports, the state is increasingly withdrawing the subsidy for football infrastructure, motivating the lack of efficiency and performance, thus excluding any of the other social function of the sport. Ecaterina Andronescu was one of the most ardent opponents of the SSCs. During her mandate at the Ministry, she repeatedly discussed the need to resize these clubs, depending on the sports performance obtained. But another minister took her place until she got to impose her policies. However, the already limited budgets of institutions are shrinking year after year, leaving them without administrators for sports bases, with buildings for which they can't afford renovations, and with teachers forced to devote their time to private clubs, in order to earn some extra income.

The disappearance of the sports bases and the privatisation of school grounds create additional problems for these clubs, which must seek places to train their children farther away. Except for the aforementioned School Sports Club No. 1, the others are forced to squeeze in the players in the renovated spaces belonging to other schools, between the official P.E. hours and the hours when the space is rented out, or to use what's left of Bucharest companies' sports bases, which are increasingly less and poorly maintained. Mălăelea says that, after 1990, Bucharest lost 42 large sporting grounds, which disappeared along with the privatisation of the units that managed them. Thus, clubs need to move further and further away from their headquarters in order to carry out their activity, which makes it difficult for many children to gain access to. For many parents, it is difficult to join their children for daily training, which, although organised by the local school club, ends up taking place in other neighbourhoods.

Andrei Mihail

The social mobility that football made possible is also restricted by switching to professional football. Tiberiu Mălăelea notes that this is still appealing to children coming from low-income families. No high performance footballer, he says, has been raised in Bucharest by private football schools so far. The problems for those with life-long hopes of making a living from football start at 16, the age when a teenager has the opportunity to become a professional in any team that plays in one of the first three leagues in the country. But as professional football is no longer profitable at a low level, the number of teams that could legitimise a young player has dropped dramatically. In League 3, for example, there are currently four clubs in and around Bucharest. By comparison, in the 1990-1991 season of the former C Division, the 5th Series, to which Bucharest was also included, comprised 13 teams from the capital and its proximity.

"Football isn't what it used to be during my days when we practised sports for free and ran like crazy with our backpacks. Now it's for money!", Gabriela Popescu from V.K. Soccer deplores the situation. The de-industrialisation, together with the withdrawal of state subsidies for school sports gives more power to clubs that speculate the children's need for physical activity and development. By being privatised this way, children's football becomes a commodity which is being monetised by the recently established schools. Football gradually isolates those who can not afford it, to become a kind of gated community with prohibited access to those who do not pay the entrance fee.

Now It's for Money

The New Old Teams
Short Guide to Football in Late Postcommunism

Petrică Mogoș

Romanian football is a more than suitable image of how the processes of post-revolutionary privatisation have informed the entire society on its way to a Western kind of neoliberalism.

As a symbolic, yet wholly representative, object in the public sphere, football leads the way in the structural reconfiguration inflicted upon the local sociopolitical dimension in the last nearly 30 years. Even though, in this whole system topped by poverty, stratification and social exclusion, football seems to be the least of problems, the capitalism's capacity to consume and metabolise any apparently (or, at most, formerly) subversive instrument, to convert any element with dissident potential into a commodified product, must not be ignored. Football itself thus became a useful tool for understanding economical and social-political phenomena, but also for decrypting the relationship between the sporting level and the private sphere in the context of postcommunist neoliberalism.

Romanian Football Seen Through the Lens of Privatisation

Neoliberal politics – including, among others, those of privatisation, excessive mercantilisation/commodification/commercialisation, or maximising profits – present themselves as solutions that appear to be absolutely reasonable: a single resolution, interpreted by the majority as essentially normative, even banal, yet serves *de facto* the interests of the *status quo*. Or, pursuing the application of Gramscian hegemony, become solutions that are scoured and chewed in the public discourse until earning the rank of *sensus communis*. In this instance, the transition towards capitalism has lead to a colonisation of the way of thinking, hence to a synchronisation of discourses and practices, one that surpasses the purely symbolic level, with Western, neoliberal space. Neoliberalism, also deeply embedded within sport, presents itself, therefore, as the only possible reality, the sole version of a truth that deserves to – and must! – be embraced. Any alternative to this universe becomes an utopia that cannot and, of course, should not be achieved. In East European football, the privatisation mechanisms have become determinant, ubiquitious phenomena, depicted as absolutely necessary to ensure a competitive, *ergo* healthy market, and, eventually, the very survival of the clubs. Aspiring in this way towards a neoliberal anti-utopianism, which leaves no loopholes, the collectivity is subject to mass errosion, while society remains formed only of individuals hunting down their own best interest – in our case, supporter-citizens turned into consumer-citizens, dedicated football players turned into opportunistic football players, or emotionally involved leaders turned into exclusively profit-oriented owners.

Following these emergent aspects in Romanian society, what social constituent is more representative of these existing transformations, if not football that is seen as a unit in constant correlation with the Western space?! Football, with its identitarily battered clubs, with histories that are either defunct, either metamorphosed in absurd mutant hybrids, with exploited and unpaid players, merely driven by vows of financial gains and/or by the promise of a very lucrative transfer abroad, with club owners determined to buy success or, on the contrary, obtain it through the minimum effort, with supporters alienated by paradigm changes, the latter becoming, from the inherent purpose of football, years ago, to a mere means of stimulating consumerist habits in contemporaneity...

Considering that at the root of these changes lies the transition to a neoliberal capitalism, this article must be understood as an attempt to briefly categorise the mechanisms that propel privatisation processes. The purpose of these classifications – otherwise, non-exhaustive and mutually conditioned in their entirety – is not to draw general conclusions regarding who lies behind the masks of the new old teams, or who controls at present their history, brand, track record, bearing in mind that such an approach cannot produce a result that is veracious or agreed upon by all parties. Furthermore, considering the fact that each actor, whether direct participant or latent observer – the club, the player, the owner, the supporter, the state –, traced their own faith according to local and regional circumstances, those of neoliberal postcommunism, I will not focus on a single case study. Instead, this article intends to deconstruct neoliberal patterns through an archeology of the privatisation operations that infested the indigenous football, and, in the following, to dwell on privatisation as angst, as hedonist hobby, but also on the answers to privatisation through counter-hegemonic practices.

Two Case Studies: Steaua and Rapid

Immediately after 1989, the teams that were previously attached to the various state apparatuses could see on their own how the smiling opportunity of privatisation looked like. As the implementation of a new hybrid socioeconomical model occured in the middle of a barren ideological space, deliberately sanitised of its own Communist past, sizeable connections between the phenomenon of privatisation and the general crisis of East European Reformism could be observed. This transition was based, among other things, on the renegotiation of the relationship between the state and (the varied forms of) capital, on the overexploitation and precarisation of work, on the deregulation of industries and the introduction of fiscal reforms that minimised legal obstacles in the pursuit of profit. In most cases, such massive restructurings led to a legislative void that transformed the state of insolvence into a redeeming circumstance, into a lucrative finality for club owners.

From the very beginning it must be mentioned that Romanian privatisation lacked an absolute radicalism, following a rather slow, gradual process of implementation, not abrupt, so as to perfectly recall of the shock doctrine. Through such operations, which stimulated alienating identitary crises, the ownership of clubs was transferred from the jurisdiction of fan communities – that, although symbolic in many cases, exerted a considerable influence on decisions taken by the management – to businessmen, especially, who are not concerned with the aspirations of the stands.

Among the most publicised examples, in which privatisation induces a kind of troubled identitary angst, are legal and existential crises, such as the case of Steaua, and gradual phenomena of disappearence and reappearence through insolvency, bankruptcy, dissolution, rebirth, as in the case of Rapid. In the first conjuncture, that moved a perpetual legal epic, the team

Petrică Mogoș

fractured in two conflictual entities: the state, represented by the MApN [Ministry of National Defence] and supported by the majority of the former glories and by the ultras, and the private, represented by the current leadership, by people that are loyal to the owner, and supported by the younger generation. In spite (or, more likely, because) of a common desire for fast earnings, both sides involved in the great schism share, in discourse and practice, similar mechanisms: from overinterpreting legislation, patching up history so as to fit their own narrative, to employing the tentacles of power to destabilise and subvert the opponent. In any case, during this fight that, since long before, holds no more connection with the sport, a crucial question seems to have been left out by the two parties: in the context of excluding supporters from the equation, is the sporting (and, accordingly, economical) success worth the price paid for the identity crisis?

The following iconic process that pertains to the identitary dimension, that of Rapid, unrolled in several catastrophic episodes: financial liabilities and losses, fights with the revenue authority, bizarre swaps between creditor owners and condemned owners, damages, confiscations and lawsuits, huge debts and complete dilapidation, bankruptcy and dwindling, re-emergence and confusion. Following these more or less chronological steps, identity disorder reached a point where, in the post-privatisation/post-bankruptcy era, there were no less than five initiatives, from associations of supporters or unionists, to the municipal council of Sector 1 [Bucharest], all self-invested as legitimate continuers of the former Rapid. In the formation of these ghostly teams, rhetorical battle transcends once again mere trailing in the collective memory, having little to do with pleasing the befuddled fans. Both in the case of Steaua and in the case of Rapid, the ridiculous media show serves the interests of political-bureaucratic clans that, at some point, will secure the winning stamp, without it bringing any benefit for emotionally involved supporters. Thus, the faith of these cynical mutants will, probably, be settled through political will, will that shall remain the decisive agent in determining losers and winners.

Football As Source of Power

In exchange for a simple custody based exclusively on the defence of community interests, the new status quo pursues the growth of capital through any means. Therefore, clubs take on abilities that are adjacent to their primitive, yet primordial purpose in neoliberal capitalism – accumulation and maximisation of profits. Following the ideas of Pierre Bourdieu, capital transcends mere monetary matters, that, unquestionably, remain central and manifest themselves socially, politically, or through media, thus clubs are turning into literal trampolines that bring various benefits to those from the ruling class.

Out of opportunism or fortunate circumstances, numerous oligarchs were clever enough to stimulate initating the process of privatising teams with pedigree. Most likely, their real motives seldom had to do with the emotional connection with the administrated teams, pertaining, more likely, to a lust for personal enrichment, the growth or conservation of a goodwill – that, most of the time, increases/decreases proportionally with the success of the team – and, not in the least, to serving as a springboard for a future political career. Like the capitalist system itself, stimulating a hierarchisation by material criteria under the guidance of a supposed legitimising meritocracy, football too is hermetically laid into a genuine pyramid structure: at the top – the owner, at the bottom – the supporter. In such hierarhical models centered on leadership we can observe the inauguration, most often self-induced, of the cult of personality, in which capital infusions justify and forgive any kind of slip. The superstratification of the system and the absolute subordonation by the ruling class also sparks the burst of related phenomena – the liberating cult of capital and of the private space: "I put in money, I do what I want!".

Through their anchorage in the sports spectacle and, thus, in the social imagination, the upstarts of the transition strengthen their symbolic capital, using it most often for their own purposes, whether we mean using their clubs as personal toys, or refer to the usage of goodwill to enter politics. We can observe that, for many of the post revolutionary riches, the phenomenon of privatisating teams with pedigree is equivalent with the opportunity to step into the spotlights, playing on/for lots of money, to plunge deep in their own bourgeois-hedonist hobbies. All this playing, once it reaches its peak (regardless of its failure or success), ends in waiving leadership and throwing the club into an administrative and financial limbo without favourable perspectives. The case of Unirea Urziceni, one as radical as it is iconic for the agitating forces of the private space, remained in history as having, perhaps, the steepest rising and the most unexpected undoing: promoted into the first league in 2006, its winner, turned into the representantive of the smallest city in the history of Champions League in 2009, dissolved in 2011. Following this path that goes beyond the mere features of sports, the received money was put into the real estate projects of the owner [from Ialomița county]. In the year Unirea disappeared, the torch was picked up by the rising/falling of Oțelul Galați, who surprisingly won the title of national champion in 2011, qualified in the groups of the same European competition and dissolved in 2016. If the success of the trophy pro-

Petrică Mogoș

pelled the former owner into the city mayoral office in 2012, afterwards the team became the propriety of an insurance company owner, who charged the club with rates that were bringing profit to his own nearly bankrupt company. It seems that, judging after these facts, in the era of post-privatisation, the road from apogee to perigee lasts no more than five years.

More than that, a brief archaeology of the last three decades shows us that football stadiums, and especially their stands, can serve as popularisation platforms for successful political characters. But, since sports events most often carry a bigger interest than politics, providing for many the illusion of direct participation, so do the figures involded in football seem more real than political ones, offering personalities the masses can identify with. In this context, an interesting aspect is represented by the ubiquity of neoliberal manifestations, where such an omnipresence of discourses and practices, that are equally accelerating and blurring the relationship between the private, politics, and football, is proved by the interdependent character of the patterns of privatisation. Thereby, the aforementioned ownerships of Steaua and Rapid, identitarily devastated, have also been directly involved in the phenomenon of privatisation as springboard: in the last decade, both clubs spawned parliamentaries, presidential candidates, party leaders, deputy prime ministers, senators.

Between the Popcornisation of the Stadiums and the New Antihegemonic Models

The path of free regulations, on which autochthonous football stands at the moment, draws consequences on several levels. The considerable financial expansion is led, one way or another, by the commercial exploitation of a loyalty towards the brand and the history of the club. In the case where this brand is genuine, it is wholly assumed by fans, and through an efficient mechanism of sudden valorisation of the collective identity and of sustaining a common cause, 'the benefit of the team', supporters either surrender to the pressure exerted by the new owners or quit for good. After all, the cost of the incapacity to compete with the other clubs that invest, and by investing attain success, may be catastrophic both for the fans' pride and for the treasury of the club. Nonetheless, debts often become insurmountable and threaten with insolvency, bankruptcy or the perishing of the team. Such transformations – and others, such as the high wages of football players compared to other professions, but also hypocritically crucifying them for it – represent but a consequence of the complete subordonation of Romanian football to the discourses and practices of the post-Fordist era.

The New Old Teams

At the same time, just as the older, yet nostalgic and knowing, public gradually fades, neoliberalism encourages the appearence of emerging niches of supporters: if some declare themselves unsatisfied and disappointed, preferring to stay home, others enjoy the gentrification and 'popcornisation' of stadiums, where the experience in the stadium began to focus on the hotdog and cup of cola bought during break time. As the model of the old fanbase, oriented on the representation of the community and working class, fades away, the proliferation of technology leads, among other things, to alienating fans, who witness their own metamorphosis from supporters to consumers of online content.

Finally, privatisation processes have been countered, at least on a symbolic level, by the deployment of certain supporter organisations in counterhegemonic practices, by the attempt to decolonise and liberate teams from the claws of the private space. Thus, fans cease to claim any longer identities that are lost in the bureaucratic thicket and set up, on the ruins of the old teams or new teams. Showing that supporters do not have owners and that football needs to be there where they, and not the mayors or landowners, are, such fans have revived the old remains of significant historical teams, such as Oțelul, Petrolul, Argeșul, Timișoara, or Farul. Although classifying these initiatives among activities with dissident and anticapitalist potential could represent an exageration, such organisations could produce in the future a microcosmos that is alternative to current normative structures. Through the establishment of entities with a less doubtful authenticity, such initiatives have the capacity to reclaim at least the importance of the supporters within the sporting life of the loved club, but also to provide new perspectives with favorable potential, in order to destabilise the hegemony of fanatic capitalism. The tradition of historical clubs must go on, bearing in mind that, at least through a symbolic dimension, this phenomenon announces a struggle that may take on, here and there, a class character, which may turn football from its path to maximising the profits for private third parties back to the interests of the local community.

illustration: Anna Grozavu

Petrică Mogoș

Ion Grigorescu
Clubul Sportiv Rapid, 1973
Litho on canvas, 130 × 97 cm, from the *16 Februarie 1933 – 1973* exhibition
Courtesy of The Visual Art Museum Galați Collection

I don't think sport belongs to anyone

Interview with Violeta Beclea-Szekely

Sorin Popescu: My main interest for this dialogue starts from an intervention you made during the *Sports Heritage. Urban Sport Bases of the 20th century* conference. Speaking of space and memory, what memories do you have of the places where you practiced running over the years and what image pops into your mind when you think about the transformations of those places? Or, in other words, privatisation and development, what remains and what disappears?

> **Violeta Beclea-Szekely:** I started out in Suceava. The stadium there, Areni, was mainly for football, but there was a running track there too. I started out practising on slag, and I ran on that slag track till I got sick and tired of it! And then I went to compete, on a rubber track. But I never complained: "Oh, I never trained on rubber, so that's why I didn't make it." On the contrary, you would train in harsher conditions and you'd perform better on synthetic surfaces. This is something I tell these days to kids who complain all the time: for better or for worse, compared to my time, there are more proper sport facilities available nowadays.
>
> The idea was that these surfaces were very well kept. Locally, at our club, there was someone whose job was to scratch the slag so it didn't spoil. The town hall would occasionally bring slag as well, and so everything was well kept. I was just there recently, after decades – the field looks terrible. The track is no longer a track, it could be a wild field just as well. I'm still adamant that sport facilities should be administered by the direct beneficiaries, because they are the only ones capable of tending to them.

What does "direct beneficiaries" mean?

> The federations, clubs and sports' associations should run the sport facilities, basically the structures that represent sport and bring players together. Probably as soon as sport becomes de-

centralised, as some would have it, the facilities will fall under the town hall's administration. Yet, I wouldn't have things this way because I'd love to see them run by the direct beneficiaries, with local support from the town hall for refurbishment and maintenance.

Do you see these beneficiaries as able to do management work?

I see them as administrators. Just a few days ago I was talking with the coach for the Olympic female boxing team, and he was telling me that the hall at "23" (– *the former "23 August" sports centre*), which is under the administration of The Ministry of Youth and Sport, is used mainly for extra-peformative activities. All sorts of companies rent it for football. And so we ended up discussing the Viitorului Stadium, the one with the rubber running track that is also in the Lia Manoliu area. Anyone can walk on it, from moms with strollers to kids with dogs. If it were under the Athletic Federation, things would have been different. Maybe it could have had a programme oriented towards performance, with time slots divided between sport activities and leisure. But, unfortunately, it is not so. And I hardly think that the current programme is actually geared towards self-sustainment through renting out to private persons.

I'm curious to find out more about what property means in sport. To whom does sport belong to? Who is responsible to whom and why? There are privately owned and state-owned sport clubs, municipal clubs, clubs financed by the Ministry and by other institutions...

I don't think sport belongs to anyone. I mean sport in the sense of sport discipline. On a hierarchical level, it goes like this: clubs are under a federation, which is under the Ministry, and the sports associations are affiliated to the federations. All federations are members of the Romanian Olympic and Sports Committee (COSR) for representation at the Olympic Games.

I think sport is a product of the people, the nation, taking into account all these entities. With this chain of command, federations are independent organisations, even though they are state funded.

There are also sport disciplines where private clubs function well, especially for team sports. On another scale, private

I don't think sport belongs to anyone

> clubs function also in running, fencing, fighting or judo. They don't necessarily have their own logistics, they still use the public sports centres. By paying rent you can train anywhere. The benefits private clubs bring are that they open up the area of performance and increase the number of participants in the respective sport discipline.

Compared to the time before the Revolution, when everything was centralised and controlled by the state apparatus, what is the state of sport facilities today?

> It's obvious that, overwhelmingly, the infrastructure is not favourable for high performance anymore. In some cases, where sport centres have been modified and refurbished, there is some evolution from the bygone era. But when it comes to numbers, we're miles away. Perhaps if there were fewer sports centres being closed down, we would have been richer today. A lot of sport disciplines are impoverished due to disappearing centres.
>
> If we were to talk about the centres that closed down after 1989, I couldn't give you an accurate percentage because, unfortunately, no state institution has info on this, not even in the capital, which is not right at all. I think it is the Ministry's job to produce these statistics.
>
> During my evolution I ended up training in Bucharest at some point. Speaking of the facilities here, they've suffered major changes. If Viitorului stadium had a slag track, now it's soft rubber. Same with Piatra Arsă. Centres have evolved – I'm strictly talking about the places where I trained, not those which became targets for businessmen – with the exception of the one where I started, which looks terrible now. I've heard of an attempt to have a mall built there, in Suceava, which turned out to be unsuccessful.

Do you think these changes in quality, but also quantity, have reflected also in sports performance? What was the state of things before 1989? What about after?

> The situation is the same for both people within the sports disciplines as well as those outside them: sport is in a free-fall. Moreover, I will say this is the society's level, with sport being nothing more that its mirror. We are all free-falling.

Interview with Violeta Beclea-Szekely

Are there many sports centres that changed their use, beyond the places you have personally trained at?

> There are a few. In Bucharest, there's Voinicelul, Metalul Sports Club's centre, on the outskirts of Pantelimon, as you exit the city. Once used to be a slag stadium there, but now it's a super market. CS Metalul closed down at some point and lost their sports centre. Or maybe they've sold it.
>
> Now we are confronting with the situation of BNR sports centre in Cotroceni, left in disrepair. It's probably no accident, though. I hope people in sport will do all they can to save it. It's an enormous centre, right in the middle of the city. There's probably big interest from the real estate and I can imagine that someone important has been eyeing the place.

How are these spaces protected by the law?

> The law is favourable, protecting sport heritage: if you demolish a centre, you have to build a new one there or elsewhere. We, the athletes, were confronted with the situation where 'Lia Manoliu' stadium, which also had a running track, was transformed exclusively into a football stadium, while we were being promised there would be a new running stadium in return. Nothing got built yet. It's easy to understand how closing down sports centres impacts on children who might wish to play sports. For example, in that part of Bucharest (*near the former sport club Metalul*) a lot of people complain about not knowing where to take their kids to. There is no space for practising, and I don't mean a proper club, but a favourable space, a stadium or sports hall. And so, younger generations are deprived of places where they could consume their energy, and why not, get selected for high performance. We often complain that the selection process is not what it used to be, but one of the main reasons for that is the lack of facilities.

Constantin Popovici, a diver, trained by diving onto mattresses. Adrian Solano, a skier, trained during the summer with an improvised device with wheels. The late Maria Cioncan was so happy she won bronze at the Olympics as if she had won gold, saying she had finally beaten poverty. They are athletes who didn't practice under proper conditions but managed to reach high performance. How do these examples speak of the condition of the athlete?

I don't think sport belongs to anyone

Across the street from the Athletics Federation, there is a centre called Club Triumph which was, I think, the first centre for artistic gymnastics in the country. I went in out of curiosity, it had a broken roof. Some very cute little girls were training there for rhythmic gymnastics. When the parents saw me come in, they rushed over: "Are you going to fix our hall?" – "Well actually, I am with the COSR, not the Ministry, I'm not even in the club that owns the centre." They told me they use buckets when it rains, and that there is no central heating even. A moment like this reminds me there are probably thousands of cases like this across the country. But paradoxically, the satisfaction is greater when you reach high performance under these conditions, when you defeat your context and overcome your condition. We didn't have an indoor running track, but we brought out European and world champions in this discipline. I remember we used to train at the Felix Baths, on the snow. The snow would squeak under our feet, we would shovel it aside and make a corridor before training. Then we would go to indoor competitions and take all the medals. All the competitors were tanned, we were all white. Those were different times, different motivations, different determination. I don't know what in the world is going on today! For a few years now, we've been talking about the generational shift. Perhaps the new generations that will carry on will rise to the level of those before them. Rowing succeeded, it seems!

The fact that some athletes manage to outdo themselves is due strictly to their will, perseverance, tenacity and their work. I don't believe, however, that we have reached an era where sport performance will be increasingly individual, devoid of context, of a community strategy or tradition. We have to invest in sport facilities. These will benefit not only the performers, but also society and the community.

The athletes mentioned earlier are, without a doubt, illustrating the precariousness of the infrastructure. I hope that the state will take care to build adequate sports facilities, but these are directly proportional to the standard of living and the education system. These should grow and develop.

Interview with Violeta Beclea-Szekely

The states that have invested in sports are the ones winning today. In the old days, many of them were behind us, the ones from the East. I think they invested in infrastructure for one reason only: the health of society and the education of young people. And that's were high performance comes from! It is completely different when you have sports facilities within every university and high school.

People say I have a treasure chest. It's actually a small trolley bag filled with newspapers, diplomas, filmed footage and a personal archive to keep me company when I'm old.

Coming back to an earlier question, is there a trend of stadiums without a running track? For example, supporters of the Dinamo football team lobbied to build the new stadium without a track. Is there any antipathy towards other sports or is it the spectacle that dictates this?
Perhaps this trend is dictated by the fact that the supporters want to be closer to the field and to the players. A running track with many lanes keeps them farther from the game. But it's admirable that supporters manage to change such things, that

I don't think sport belongs to anyone

> football has such a large number of supporters, that they can modify or make their contribution to how a stadium will be built, with or without a running track. In other sports this does not happen. If we were to observe the results at an international level, many other sports have better results and would be deserving of support from the fans.

Is this an asymmetrical and populist relationship?

> I think it's a reaction of admiration from people who understand this sport. From a young age, the first contact with sports is football. You have a ball, you kick it. Even a toddler who can't walk will do the same thing. Maybe this is why it is a better understood sport, a popular sport, a sport with social connotations of coagulation around the phenomenon, which is not the case with other sports. That is why it is said that football is football, and all the others are just sports. With football, people meet and socialise. At other athletics events the stadiums are unfortunately empty. This absence felt more strongly in individual sports.

This is also true for the media coverage. TV stations broadcast football much more often that other sports.

> Very few sports other than football are televised; some sports, not at all. Only a few minutes during the Olympics, if you are lucky enough to compete in a trial that is being broadcast. There is no interest. But when it comes to football, stations fight over broadcasting rights, and this high interest, the existence of a large number of spectators and viewers, generates money. The keyword here is money! TV stations will never film an athletics championship from start to finish. I don't think I've seen more than five minutes of a National Athletics Championship on TV. And this was on TVR 2 (national channel), not 1. Other TV stations don't air even this much. In order to attract the audience, viewers need to be given as much information, as many pictures, as many contests as possible.

> Sports journalists are probably extinct as well. There are no nationally distributed magazines, except for the Gazeta Sporturilor, which has also reduced its print run. ProSport is now available only online. The Sports Department from Antena 3 (TV station) also disappeared. I don't know what happened to all those journalists, where they went...

Interview with Violeta Beclea-Szekely

There is no more relevant sports analysis because there are no more specialists. Now, sports commentators comment on everything, but none of them are capable or ready to go into detail on a particular sport, because they are not specialised. We can talk about the aspect of global marketing in sports - we comment on everything. But as things stand, I do not think fans can find out, beyond the names of the athletes, a great deal of things about a certain sport, because it is quite difficult to get acquainted with its history, with the athletes competing, with the techniques of approaching the competition, with tactics. The element of emotion is not identified in the broadcasts either. In order to know a sport you have to go beyond the internet research level. You have to see live training and junior competitions. If you don't, you can't really comment on anything. From my point of view, these kind of commentators are spectators who think out loud.

At local level there are problems with sports administration. From your point of view, what is the relationship between those who hold the power and the way sports are carried out at school, amateur and professional level?

I wouldn't say there is a relationship. I'm talking about the Ministry of Sport, the Ministry of Education, the important institutions. They should have a common protocol in order to enable high performance. I don't think the local authorities are ready to take over the mass and performance sports activities, in an attempt to decentralise sport. Over time, probably, we will witness the disappearance of some sport disciplines altogether. In this respect, the individual sports are the most vulnerable. The city halls are not yet prepared to take on everything that sports on a local level entail. Their main interest would probably lie in the cohesion between the public and the athletes rather than the sports activities themselves - so, in team sports. We must admit that team sports succeed in creating a following for the sports' movement. Spectators behave differently to a game of handball, basketball or volleyball, etc. as opposed to athletics. People feel like belonging to a team and associate it with a form of patriotism. "I am also Romanian", "I am also ...", and this team represents us locally. It's an undeniable truth.

I don't think sport belongs to anyone

> Sports administration is a matter of depth, it is necessary to involve several factors. I'm not just talking about the Ministry, the one that ultimately generates the strategy. Besides it, the COSR, the Ministries of Education, of Internal Affairs, of Health must also come together. There used to be a protocol between these ministries in the past. Beyond that, it is also necessary to implement the strategy at school level, because that is the very basis where selection starts. That is why the Ministry of Education is needed. I'm talking about Physical Education classes and inter-school competitions, which don't exist anymore. This is how the selection is made. Otherwise, how would we know if there are any potential athletes, with inclination towards one sport or another, if there is no place for them to showcase their qualities? In the old days, big club coaches would travel to make selections. For example, Dinamo came to my village for selecting handball players. I was running fast between the goals but didn't handle the ball too well. There probably isn't any more funding for this kind of activity, because it involves transportation, accommodation, meals and a schedule. What happens to the kids who get selected? You have to provide them with school, accommodation and so on. There are many things that need to be resolved.

Among them, the *Physical Educations and Sports Manual*, a 2017 novelty...

> I find the form less than desirable and I still think Physical Education is more of a practical discipline. It's true that at the University of Physical Education and Sport there are also theoretical classes. Athletics, moreover, is a sport that is mastered with the help of theory. But this manual has been received as a joke because there is also a problem of expression. It can be improved, it could become a good product, but I don't think that's the priority right now. More important is that physical education classes are taken seriously.

Within this context, how do you see the effects of the recent amendment of the Law on Physical Education and Sport?

> The amendment provides that city halls allocate up to 5% of their budget to sports activities. I think it would have been more beneficial for the sports to specify the exact percentage

Interview with Violeta Beclea-Szekely

of the allocation. It's a good law that can help communities grow by investing in a sports discipline specific to them. Every place has its own tradition in a certain sport. We'll see what happens next year, when the law will be implemented. It remains to be seen how each town hall will interpret this maximum of 5 percent.

Starting from the topic of high-performance sport to enter the recreational level, of public sports, how do you think this landscape looks today?

At least in Bucharest, and if it doesn't happen here, it certainly doesn't happen anywhere else, there is a shortage of spaces dedicated to mass sport. If it were otherwise, it would mean that parks everywhere would have running tracks, mini-basketball and football fields, just like abroad. In our cities it is much harder because we are suffocated by buildings. But of course, if there's a will, there's a way. But on the other hand, as a nation, we aren't that physically active. Moreover, new neighbourhoods are being built and even now, in the 21st century, basic needs are being disregarded. There is still no communication between authorities and developers about the proper way to build and the future needs of the community.

What's on an athlete's mind when running?

Training sessions mean much more than running in a competition, when you can't really think about anything at all. Each moment triggers what happens next in the race, and then you must act immediately. When I was running, I would look at the display panels – there were timers for every 100 metres – I wanted to see what's the tempo of the race, I would look at the big screen to see the opponents' arrangement: who is the most dangerous, what is she up to, etc. A lot of things going through my head. You weren't lining up at the starting line thinking: "Wow! Am I gonna win, or not?" No, each moment triggers the next. Most of the time I had the impression that I had the race prepared, at least mentally, but things did not happen as I had intended.

As you're preparing, you have all the coordinates – who are your opponents, what their time is, what your time is, what their strengths are – and you relate to them, but it never goes

I don't think sport belongs to anyone

> as planned. The race is decided in every moment. If everything were as clean cut as the coordinates might indicate and these are relevant indeed, it would mean to stay home and get the medal in the mailbox. In addition to strategy, creativity also plays a role, as well as the Day. The Day is crucial, a lot depends on it. There were years when I was in the world rankings, but I didn't win the Olympics. I finished in 2nd place, although I had the best performance of the year. Until that moment I had won all the races, and after the Olympics I kept winning. Nothing is predefined or predetermined, that moment is the moment of truth. It depends on your Day. Everyone trains just as hard, everyone is talented, but the Day is what determines the winner.

How has the general condition of the Romanian athlete changed since when you first started out?

> I started in 1980 and I was fortunate enough to make the national senior group that same year, me, a junior with 6-8 months of experience. Mr. Ion Puică, who was the Romanian seniors' division coach, noticed me. I had the luck of growing up with Maricica Puică, Natalia Mărășescu, Doina Melinte, Fița Lovin ... They were the perfect role models for me. As a junior I was in the School Sports Club in Suceava, then at CSM Suceava and, after finishing my studies in Suceava, in 1989, I moved to Bucharest, where I competed under the colours of Rapid club. I was also courted by Dinamo and Steaua, but I chose Rapid because they gave me my apartment keys on the spot. This was before the Revolution, I think I caught the last train. Now, something like this is no longer possible. At that time there were houses allocated to the state companies; the workers and the employees were given a house and so were the athletes. Clubs were allocated a certain number of houses. However, with the Revolution, this system ceased. Also building new infrastructure went at a slower pace, the state no longer pursued a social policy, whose beneficiaries used to be athletes as well. Today, the housing problem is a pressing one.

You switched from the running track to an office job, as a marketing director for the Romanian Olympic and Sports Committee. What is your relationship with such a space?

> I have 12 years of experience working in an office, and yet I

am still not very comfortable with a closed space. For 23 years my activity took place outdoors. However, I can't complain because we have an extraordinary team. The environment in which you are, the colleagues you have matter a great deal. I went from one extreme to the other, from an outdoor space to a fish tank, but it's nice. The fact that you have the chance to do something for sports and remain in this profession after finishing your high-performance career is a great thing. It is important to give something back to the sport that shaped you as a person, which gave you status. I am fully admitting to being a product of athletics, just like Ionela Țârlea (former athlete, today a colleague at the office).

There are some disputes regarding the presence of athletes within the administrative structures of sport.

There are some finer details to what a certain field is all about, that only someone from the inside can fully comprehend. My experience in sports is one of the main reasons why I'm here. We, the athletes, can create a connection between sport and its administration, we are the best qualified to translate our needs to the rigid administration jargon.

I don't think sport belongs to anyone

The System Against the System – Holland v U.S.S.R. in Euro 88

Declan Clarke

It all began with an Irishman. Or to be more precise, it all began with an Irishman who had the great misfortune to be born in England. To be more precise still, it all began with Jimmy Hogan.

When Sándor Barcs met the English press after the *Match of the Century* in Wembley stadium he laid it out for the shell-shocked scribes. Barcs was president of the Hungarian Football Federation, and England had just been battered 6-3. It was 1953, and the best football team in the world had just showed up at the home of football and exposed in excruciating detail how far the inventors of the game had been left behind.

At the time, the idea that Hungary, or anyone, could beat England at Wembley was absurd. Ireland had already become the first team to defeat England on home soil when they beat them 2-0 at Goodison Park in September 1949. But that was put down as a freak incident. It didn't count. It was only Ireland, and it wasn't at Wembley. It wasn't a real match. Hubris and the England football team have always been cozy bedfellows.

But then Hungary came. It only took one minute for Nándor Hidekuti to usher in modernity. It's not odd that a number 9 would score early, but what was so revolutionary was where the number 9, Hidekuti, was positioned. In 1953 there was only one formation in town, the W-M. Or, in today's parlance, a 3-2-2-3. Every team in the business used this formation, except Hungary. They used a 4-2-4 formation. What was even more radical, was that the number 9 was playing *behind* the front four. This meant the striker was simultaneously playing as a playmaker, and using his movement off

Jimmy Hogan

the ball to create space further back from which he could shoot or dink defence flummoxing passes to the four attacking players interchanging positions in front of him. But, should a shooting chance emerge, as a number 9, he was the perfect candidate to take it.

With the genius and guile of Lionel Messi, the idea of the false 9 is common in more in-depth football analysis in 2019. But even in 2019 the false 9 does not play behind a front four. In 1953, this was splitting-the-atom stuff. It still is. And it didn't stop there. The goal from the match that echoes loudest still was Hungary's third and Ferenc Puskás' first. Hidekuti had already bagged a second when "the outside left, Cizbor, way over on the right wing" – as Kenneth Wolstenholme commentating for the BBC described it - found Puskás in the box. The England right-half Billy Wright rushed to close down Hungary's number 10. As he slid in to clear the ball, Puskás, as if killing time at a bus stop, gently rolled the sole of his boot over the ball and pulled it back. Wright slid through the void of space where the ball had been, and kept on going. Puskás then turned and rifled a shot straight past the flailing Gil Merrick. Modern football had arrived.

Hidekuti got a hat-trick, Puskás got a brace, and Hungary took their foot off the gas after 50 minutes because it was just getting embarrassing. In the press room afterwards, Barcs explained:

"Jimmy Hogan taught us everything we know about football."

THE ORIGIN OF THE SPECIES

Jimmy Hogan had ideas. Jimmy Hogan travelled. Jimmy Hogan was a football coach, but he couldn't get work in England, so he looked for work abroad. Football was in its infancy, and football coaching even more so. In the 21st Century, mainland Europeans still describe the English game as 'kick and rush'. Is it fun? Sure. Is it sophisticated? Hardly. New ideas don't grow in English football – they're always imported. Jimmy Hogan seems to have embodied this tendency from the offset.

Hogan's idea was that a fluid interchanging of positions on the field could create an amorphous flow of football that would force the opposing team out of shape. This space could then be immediately occupied by attackers who could compound the advantage of possession and numbers in the opposition half to lethal effect. No one was buying in England. In 1910, Jimmy Hogan became the Dutch national football team manager. He then moved to club management in Austria before becoming manager of MTK

Budapest in 1914. It was during these travels that Hogan sewed the seeds of his vision, a vision that would have its last sigh in the final of the European Championship in 1988.

A HUNGER FOR NEW IDEAS

In the wake of the Wembley match, there was a desire to know more about who this team were and how they came to play as they did. Their visionary coach, Gustáv Sebes, was a political man and a man of principle. He famously described the style of play as 'socialist football' – with every team member working for the entire unit, and no individual taking precedence. When the England team travelled to Budapest for a rematch six months later in the newly constructed Népstadion, they were annihilated 7-1. Hungary were now considered the best team in the world, and even the English knew that tradition had made way for the future. This style of football and this magnificent team, did not just appear out of the ether. As is invariably the case with such things, it was a mixture of circumstance, luck, and vision.

The circumstance was that in the 1940s Hungary had a strong league set up and a good standard of football was played in the country. Their two main clubs, Ferencváros and Magyar Testgyakorlók Köre Hungária FC – MTK for short - were on a par with the best teams in Europe. The luck was provided by a number of extraordinarily gifted players emerging at the same time: Ferenc Puskás, Sandór Kocsis, Nándor Hidegkuti, József Bozsik, Zoltán Czibor, László Budai, and Gyula Grosics all had the capacity to star in a top-level team, and all still rank amongst the true greats of the game. The vision came from Gustáv Sebes. Sebes was a committed communist and Trade-Union activist. He genuinely believed that if football followed socialism, a better, more egalitarian, more beautiful type of play would be achieved. He took this fervent vision into his approach to the game, and fortunately for him, a committed communist was just what the hard-line Stalinist government of Mátyás Rákosi had in mind when they were looking to appoint a national manager in 1949. Given free reign, Sebes had noted that recent international teams that had been dominant tended to draw the majority of their players from two national club sides. This meant that the players were already familiar with one another, and made more advanced

Gustáv Sebes

Declan Clarke

coaching easier to achieve when the players met up at international level. He compounded this advantage by creating a new club team.

Due to their association with the Hungarian fascist movement, Ferencváros were suppressed as a club in the Hungarian People's Republic. The Jewish team – MTK, had lost much of their support and personnel to the Holocaust, and the Hungarian secret police had taken over the club. Looking for a team to fit the project, the government took the small club Kispet, turned it into the army team, and re-branded it Honvéd. The army could induct any civilian into its ranks, so Sebes was able to use this method to recruit the players he wanted, and oversee their development. Honvéd went on to form the trunk and branches of the national side, and is still the most internationally recognised Hungarian club side.

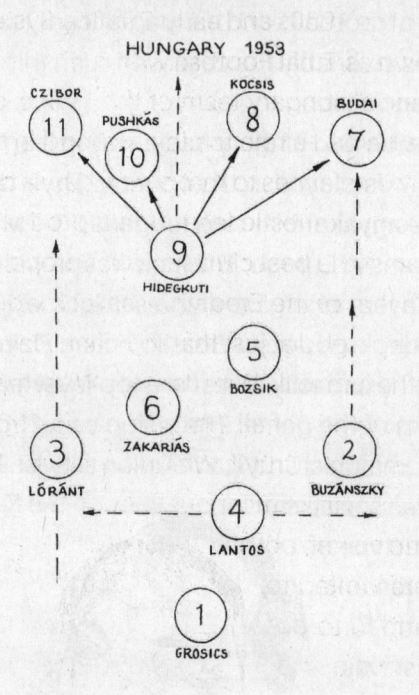

His team first showcased their potential, and excited crowds with their interchanging play at the 1952 Helsinki Olympics, which they went on to win. By the World Cup in 1954, they were *the* team on the world stage. They coasted through a group of West Germany, Turkey, and South Korea with an aggregate score of 17-3.

In the quarter finals, they faced the runners-up of the previous World Cup, Brazil, whom they swatted aside 4-2. Next came reigning champions Uruguay. Two late Juan Hohberg goals forced extra time, but Sándor Kocsis scored twice and Hungary again galloped away 4-2 winners.

The final, against West Germany, a depleted version of which had been crushed 8-3 in the group phase, was all set to be the crowning glory of this revolutionary side. An incarnation of Jimmy Hogan's System was about to win its first World Cup. Puskás and Czibor scored two inside the opening eight minutes, and it looked as if another eight goal blitz was in the post. But then, something that creeps into every great team appeared, even teams that their coach believe are modelled on socialism; hubris. Hungary got complacent, and by the 18th minute the score was 2-2. Hungary dominated the game, but for once, the team that had scored 25 times in the previous five matches,

The System Against the System

couldn't score. They bombarded the West Germany goal, but the ball just wouldn't cross the line. Then, having only had one chance in the second half, West Germany scored with six minutes to go. Puskás scored an equaliser, but it was ruled offside – a decision that embittered the player into old age.

Hungary, and the System, had lost. After the World Cup, Hungary went on an eighteen match unbeaten run. The Magnificent Magyars team only lost one match in six years, but that match, against inferior opposition, just happened to be the World Cup final.

THE SYSTEM TRIES AGAIN

As mentioned, Jimmy Hogan had been national team manager of Holland, in 1910, before moving to Hungary to develop his coaching method. The System took root in Holland too, and the Oranje would go on to become its most famous exponents. Under Rinus Michels in the 1960s and early '70s, the System was adjusted slightly, and became known as Total Football.

As had happened with the majestic Hungary team of the 1950s, our old friends circumstances, luck, and vision had a role to play. Holland in the mid 1960s found itself in very similar circumstances to that of Hungary a decade previously - it had developed a strong domestic league that produced teams who could compete and win against the best club sides in Europe. As the standard of Dutch players rose with that of the Eredivisie, as luck would have it, a number of world-class players emerged at just that moment. Players like Johnny Rep, Johan Neeskens, Rob Resenbrink, Wim Jansen, Willem van Hanegem, and Ruud Krol. But most importantly of all, Holland of the 1960s had its own Ferenc Puskás. His name was Johan Cruyff. While not very similar in physical stature, Puskás and Cruyff had many similar qualities on the field. Both were gifted with sublime touch and vision, both were on field leaders that other players looked to, and took direction from, and both seemed to do things with the ball that looked both simple and extraordinarily complex at the same time. Maybe it was just that they both made the extraordinarily complex look simple.

A case in point with regard to the similarities between the two is the football standard "Cruyff Turn". The Cruyff Turn entered the football dictionary on June 19th, 1974 during a World Cup. Holland were playing a decent Sweden side in their second

Rinus Michels

Declan Clarke

group stage match. Cruyff was just outside the box on the left wing when he received the ball. He was being closely marked by Sweden's Jan Olsson. Cruyff received a high crossfield pass that he controlled immaculately with his left foot, and then, having shifted his weight, attempted to cross it into the box with his right. As Olsson; everyone else on the pitch; everyone in the stadium; everyone watching on telly; and everyone who has watched it replayed since, moved with the momentum of Cruyff's right foot towards the right of the field, the Dutchman played the ball back down the left flank behind Olsson – and behind himself – and ran on to it to deliver a *right* footed cross in from the *left* hand corner of the box. The crowd roared as if a goal had been scored, and even though it didn't lead to a goal, it had the significance of ten goals. Maybe a hundred.

The Cruyff Turn is a football standard now, and about the only thing that compares in terms of simplicity of movement embodying an enormous football shift, is Puskás' ball roll against England that left Billy Wright prone. Puskás was so far ahead of the curve that people didn't even think you could give such a thing a name, but before the Cruyff Turn there was the Puskás Sole Slide. The technical similarities are in perfect synchronicity. Perhaps worthy of note is that Puskás' wizardry actually produced a goal. Maybe Cruyff should have just tried to belt it in from an impossible angle, but such a thing had never been done. It would be though, and also by a Dutchman...

But, back to the final link in the chain: vision. The vision for what would become the 1974 Dutch team came from Renus Michels. Michels was appointed coach of Ajax in 1964. A former Ajax striker who had scored 122 times in 264 appearances, Michels had a kinship for the club, and clearly, a fondness for goals.

Ajax were down on their luck and at the bottom of the table. Renus Michels strode into the club and transformed them utterly within less than a decade. With the Dutch league having just turned professional, players were only now able to train and play full time. Michels took full advantage of this and had his players train four times a day. He wanted maximum fitness from his squad, and sought to use this to up the tempo of their on-field play. Michels had a very authoritarian approach, not unlike that of Sebes, but, unlike Sebes, he was eager to have communication throughout the team, and welcomed the input of the players in terms of how the flow of play evolved. An example of the impact this had is in how their high defensive line emerged, and how it in turn evolved into the Total Football System.

Johan Neeskens used to press relentlessly, and frequently. When he had driven his man back into his own half, he would continue to pursue him until, left with no option, the disheveled player would pass it back to his keeper. At some unspecified point, the defensive line moved forward with Neeskens, innately understanding that a forward defensive line that harassed the ball back into the attacking team's third would hugely reduce the field of play. A misplaced pass suddenly had eleven men swarming in on goal; a ball over the top was offside, allowing the Ajax team to regroup.

Together they developed this efficient and effective style of play. Why run the length of the field to attack, and then run back again to defend? Could not the consumption of energy be more efficiently modulated? If the defender overlapped the winger in attack, surely it made more sense for the winger to drop back to defence to shield against a potential counter attack, and then switch back again at the most opportune moment. It sounds simple, it *is* simple, in theory – but in practice?

Ajax honed this method to such a degree that they dominated the Eredivisie in thrilling fashion, winning titles in 1966, '67, '68, '69, '70, '72, and '73. But it was in the European Cup where they really made their mark. Ajax won three successive European Cups between 1971 and 1973, and they did so with jaw dropping eloquence and grace. This was a type of football the European Cup had not seen before, and they seemed to do it on auto-pilot. Michels left for Barcelona after the first European Cup win, but the System as he had embedded it continued with Cruyff as his on field successor. As Michels' replacement, the more withdrawn but nonetheless wise Romanian Stefan Kovács, took an 'if-it-ain't-broke-don't-fix-it' approach to keeping the Ajax momentum flowing. They won two more European Cups and two more Eredivise titles under his watch.

But it wasn't just about Ajax – Feyenoord were thriving too. They won the league when Ajax didn't in '71 and '74, and the European Cup in 1970 before Ajax got their treble.

As the 1974 World Cup approached, Rinus Michels was installed as the Holland manager after they had qualified for the tournament. This was to be the gilding of Dutch football dominance, and where better to do it than in West Germany – the recent wartime enemy.

Reigning champions Brazil were the favourites, and West Germany – third placed in 1970 – had home advantage, but the football world was looking to the Dutch, and to Johan Cruyff in particular. Their new vision of football was so revolutionary, that their goalkeeper wore the number 8 jersey – traditionally the number of an attacking midfielder. If Hungary split the atom, this Holland team was first contact with an alien life form.

Declan Clarke

It started well. Johnny Rep scored two to beat Uruguay, a draw with Sweden brought a football monument with Cruyff's dilettantism against Ollson, and Bulgaria were eclipsed 4-1 in the final group match. And then it got better.

The format at the time meant a second group phase determined the finalists. Holland's group housed Brazil, East Germany, and Argentina. Argentina were beaten 4-0, and East Germany 2-0. July 3rd, 1974 saw what was in effect the semi-final. Holland against the reigning champions Brazil. This was Holland's moment, and take it they did.

Brazil, the great Brazil, were reduced to an erratic performance that involved hacking opposition players down such was the extent of their bewilderment at the Dutch finesse. Holland's high defensive line meant that each time Brazil played a through ball they were offside, usually about ten yards into the Dutch half. When attacking, Holland interchanged positions to an extent never before seen then or since. Cruyff played in both wing-back positions, across central midfield, and as a centre forward. Neeskens scored the first when fed by Cruyff from the right wing, and Cruyff scored an acrobatic, high speed floating star second from a classic centre forward position, after three swift passes from the left-back position, played in the actual left-back, Ruud Krol, on the edge of the box to sail in the cross.

Not since the publication of James Joyce's *Ulysses* had the textbook of what could be done been so categorically torn asunder. The nail in the coffin was when Neeskens jaunted diagonally through the midfield and was lumberjacked by Luis Pereira who was already on a yellow card. He received a straight red, and the idolised Brazil were marched out of the tournament. No one could see past Holland as inevitable champions.

But history is unkind. Holland showed up in Munich on the Sunday morning with an aura about them. West Germany may have been the home team, but football's team was Holland. The Oranje could do what the Might Mygars could not. The System would prevail.

The System Against the System

And so it initially proved. It only took a minute for Holland to score against West Germany in the final. From tip off, Holland splayed the ball around seventeen times until their deepest lying player, Johan Cruyff, collected the ball at the half way line. He then ran straight to goal, and was eventually clipped by Uli Hoeneß. Penalty. Germany were yet to touch the ball. The closest they had come was Hoeneß's boot hitting Cruyff's shin. Neesken's fired the penalty kick straight down the middle, and Holland had made World Cup history by scoring the earliest ever goal, and the only goal scored without the opposition touching the ball. 1-0 up in a World Cup final after 80 seconds. So far, so Holland 1974. And then, hubris crept in.

Whatever it is about the System, no matter how democratic, no matter how egalitarian, no matter how socialist, no matter how pure, it always gives way to hubris. As Johnny Rep put it when interviewed by David Winner in his authoritative book *Brilliant Orange: The Neurotic Genius of Dutch Football*:

> "We wanted to make fun of the Germans. We didn't think about it
> but we did, passing the ball around and around.
> We forgot to score the second goal."

For twenty minutes, Holland toyed with the Germans, they could have scored more, but they didn't. Then the pragmatic West Germany got their own 'penalty' – the result of a Steven Gerrard-esque dive from Bernd Hölzenbein – and Paul Breitner converted it. Impossibly, it was 1-1. After that, West Germany finally came into the game, and looked to get the ball to their lethal weapon, Gerd Müller, arguably the most clinical centre forward in the box of all time. Müller scored 68 times in 62 appearances for West Germany, so, inevitably, he scored. Holland were 2-1 down having been cruising to victory. They had left it too late. Rather than killing off West Germany at the start, Holland were now chasing the game. The next 45 minutes saw wave after wave after wave after wave of Dutch attack, but no goal. The System had lost again. The second World Cup final had slipped by, and largely for similar reasons. In Holland, it is still known as the 'Lost Final'. In football too. Holland, like Hungary, would become one of the best teams not to win a World Cup.

THE SYSTEM FAILS AGAIN

In 1978, Holland again reached the World Cup final. Many of the same players were there – Rep, Neeskens, Krol, Rensenbrink, Jansen – but Michels and Cruyff were not. Ernst Happel was the manager, but so deep set was the Dutch system when he took over, that he struggled to get the respect of the players.

Declan Clarke

He only managed to do so after one day in training he lined up a series of balls on the 18-yard line and chipped each consecutively onto the bar. Then, finally, the players listened.

They haltingly played their way through the first group phase, Archie Gemmil memorably scoring a World Cup wonder goal for Scotland to push them to the limit, but, when the business end of the tournament came they delivered. They beat Austria 5-1, drew with old foes West Germany 2-2, and beat Italy 2-1 with a comprehensive performance and one of the greatest long range goals ever scored, when Arie Haan sent a Soyuz rocket into the outer reaches of known space, much to the shock of Dino Zoff.

Then came the final, again against a home nation – this time Argentina. The atmosphere in the Estadio Monumental was intense, and armed troops from the right wing military junta lined the stadium. Conspiracies abound about the match, and Argentina certainly used their home advantage, but ultimately, the on-field play was more even than in 1974. Holland had several chances to score, but didn't take them. Argentina won in extra time by three goals to one. The System had failed yet again, and it would disappear from international football for another decade.

THE SYSTEM EATS ITSELF

If Gustáv Sebes had described the System as 'socialist football', and Rinus Michels had described it as Total Football, it indicated something very clear about Europe at that time. Europe was divided into two halves. East and West. Almost everything that happened in Europe as of 1945 was defined in these terms. Now, the distinction is made clearly and simply: East was bad; West was good; East was inferior, West was superior; East lost, West won. And the winners write the history. But before 1989, the game was still being played, and no one knew who was going to win.

Valeriy Lobanovskyi

This ideological battle was played on all fronts, and invariably, to the most petty of rules. Such is the way of high stakes competition. If Western Europe had been dominating World Cups – only Hungary in '54 and Czechoslovakia in '62 had made finals – the Euros had been a much more even playing field. The U.S.S.R. had beaten Yugoslavia in its first incarnation in 1960. Spain beat the champions in 1964, and Italy beat Yugoslavia in 1968. West Germany

The System Against the System

beat the U.S.S.R. in 1972, but were famously beaten by Czechoslovakia in 1976 through a legendary penalty by Antonín Panenka in the shoot-out.

Central and East Europe had a football renaissance in the post war period. In communist countries, clubs were state owned, and often attached to different state bodies, usually recognisable in their names. For example, clubs called 'Dynamo' – such as Moscow, Kyiv, Bucharest, Berlin, Dresden, Tirana, Tbilisi, Sofia, Minsk, Tallinn, and Zagreb – were notoriously attached to the state security. Not surprisingly, these teams tended to win a lot. The state sponsored management of the football leagues allowed players to develop at club level, and as seen with Sebes at Honvéd, this could be translated impressively into the national side.

One manager in particular, could be seen to have continued the tradition of the Sebes and the Hungary system – Valeriy Lobanovskyi. Lobanovskyi had come through the youth set-up at Dynamo Kyiv, and played the bulk of his career at the club. He entered management a year after retiring, and four years later, in 1969, was appointed manager of Dynamo Kyiv. Dynamo played in the Soviet Top League, and under Lobanovskyi, they became a winning force, breaking the heretofore Russian domination of the Soviet Top League.

Since the Soviet Top League had been established in 1936, only four teams from outside Moscow had won it. Dynamo Kyiv had been the first in 1961. Dinamo Tbilisi had brought Georgia its first title in 1964, before Kyiv won a treble of titles between '66 and '68. The shifting sands of the Soviet republics continued as Kyiv won a fifth in '71, Ukraine got it's second club winner through Zorya Voroshilovgrad in '72, and Ararat Yerevan became the only Armenian winners in '73. When Lobanovskyi took charge of Kyiv the conditions were perfect for him to impose his philosophy on the club. Seen across Ukraine as national representatives amongst the Soviet republics, and more specifically, representatives against Moscow – Kyiv had enormous support with the Soviet fan base, and more importantly, among the political establishment. Volodymyr Scherbytskyi was the club patron through the 1970s and 80s. He was also the leader of the Ukranian Communist Party[1], which helped.

While Rinus Michels had an openness with his players, and would encourage their input on tactical development, Lobanovskyi had a more authoritarian approach. He alone had the vision, and he instructed players to undertake his precise instructions on the field. At its core, Lobanovskyi's version of the System differed little from that of Sebes or Michels. When not in possession, compress the field of play and try to win back the ball as quickly as possible. When in possession, stretch the field of play as much as possible,

Declan Clarke

and use the positional interchanging of players on the field to make this more effective while confusing the opposition. Then exploit the space that opens up with ruthless efficiency. This required enormous amounts of energy, so Lobanovskyi coached his players to be both incredibly fit, but also very intelligent and selective in their use of this fitness. Pointless, inefficient running was not encouraged.

Additionally, Lobanovskyi was not open to the idea that the players could improvise around the System with their talents – he was more interested in refining the movement and positional interchanging so that they functioned immaculately, and flawlessly, like a beautiful, intelligent organism. The players were the cells in this organism, and the cells had their function – there was little tolerance for malfunction.

Between 1974 and 1986, under Lobanovskyi Dynamo Kyiv won seven Soviet Top League titles, five Soviet Cups, and in 1975, the UEFA Cup Winners Cup.

Just prior to the 1986 World Cup, Lobanovskyi was asked to manage the U.S.S.R., a job he undertook while concurrently managing Dynamo Kyiv. He did what Sebes and Michels before him had done, and picked a team made up largely of his recent Dynamo champions. The U.S.S.R. topped their group, but went out in the first knockout round to eventual semi finalists Belgium. Lobanovskyi then took the team into qualification for the European Championships.

If the Soviet Union were improving in the 1980s in qualifying for both World Cups, Holland had fallen off the international map in the wake of 1978. They had qualified for Euro 1980, but had failed to get out of the group. After that, they disappeared without a trace, failing to qualify for three international competitions in a row. But hope was near.

A generation of players who had been born around 1962, and who would have watched the great Ajax team win their treble of European Cups in the early 1970s, and seen their national side come oh-so-close in '74 and '78, were all coming of age in the lead up to Euro 88. Players like Ronald and Erwin Koeman, Jan Wouters, Berry van Aerle, but most importantly of all, the holy trinity of Frank Rijkaard, Marco van Basten, and the then most expensive player in the world, Ruud Guillet. Before qualification for Euro 88, Rinus Michels was appointed manager of Holland.

The majority of the squad had played together and won titles at Ajax or PSV – or both as did Ronald Koeman and Gerald Vanenburg, in the 1980s. Marco van Basten and Ruud Guillet had just become teammates at AC Milan at the beginning of the 1987-88 season where they were fresh from winning the *scudetto*. More remarkable still, almost the entire squad had played alongside Cruyff, been managed by Cruyff, or experienced both. Ruud Guillet had won the Dutch league and cup double alongside him in his final season as a player at Feyenoord – Cruyff taking sweet revenge on Ajax for not extending his playing contract by signing for their biggest rivals. Additionally, five of the Dutch squad had just won the European Cup with PSV. The System was back, and Euro 88 in West Germany was to be its stage.

As if that was not enticing enough, the draw made it even more exciting. Lobanovskyi's Soviet Union and Michels' Holland were drawn in the same group, a group of death if ever there was one. England and an exciting Republic of Ireland team managed by Jack Charlton filled out the deck.

As per usual prior to an international competition, England installed themselves as pre-tournament favourites. Their opening group match against the Republic of Ireland was seen as a warm up for Holland and the U.S.S.R. It only took five minutes for that bubble to burst. Ray Houghton scored early, and the Irish defence, ridiculed by Brian Clough in the pre-match commentary, shut England out for the rest of the game.

Next up, Lobanovskyi and Michels' teams met. The System would face the System.

The U.S.S.R. team that lined up against Holland on June 12th, 1988, contained eight players who had just won the Soviet Top League under Lobanovskyi at Dynamo: Volodymyr Bezsonov, Oleh Kuznetsov, Anatoliy Demyanenko, Oleksandr Zavarov, Oleksiy Mykhaylychenko, Vasyl Rats, Igor Belanov, and Oleh Protasov. This match was pretty much Lobanovskyi's Dynamo Kyiv against Michels's Holland. While Moscow tended to prefer teams that represented a broad spectrum of Soviet republics, Moscow also wasn't stupid. Lobanovskyi knew what he was doing, and his Dynamo players knew best how to implement it. Michels picked the Holland side everyone expected, save for one player. He opted for John Bosman ahead of Milan star Marco van Basten, the latter deemed not fully match fit.

At the time, the match wasn't viewed the way it can be done now. People in Western Europe didn't pay any attention to the Soviet Top League, and little was known of Lobanovskyi and his Dynamo team. The Soviets were viewed as a decent enough side, but most thought Holland would prevail. They didn't.

Michels had informed his team about the threat the Soviets posed, particularly their ability to counter-attack at speed, but the players didn't heed his warning. A good flowing match, with both teams playing well, was decided early in the second half. Igor Belanov collected the ball on the right by the

Declan Clarke

edge of the Dutch box. As the Dutch back line and midfield turned to close down the space, Belanov waited for Vasyl Rats to continue his run down the left wing, and then sailed the ball over the box. Rats caught it on the half volley and slammed it into the far right hand corner of the goal. Holland had some half chances thereafter, but were not able to out-manoeuvre Lobanovskyi's fluidly morphing organism. The Dutch opened their Euro 88 account with a 1-0 defeat. Lobanovskyi 1, Michels 0.

On June 15th, both teams played again. Holland faced a shell-shocked England, with both teams in need of a victory to stay in the competition. Group leaders U.S.S.R. and Ireland, were facing each other looking to secure progression to the semi-finals.

Having perhaps been afraid to gamble on Van Basten's fitness in the opening match, Michels doubled down and picked Van Basten from the start. He also refrained from lambasting his team, and instead gave them encouragement. "It will come", he told them. And come it did.

Just as halftime approached, Guillet sped down the left wing and chipped an early right footed cross into the centre of the England box for the waiting Van Basten. Van Basten did what Cruyff and Puskás had done before him. In fact, the goal was almost a perfect blend of Cruyff's 'turn' against Sweden in 1974, and Puskás' goal against England in 1953. With his back to goal and adjacent to the penalty spot, and with Tony Adams closely marking him, Van Basten trapped the ball with his left foot and used his right to play the ball behind both Adams and himself towards the left of goal. He ran into the space that he had created and clinically stroked the ball into the right of goal as Adams flailed and Gary Stevens slid in just that bit too late.

Bryan Robson equalised, but Van Basten was not done. Fed again, beautifully, by Guillet, he sent the ball to almost exactly the same spot in the goal, this time as he ran from the left on to Guillet's pass. His hat-trick came with a training ground standard that the team had rehearsed endlessly. A corner, flicked on by Kieft, was buried from the goalmouth.

Later that day, the U.S.S.R. faced Ireland. Sometimes the occasion, and the quality of the opposition, brings out the best in players. Jack Charlton knew how Lobanovskyi's team graced the field of play, so he counseled his players to "put it in the corners, and go up and attack them" as Ronnie Whelan recounted during a television interview many years later. But Ireland, though not thought of as a 'footballing' team, contained top level players like Paul McGrath, Kevin Moran, Ray Houghton, Frank Stapleton, and John Aldridge. As Whelan put it: "On that night I don't know what happened to that team. We had a lot of gifted footballers that could play. That afternoon we decided to play. Jack didn't tell us to go out and play... but we played some tremendous football that afternoon."[2]

None more so than Whelan himself. He scored a spectacular left-footed volley from the edge of the box from an unfeasibly long throw-in by Mick McCarthy. In the same interview Whelan remarked, "I don't even know why I was there, that wasn't my position to be in." Maybe the fluid interchanging of positions by the Soviet Union rubbed off on the Ireland team, and faced with a footballing challenge, they rose to it.

The Soviets played equally well, and when they levelled the score through Protasov in the 74th minute, it was deserved. A calm and skillful finish from the left, after a rapid transition from defence to attack. With England out of the picture, the U.S.S.R., Ireland, and Holland would need the final match to determine who would progress.

The final group matches were played concurrently, and as the Soviet Union lined out against England before the match, another iconographic element of this tournament, albeit one long forgotten to history, was on display. The Soviet away kit. The first time it had been worn in the tournament. It was a red version of Holland's now legendary 1988 Adidas jersey. Both teams had the same kit manufacturer, and Adidas had provided both teams with the same iconic geometric chiaroscuro patterned jersey. A postmodern design classic. Retrospectively, it seems apt that these two teams should have been adorned in the same classic pattern, suggesting their unique pattern of football, a pattern not seen since.

England, already out, were down and out inside three minutes. Sergei Aleinikov dispossessed Glenn Hoddle as he advanced with the ball from the England area, drove into the box, and slotted the ball in to the left hand corner of goal. Protasov nearly made it two shortly thereafter, as the U.S.S.R.'s rapid interchanging of positions was slicing through England with ease. England rallied and Adams restored a modicum of dignity heading in a Hoddle free kick. A Barnes cross was shortly thereafter headed over an open goal by Trevor Steven, and that was all the encouragement the Soviet Union needed. They scored in the 28th minute, Mykhayilchenko heading in after running deep from midfield in another flowing attack. The substitute Viktor Pasulko blessed the grave when tapping in another team goal. The Soviets were through, and England finished alongside Denmark as tournament whipping boys.

Holland's game was far less one sided. Ireland were a point to the

Declan Clarke

good against the Dutch, and a win or draw would see them through. Holland had to win. Ireland came out swinging. Having won a corner, Paul McGrath rose and powered a header towards goal as Guillet and Wouters looked on. It hit the post, bounced onto Vanenburg's back, who was on the line, and went back into the goalmouth where Ray Houghton tried desperately to nudge it over the line. Somehow, impossibly, Van Breukelen managed to block it and smother the ball. Amazingly, Ireland were not in the lead. Holland attacked relentlessly, but couldn't break down the Irish defence. The match looked certain to be a draw when McGrath headed yet another ball clear of the box in the 82nd minute. It landed for Ronald Koeman, who scuffed his long range attempt, which, in turn, fell to the offside Kieft, who headed the ball past Bonner in the Irish goal. 1-0, and so it remained. Holland, so unlucky in the past, cashed in all their lucky chips at once. Ireland, the surprise package of the tournament, were out, and Holland would get to try the System one more time against their loathed rivals West Germany.

WEST GERMANY V HOLLAND. AGAIN.

It was in the Olympiastadion in Munich, fourteen years previously that Rinus Michals and the great footballing philosophy of the Dutch had been put to the sword. The Lost Final – a trauma for the Dutch even now, over forty years later. This time it was the Volksparkstadion, Hamburg. The man who had lifted the World Cup trophy that day in Munich, Franz Beckenbauer, was now the West Germany manager.

That final, and the spectre of the War, overshadowed the pre-match build up.

Aside from those deluded folk residing in the British Isles, West Germany were everyone's pre- tournament favourites. Beaten by Diego Maradona, and, of course, Argentina, in the World Cup final of '86, the West Germans also had home advantage in Euro 88. The team was alright too. Jürgen Klinsmann, Rudi Völler, Andreas Brehme, Lothar Matthäus – experience and quality throughout. In Völler, and more notoriously so in Klinsmann, they had centre forwards who were experts in the dark art of 'influencing' referees, a compelling tactic when playing with home crowd advantage.

Unsurprisingly, the match was a tempestuous and untidy affair. The crowd atmosphere was tense, with many a war themed chant, and tackles tended to leave one or both players flat on their backs. Klinsmann was left felled on the turf after running onto a through ball and meeting only Hans van Breukelen's shoulder on the edge of the box. Van Breukelen then leaned over the writhing Klinsmann and roared.

The System Against the System

Early in the second half, Klinsmann got his revenge in inimitable Klinsmann fashion. He gathered the ball in the centre circle, turned, and accelerated away from Van Tiggelen. As he dribbled into the box, he waited for Rijkaard to make a challenge. As soon as he did, Klinsmann hit the deck. The reaction of Rinus Michels embodied perfectly what most people thought of the decision, a decision as soft as the challenge. Matthäus converted, but Romanian referee Ioan Igna evened the scores and the feeling of injustice, by giving Holland an equally absurd penalty twenty minutes later. A long ball from behind the halfway line – even Total Football must be expedient at times – found Van Basten, who feinted left, then turned right, but as he ran in to the box he was shepherded away from goal by Jürgen Kohler. As Kohler made his tackle he disposed Van Basten of the ball and van Basten simply fell over, either through momentum or duplicity. Penalty. This time Ronald Koeman converted.

Then, with 15 minutes to go, Holland finally began to play like a Rinus Michels team. From goal the ball was rolled to Van Tiggelen, who squared it to Ronald Koeman. Koeman advanced and picked out Wouters in the space he had moved to around 40 yards out. Wouters played a ball straight into the box that Van Basten ran on to and, with perfect centre forward play, slid in to guide the ball past Kolher and Immel into the far side of the goal. Holland had beaten West Germany, in West Germany, and were now in the final.

THE FOOTBALL OF THE NEXT CENTURY

The next day, the U.S.S.R. faced Italy. This was a far less combative affair than that of the previous day, and Lobanovskyi's team eased into the final with an emphatic display of their fluidity of movement and almost psychic understanding of each other. An Italy defence containing Franco Baresi and Paolo Maldini managed to shut them out for the first half, but the U.S.S.R. started the second half at a higher tempo, and scored twice in four minutes. Lytovchenko opened the scoring with a wonderful mazey run into the Italy box before finishing with his right, having had his first attempt blocked. The second goal, was a classic Lobanovskyi era U.S.S.R. goal – the ball was released quickly from defence, found width at pace from the wing, before being whipped in to the newly created space that had emerged in front of the opposition goal. Zavarov's drive down the wing and perfectly weighted pass distracted Baresi enough to let Protasov run into the chasm of space he left behind him, and as Maldini belatedly chased after Protasov the damage was done – the number 10 chipped Walter Zenga at his far post to put the Soviet Union two goals ahead. Afterwards, Italy coach Azeglio Vicini said that the Soviets played, "the football of the next century".

Declan Clarke

But it didn't come without a cost. Lobanovskyi's team had been picking up injuries through the tournament. Additionally, Oleh Kuznetsov, who had marked Gianluca Vialli out of the match, would not make the final due to a second, and harsh, yellow card he had received in the second minute. Volodymyr Bezsonov had had to be substituted through injury in the first half, meaning the U.S.S.R. would go into the final without their two first choice centre-halves. Centre forward Igor Belanov had missed the semi final due to a thigh injury, meaning Lobanovskyi had played a 4-3-2-1 formation, but Oleh Protasov had also picked up an injury in the Italy game, meaning the team were far from fit and much depleted three days before the final – the fourth Euro final the Soviet Union had reached.

THE SYSTEM FINALLY FACES ITSELF –
The Euro 88 Final.

Just how iconic this final would become was not felt in the build up. Sure, Michels was back in a final with a Holland team that had excited a good competition – there had been no 0-0 draws and no penalty shoot-outs. Euro 88 was the most emphatic argument against expansion of the tournament format. Six strong sides and Denmark and England had played superb quality football, and the best two teams by far had reached the final. But no one was talking about the System, and no one imagined that this would be its great farewell.

Somehow, it seems looking back, the System was tied to the division of Europe. No one could foresee then that by Euro 92, the U.S.S.R., the Union of Soviet Socialist Republics would be competing as CIS – the Commonwealth of Independent States, and that shortly thereafter that Commonwealth would become twelve different European states. The System that developed as nation state Europe found its footing between two World Wars, the System that developed in Hungary under a repressive Communist leadership ruled de facto from Moscow, the System that flourished under a progressive socialist government in Holland during the 1960s, before reconfiguring itself in the Soviet Republic of Ukraine as a nascent expression of the coming deconstruction of the Soviet model, was about to have its last gasp of air in the final of the European Championship. No one could have predicted the monumental reconfiguration of Europe that was on the brink of coming into being.

Rinus Michels

In Euro 96, The People's Republic of Bulgaria would face The Socialist Republic of Romania as simply Bulgaria v Romania. Half of Czechoslovakia would face East and West Germany combined as the Czech Republic v Germany in their opening Group C game. A constituent Republic of the Socialist Federal Republic of Yugoslavia would complete in Group D as Croatia. The U.S.S.R. were now just Russia, and they would be beaten comfortably by Italy in their opening match. That is now, this was then.

With only one name on the ballot sheet, the System couldn't lose. The only question was which version of the System would win – that 'socialist' football of the European East or the Total Football of the European West?

The U.S.S.R. was seriously weakened, and though they had beaten Holland only ten days prior, they now had a central midfielder, Sergei Aleinikov, and a libero in Vagiz Khidiyatullin partnering for the first time at centre-half, and unlike Bezsonov and Kuznetsov, they were not club team mates. Both centre forwards were carrying injuries, so the fluidity that hard marked the Soviet's play thus far was dramatically reduced. The Netherlands, on the other hand, were in prime condition. They had kept the same team almost throughout the tournament, and had no injuries or suspensions to their key players.

Like most finals, it was cagey to begin with. The first chance of note came after half an hour from a Holland free kick. Guillet chipped it towards the top of the goal, but it was central, and Rinat Dasayev comfortably, though acrobatically, tipped it over. The U.S.S.R. cleared the corner, but Erwin Koeman collected and returned it into the box, Van Basten headed it back across the goalmouth, and Guillet powered a bullet of a header into goal. The whiplash inducing force of the strike emphasised by the rapid surge forward of Guillet's famous dreadlocks as he connected with Van Basten's cushioned cross. 1-0.

The Soviets now had to chase the game, allowing Holland to play a more counterattacking game, turning Lobanovskyi's preferred implementation of the System against his team. Early in the second half, Khidiyatullin played a long ball out from defence along the ground to Zavarov, who struggled to control it allowing Van Tiggelen to steal possession. As Holland rapidly swept up-field, the ball was played to Mühren, who took his time on the left wing before lobbing in a high slow ball to almost the opposite edge of the 18-yard box, about two yards from the touchline. Vasyl Rats and Van Basten chased it, but the ball was clearly headed out of play, Rats even reducing his speed at the last. But Van Basten tried the unthinkable, the lashed at the ball with his right foot, and unthinkably, he volleyed it over Rats, over Dasayev in goal, and from a ridiculous, geometry defying angle, sent the ball into the left

Declan Clarke

hand side netting of the goal. If Diego Maradona's *Goal of the Century* is the greatest World Cup goal ever scored, Van Basten's volley in undoubtedly the best Euro goal ever scored. Simply stunning. A goal of pure instinct, and pure class, by a unique player at the top of his game. Rinus Michels couldn't believe it, and he wiped his eyes with his hand after watching it go in. The U.S.S.R. had a penalty late on after Van Breukelen cleared out Gotsmanov as he chased a loose ball in the box. Belanov sent it low and hard to the left, but Van Breukelen, recalling a similar penalty that the number 11 had scored against France in the 86 World Cup, dived to his right and saved it. And that was that. The System had finally won. But, in the same breath, the System had lost again.

EPILOGUE

Since that final in June 1988, the System has disappeared. The collapse of communism saw a collapse of the football league structures across Central and Eastern Europe. As state funds dried up, teams had to sell their best players to maintain economic stability in a deeply unstable economic climate. Consequently, the standard of football diminished and club teams appeared less and less in a constantly expanding European Cup that became a league in 1992. The coefficient system that UEFA introduced allowed teams from stronger leagues, namely those from Western Europe, who were not champions to compete in the competition. Thus, slowly the former communist teams were muscled out of top European competition, and their league standards plummeted.

At club level, the last gasp of the System came, as you might expect, from the last great team that Valeriy Lobanovskyi built at Dynamo Kyiv. As the Soviet Top League became redundant, the Ukrainian Premier League was formed in 1991. After stints as manager of UAE and Kuwait, Lobanovskyi returned to Dynamo for one last spell in 1997. He won five consecutive league titles and three Ukrainian Cups. But perhaps most memorable, is how they competed in the Champion's League, the semi-finals of which they reached in 1999. His key player, Andriy Shevchenko went to AC Milan after that season, and his team was broken up. 1999 was the last time a team from the former Soviet Union or Eastern Europe reached that stage of the competition. Since then, only Shaktar Donetsk have managed to reach the quarter-finals of Europe's top club competition, in 2010/11, where they were thrashed 6-1 by Barcelona on aggregate.

The System has been replaced by a different type of football, in a different era of football. Tiki-taka, kick and rush excitement, merchandising and €100m transfer fees are what now provide the entertainment. And some of it is indeed that. Few could argue that recent Barcelona or Bayern Munich teams, and in the last two years Manchester City and Liverpool, have not produced joyously fluid attacking football at times. But none of these teams play with the fluidity and abandon of the System.

The tiki-taka of Barcelona and Spain, rather than requiring players to adapt their skills and interchange positions, is about building a team of number 8's. It's about smothering the game with possession and passes, preventing the other team from touching the ball as much as possible. Rather than inspire players to understand how to play in different positions, it demands that players play in the exact same position, in the exact same manner.

Bayern Munich and Germany's counterattacking game is all about physicality, athleticism, and, undeniably skill. It can be highly entertaining - arguably the Bayern Munich of Jupp Heynckes that won the Treble in 2012-13 was the most exciting team of the modern era. What did Heynckes get for his trouble? He was forced to make way for Pep Guardiola.

The decline of club football across half of Europe, the central and eastern half, has deeply impacted on the national teams. In June 2017, the once mighty Hungary lost to Andorra who ended their 66-match winless run in the process. Hungary, losing to Andorra. The Népstadion (People's Stadium) that was built in such haste to house the return match between Hungary and England in 1954 and which was later renamed the Ferenc Puskás stadium, was demolished in 2017. It is to be rebuilt, and is set to open in November 2019, but it will be a long while before a a home grown player worthy of the Népstadion will graceits pitch having developed their football in the Hungarian League.

Holland have continued to compete at international level, even reaching, and losing, the World Cup final in 2010. But their international players no longer play in the Eredivisie, and Ajax and PSV no longer compete at the business end of the Champions League – the young Ajax team of 2018-19 that lost the semi-final by a harsh 3-3 aggregate score to Tottenham Hotspur are the exception that proves the rule: they were broken up during the summer that followed. Holland will not get to benefit from their growing together as player at Ajax. Even the second tier Western European leagues contain feeder clubs for La Liga, the Bundesliga, and the great behemoth that is England's Premier League.

The System needed a tightly knit group of players, used to playing regularly together at club level, to be integrated into the national set up and augmented by the best other players available, preferably also playing to-

Declan Clarke

gether at club level. Surprise champions of Ligue 1 in 2016/2017, AS Monaco amply demonstrated the inherent problem only but a few mega-clubs face: of the team that won the league in May 2017, nine of them, six of whom were French nationals, were sold by the beginning of the 2017/18 league season commencing the following August. Kylian Mbappé became the most expensive teenager ever when he joined Paris Saint Germain from Monaco for a fee thought to be around €145m. In such a climate, it is no longer possible for the System, or Total Football to exist. A different type of football, for a different type of Europe, in a different type of era.

1) *Behind the Curtain*, Jonathan Wilson, Orion, London, 2006, p. 10
2) *The Late Late Show*, RTÉ One, Ireland, September 9th, 2011
illustrations: Declan Clarke

SOLIDARNOŚĆ

Matei Bejenaru

I spent my childhood and adolescence in the '70s in Suceava, a place where I attempted to understand the world through movies in cinemas, geography readings, and TV shows. Like any provincial city in in full-force industrialisation communist Romania, it was an eclectic mix of an urban-grown minority and a mass of newcomers from the nearby villages who became workers in factories and plants. There weren't that many buildings which reminded of the past, while the few houses in the centre that survived demolition were being squeezed between the sprawling apartment block neighbourhoods.

And yet something interesting happened in the middle of that decade. I don't know how, but Bucovina, the region whose capital my city was, was awarded the Golden Apple Award by the World Federation of Travel Journalists and Writers for its monasteries, and, consequently, groups of western tourists started appearing. I remember seeing these huge motorcades on the main road carrying German tourists on their way to the Romanian seaside, taking a detour to visit the monasteries in Bucovina, which was once under Austrian rule. You can imagine what surge of the imagination it was for a 10-12-year-old child to see countless Mercedes, Opels, BMWs and trailers, full of stickers, towing boats, all of these things that just didn't exist at that time, all passing before his eyes. I didn't interact with any of the Germans because it wasn't allowed, although in the cars I could see children my age...

Around the same time in Suceava a different kind of tourist was starting to show up: The Polish. They were travelling to Turkey or Bulgaria and would sleep at the motels in the city, and, like good communist brothers, they chatted with us, the locals. As far as I was able to understand, I gathered they were coming from a world materially superior to ours, they were better dressed, had Unitra cassette players produced in their own country – which we would only achieve a decade later – and their cars, Polski Fiat, looked better than our Dacia 1300. Each summer I would meet young Poles my age, and it was a joy to play football and then talk about our famous players – they had their Lato and legendary goalkeeper Tomaszevski and we had Dobrin and Balaci. After 1980, when I was in high school and listened to music and the news on Radio Free Europe, my chats with the Poles would revolve around politics. They were telling me that ever since there was a Polish pope in the Vatican, things were beginning to change in Poland, the workers in the northern seaports began organising into a free syndicate and were fighting for better living conditions, for rights and democracy. They held demonstrations in public squares and, when the *milicja* came, they took refuge in churches, where they felt protected. I was stunned listening to their stories, and I was unable to imagine something similar happening in Ceaușescu's dark Romania. In the summer of 1982 my Polish friends never made it to Suceava. General Jaruzelski had declared martial law a few months before with all its consequences. Even Radio Warszawa, which I could under certain circumstances listen to, stopped broadcasting western music. These were troubled times, but I was too inexperienced to understand them. Besides, I was busy preparing for my university entry exams and learning to dance.

In the same period, the football World Cup in Spain took place. Sadly, no games were broadcast on Romanian television, so the Romanians who lived close to the borders turned their TV antennas towards their neighbours. In northern Moldova we watched Soviet television, where we could see all the games. Sometimes the 'snowflakes' on the screen were bigger than the ball, but nevertheless, in our flat, several people would gather every night to watch the game. The Poland – USSR game, crucial for the qualifications into the semifinals, had an unexpected development, which went beyond a sporting competition. From the beginning of the match, behind the Polish goal, a number of supporters, probably Poles, displayed a huge banner that read *Solidarność*, the name of the Polish free anticommunist syndicate. Without paying

SOLIDARNOŚĆ

attention to the game, we jumped into a political discussion, admiring the bravery of the Polish workers led by Lech Wałęsa. We began piecing together the information we had heard on Radio Free Europe or Voice of America. The 1977 Jiu Valley miners' strike was mentioned...

Towards the end of the game one scene stayed with me vividly. At one point, Polish left winger Smolarek stopped moving towards the Soviet goal, and instead went to the corner flag, where he tried to protect it against the Russian defenders' charges. In the stand was the Solidarność banner. The same thing repeated a few times until the referee announced the end of the game and the Poles qualified for the semi-finals. The players wanted to show the whole world their solidarity with the free syndicate and with the will of their people to be rid of the Russians and of communism. I think the way they defied the rules of a football game watched by billions worldwide in order to send a political message was the most emotional moment in the tournament. I still wonder if it was the players' idea or if they just enacted the plan of a few specialists in manipulation and media communication.

At the end of the game I tried to imagine what was going on in the homes of the Poles who were watching the game just like we were. I found out a few things in 2005 when, in an exhibition in Łódź, I showed a video reminding of that scene in the corner in 1982. At the opening, a few older Poles invited me for a beer and told me about the delirium in the city's streets after the end of the game. When I asked them if, more than 20 years after that memorable event, they were satisfied with the new order of things they replied *no* but also said that they looked back with emotion and nostalgia to the anticommunist struggle of their youth.

images: stills from Poland-USSR World Cup match on 04.07.1982 https://www.youtube.com/watch?v=hTN_nGoz4tc

Matei Bejenaru

SINDICATUL SE MIȘCĂ DIN CE ÎN CE MAI BINE!

În ultimii ani, Asociația Fotbaliștilor Amatori și Nonamatori a inițiat câteva proiecte de anvergură

CINE SUNTEM?

Adresa: Strada Sabinelor Nr. 117, Etaj 3, Sector 5, Cod 050852 București, România
Telefon: +40 21 310.35.40; **Fax:** +40 21 310.35.48

Asociația Fotbaliștilor Amatori și Nonamatori din România – AFAN este organizația sindicală a fotbaliștilor profesioniști și amatori din România, afiliată pe plan internațional la FIFPro și pe plan național la BNS

CU CE VĂ PUTEM AJUTA?

Email: office@afan.ro; afanr2002@yahoo.com
Site: www.afan.ro
Facebook: https://www.facebook.com/afan.bucuresti

▶ AFAN reprezintă și apără drepturile și interesele fotbaliștilor profesioniști și amatori din Ligile I, II și III și din ligile inferioare de fotbal, inclusiv fotbal feminin, futsal, juniori, precum și pe cele ale antrenorilor de fotbal;

▶ AFAN acordă jucătorilor și antrenorilor consultanță la semnarea contractelor, a actelor adiționale, a acordurilor, transferurilor și a oricăror alte documente pe care un jucător/antrenor le încheie cu un club;

▶ AFAN reprezintă jucătorii și antrenorii în fața comisiilor cu atribuții jurisdicționale ale FRF (Camera Națională pentru Soluționarea Litigiilor, Comisia de Recurs și Comisia de Disciplină și Etică) pentru încetarea raporturilor contractuale, recuperarea drepturilor financiare restante, punerea în executare a hotărârilor comisiilor, etc.;

▶ AFAN reprezintă jucătorii și antrenorii români aflați sub contract cu cluburi străine și jucătorii și antrenorii străini aflați sub contract cu cluburi din România, în fața Camerei de Soluționare a Litigiilor FIFA și Tribunalului de Arbitraj Sportiv;

▶ Pentru jucătorii și antrenorii aflați sub contract cu cluburi în insolvență, AFAN întocmește și redactează cererile de înscriere la masa credală pentru recuperarea restanțelor financiare, contestațiile la înscrierea în tabelul preliminar, cererile de plată pentru recuperarea datoriilor curente, etc.;

▶ AFAN participă, în numele membrilor săi, la elaborarea și adoptarea de acte normative, instrucțiuni, regulamente și orice alte documente care se referă la drepturile jucătorilor și antrenorilor de fotbal.

▶ AFAN negociază și încheie contracte colective de muncă la nivelul Ligilor I, II și III, inferioare, fotbal feminin;

▶ AFAN urmărește organizarea unui fond de asigurări pentru accidente și boli profesionale și a unui fond de pensii pentru jucătorii de fotbal, în scopul protejării acestora pe durata activității profesionale și după încheierea acesteia;

▶ AFAN organizează evenimente destinate jucătorilor de fotbal (turnee ale fotbaliștilor fără contract, gala anuală a premiilor AFAN, etc);

▶ AFAN organizează întâlniri/seminarii cu jucătorii și antrenorii în vestiare, la cluburile lor, pentru a fi informați cu privire la drepturile și obligațiile lor și despre modificările regulamentelor Federației Române de Fotbal, proiectele AFAN, etc.

SFATURILE JURISTULUI: CITIȚI CU ATENȚIE CLAUZELE FINANCIARE!

„FIȚI UNIȚI!"

AVEȚI O FORȚĂ EXTRAORDINARĂ

AFAN, footballers' syndicate
Collage from publications, 2016

The Syndicate is moving better and better!
In the past years, The Association of Amateur and Nonamateur Footballers has initiated some major projects

Who are we?
Address: 117 Sabinelor street, 3rd floor, Sector 5, Bucharest
Postal Code: 050852, Romania
Phone: +40 21 310.35.48, Fax: +40 21 310.35.48

The Association of Amateur and Nonamateur Footballers of Romania - AFAN is the syndicalist organisation of professional and amateur footballers from Romania, internationally affiliated with FIFPro and locally with BNS (The National Syndical Block)

How can we help you?
E-mail: office@afan.ro, afanr2002@yahoo.com
Website: www.afan.ro
Facebook: https://www.facebook.com/afan.bucuresti

- AFAN represents and defends the rights and interests of professional and amateur footballers in the I, II and III leagues and in the lower football leagues, including women's football, futsal, juniors, as well as football coaches;
- AFAN undertakes consultancy in signing contracts, additional documents, agreements, transfers and for any other documents that a player/coach signs with a club;
- AFAN represents the players and coaches in front of the committees with jurisdictional attributions of the FRF (National Chamber for Dispute Resolution, the Appeals Commission and the Discipline and Ethics Commission) for the termination of contracts, the recovery of the unpaid financial rights, the execution of the committee decisions, etc.;
- AFAN represents Romanian players and coaches under contract with foreign clubs and foreign players and coaches under contract with Romanian clubs, before the FIFA Dispute Resolution Chamber and before the Sports Arbitration Tribunal; For players and coaches under contract with insolvent clubs, AFAN draws up and prepares the applications for registration at the credit table for the recovery of the financial arrears, the disputes for the registration in the preliminary table, the payment requests for the recovery of current debts, etc.;
- AFAN participates, on behalf of its members, in the elaboration and adoption of normative acts, instructions, regulations and any other documents that refer to the rights of football players and coaches.
- AFAN negotiates and concludes collective labour contracts at the level of I, II, III, inferior and women's football leagues;
- AFAN aims to organise an insurance fund for accidents and occupational injuries and a pension fund for football players, in order to protect them during the professional activity and after its conclusion;
- AFAN organises events for football players (tournaments for players without a contract, AFAN Awards Annual Gala, etc.);
- AFAN organises meetings/seminars with players and coaches at their clubs, in locker rooms, to inform them about their rights and obligations and about the changes of the regulations of the Romanian Football Federation, AFAN projects, etc.;

JURIST'S ADVICE: READ CAREFULLY THE FINANCIAL CLAUSES!
""BE UNITED!" YOU HAVE AN EXTRAORDINARY FORCE!"

LA MANO DE DIOS
Truth or dare?

Anca Verona Mihuleț

1986, Mexico: Romania did not qualify for the World Cup in Mexico; in fact, the games were not even broadcast on TV, so a lot of the information that reached us did so orally – rephrased commentaries based on fragments or brief news clips on the radio. In 1978 some of the games were shown on TV, but in 1982 the much-anticipated live broadcasts went silent.

The final of the 1986 championship, played between Argentina and West Germany, was won by Argentina in the Estadio Azteca in Mexico, 3-2.

Also in the Estadio Azteca, on June 22nd, 1986, the spectacular quarter-finals game between Argentina and England took place; Argentina won 2-1 thanks to Maradona's two historic goals. The first was in the 51st minute and was scored with his hand. It was dubbed 'the hand of God' ('la mano de Dios'). It was followed after just four minutes by the 'goal of the century', as Maradona dribbled past four English players and scored past Shilton. The famous Uruguayan commentator Victor Hugo Morales called Diego Armando Maradona the "cosmic kite" ("barrilete cosmico") as he was ecstatically commentating the game. Besides the obvious tension on the field, this game took place four years after the Falklands War between Argentina and Great Britain.

The game's tension was analysed starting from the architecture of the stadium, the rules of the game, and the language of sports commentators by Croatian artist Ana Hušman in her film *Football*, produced in 2011.

The artist travelled to Mexico City to understand the structure of the monumental stadium in which a series of important matches took place. Afterwards, together with a team of performers, she re-staged the match using the specific language of sports anchors to fragment the key moments of the game, unveiling the rhythm and dynamics of the Argentina – England rivalry. The cinematic method used was a mix of stop frame, film inserts on green screen, and longer one-take shots, highlighting the feminine voice's modulation in moments of image deconstruction, the woman's position as social commentator being a constant interest of the artist. To prepare her voice and to be able to accurately convey the mood of the imagined game, Ana Hušman worked with a diction coach, the result being, among other things, an ability to shout "Gooooaaal!!" without straining her voice and to string together long sentences in a single breath. In articulating the players' discourse, the artist used the original press statements, interviews and biographies; some older, some more recent.

In the beginning of the film, Hušman explains the structure of the football pitch, which is built in such way that the goalposts are on the north-south axis, preventing the sun's impact on the length of the field. The stands can be built in the form of an amphitheatre, a horseshoe, or a rectangle. As the explanations go into more detail, the language gets more and more abundant and more difficult to grasp, the words being directly coordinated with the player's performance.

The ball, the foot, the pitch, the forces involved in delivering a shot are described through language with emphasis on the specific verbs. The moment of the goalkeeper's blocking the ball is shot in a room with a green screen, which enables the osmosis between commentary and movement.

The colours of the simulacrum teams' equipment are bright yellow for the English and light blue for the Argentinians. Ana Hušman only represents eight players from the Argentinian team and seven from the English one, the players she considered the most visible during the match. The routine of team description and anthem singing is replaced by surprising elements from the players' confessions. We find out that goalkeeper Peter Shilton had a gambling problem after retiring from professional football, while Terry Fenwick holds the record for most yellow card penalties received in a world cup. Tunisian referee Ali Bin Nasser has always been criticised for how he adjudicated the game – it was said that a European referee would have done better. Nasser claimed he did not see Maradona's handball; due to his deficient performance as referee he never officiated such a high-level game after the tournament.

Ana Hušman brings a lot of force into her football commentator discourse when she talks about the game technique – misleading the opponent is the pretext for the anchor to intensify language, to use harsh, sometimes unpleasant words, to create confusion – kicking, pushing, gripping, or blocking the ball are just a few of the techniques for misleading the opponent. "The taste for farce is very Argentinian", said Jorge Valdano.

A basic rule for commentators is that they must not raise their voice or shout gratuitously – 'tdlne, tdlni, tdlno, tdlnu' are series of consonants ending in a vowel used to develop rhythm and speed in speech. Certain expressions must often be accompanied by gestures so that the commentator feels familiar with a particular moment, which they can then repeat, thereby gaining consistency in commentary.

Peter Reid, the manager of Thailand's team between 2008 and 2009, declared that even though football is a universal language, he could never pronounce the names of his team's players, so he would always address them by the number on their t-shirts.

Terry Butcher, one of the players who tried to stop Maradona's rush for the 'goal of the century' had a rising career as coach and manager; at the 2010 World Cup he refused to shake Maradona's hand, showing that the bitterness of that unclear defeat was still there 24 years later. Burruchaga's epiphanies on the field and the coordination between him and Batista have already gained mythical status. These magical moments of the game are described by Hušman through the movement of the players in front of the green screen and through an animation where each player's number follows the unfolding of the game.

At the end of the commentary we hear Valdano saying "football is a metaphor for the time and place you play in. Who doesn't agree with the evolution of football does not believe in the evolution of the world". Everything concludes when the fragmented information of the film is brought together and 'the hand of God' is performed by all 15 players under the controlled comments of the artist, who ends on the melodious name 'Diego Armando Maradona'.

images: Ana Hušman, *Football*, video color PAL, 4:3, 16mm transferred to digitBETA, 15'00", 2011

Anca Verona Mihuleț

Symbolic Language and Social Behaviour

An interview with Dumitru Graur

Personal realities are recomposed based on the messages filtered through the various media we come in contact with – "the medium is the message", as Marshall McLuhan presciently declared in the 1960s. Language, and communication more generally, are extensions of our actions, which function like cells, dividing, creating connections and transmitting information. I spoke about language and its use in the field of sports with journalist Dumitru Graur, a representative figure for radio and television sports commentary, currently president of the Romanian Sports Press Association.

Anca Verona Mihuleț: A debate around language in football will lead us into a discussion on sports more generally. There is a series of artists working with the idea of language, collaborating with specialists from various fields in order to study in detail the nature of expression from a creative perspective, but also from the perspective of visual culture. The image or images we use play an important role in reaching a result or finishing a demonstration. As I was researching the topic of sports language, I thought it would be useful to talk to a person who was an actual sports commentator and who, furthermore, writes, interviews and works with a specific methodology.

At the same time, I tried to find out whether there are places that prepare people to become sports commentators or where it is that you can study the language used in sports. I discovered that at Leicester University there is a module entitled *Football and Society*. Its description states that, generally, football is played in every country; sports offer a common language and a set of familiar reference points that allow for fruitful communication beyond national borders.

When the World Cup is on, the whole world watches. Nowadays women are just as interested in football as men, and women's football is quickly gaining popularity. Exploring football means exploring who you are.

Today there are glossaries of sports terms available, mostly in English. I would be interested to know if there are certain stereotypes within Romanian sports language, a certain terminology, and if we could talk about a glossary of football terms.

Dumitru Graur: First I would like to say that I'm not a linguist. What you are proposing is a linguistic question. It's true that I am the son of the famous linguist Alexandru Graur, from whom I borrowed a few methods. On the other hand, as a professional user of sports language for many years, I have got used to the vocabulary and the various sentence structures or linguistic stereotypes. At the moment, I don't think we could have a sports language dictionary. There are too few specific expressions.

In Romania, many of the expressions associated with sports language were imported from French. I know all of this from my father, with whom I discussed the topic and who explained to me that there is a series of language mistakes stemming from translations from French done at the beginning of the 20th century by people who did not know the language too well. Sports writers weren't very cultivated at the time. For instance, the phrase «de près», which means 'close to', was imported as de puțin". It is a mistake to say "de puțin". What we should say is "cu puțin pe lângă", meaning that someone narrowly missed. If you listen to sports' commentaries, you will often hear "de puțin", which became the convention.

Another mistake is "degajează mingea". "A degaja" means 'to free up' or 'to clear'. It is completely wrong to say "degajează mingea" ('clearing the ball') instead of "degajează terenul" ('clearing the field'). As soon as the ball is kicked away the players run after it, leading to a clearing of the field.

I would also add here constructions like "echipa României de handbal" or "de hochei", "de fotbal", and so on. The correct word order is "echipa de fotbal/handbal/hochei a României" ('Romania's football/handball/hockey team'), but too few commentators nowadays still use the accusative in their language.

Another thing that could be mentioned is the pronunciation of players' names from Transylvania, like Rotáriu or Cojocáriu. In the South-West they mispronounce them as Rotaríu or Cojocaríu.

Recently we reprinted *Dicționarul greșelilor de limbă* [The Dictionary of Language Mistakes] at Editura Humanitas, initially compiled by Alexandru Graur and published at Editura Academiei in 1982. The new edition is edited by Associate Professor Dr. Liviu Groza. The first edition was corrected with references to the *DOOM* (the Orthographic Dictionary of the Romanian Language) and the editor intervened next to my father's notes, sometimes contradicting him. I was surprised many times by the linguistic conclusions reached. For instance, Alexandru Graur discussed the correct pronunciation of the word 'rugby'. Should you say "ruibi" or "rugbi", also given the English pronunciation? In the new edition, according to the *DOOM*, both pronunciations are accepted, whereas Alexandru Graur thought "ruibi" was wrong and "rugbi" correct, as it corresponded to the English spelling. He also opined that we shouldn't use the term "teninsmenă" (the masculine "tenismen" with a feminine suffix), but the new edition of the *Dictionary*, citing the *DOOM*, says the term is correct, as it has become accepted through use. If we were to translate it word for word, it would be a flat-out self-contradiction.

I will mention one more word here: "scor". In the 1982 edition of the *Dictionary* it says that the English *score* initially meant 'a notch in a piece of wood' and now, in sports, it means 'the total number of points scored by both sides' and not, as it says in the Romanian Explanatory Dictionary (DEX), "the ratio between points scored by and against a given team". It is therefore a mistake to say one "scores and reduces the score" ('marchează și reduce scorul'), as the total cannot decrease by adding a new point. In the recent edition of the *Dictionary*, they present the following definition, taken from the DEX: "scor, scoruri" means 'the ratio between points scored by and against a given team in a sports competition, the result reflected by this ratio,' taken from the French «score», which completely ignores Alexandru Graur's proposed linguistic construction.

To conclude, it is not possible, in my opinion, to produce a Romanian dictionary of sports expressions, as Romanian sports language is quite poor. In sports one uses words from everyday speech when describing an event or writing a text; from time to time specific expressions are used as well, but there are very few. So this hypothetical dictionary would only be a few pages long.

The English, who invented football, but also sports language, use many specific expressions; in our case, like I said, the expressions are borrowed from other languages. We refer to a 'throw-in' as an "aut", taken directly from the English 'out'.

These last few years I've heard commentators using 'sezon' – "a făcut un contract pentru două sezoane" ('he/she made a contract for two seasons'), by which they actually mean 'for two years'. I used it differently – a sports' year was split into two seasons: winter-spring and autumn-winter; summer was the break in the middle. Recently "sezon" has started being interpreted as a whole year.

We could also mention the term "repriză". Alexandru Graur writes that "repriză" comes from the French «reprise», which means 'to recover'. In Romanian we have the established phrases "repriza întîi" ('first half') and "repriza a doua" ('second half'). Given the original meaning of the term, it is not correct to use the expression "repriza întîi", given that the game can't resume from zero. "Repriza întîi" should technically be the second part of a game. «À la reprise» means something like 'at the recovery' and refers to what we call "repriza a doua".

Language changes, and currently we are using a language that is, I would say, a bit crooked – Facebook language.

Anca Verona Mihuleț

> My father would say: nobody can influence language, language evolves like a living organism that goes where the people want.

How are sports commentators trained in Romania? How were you trained, for instance?

> There was never a school for sports commentators, everything was done informally. In my case, nobody ever told me how I should go about doing it; I had to figure it out alone by feeling. I made mistakes too, human mistakes, really, that were jumped upon with gusto by the written press. I'm referring here to my commentaries on TV. Such mistakes happen when you need to express yourself freely and extremely quickly.
>
> Before the Revolution there was the Ștefan Gheorghiu Academy, a journalism school where party activists were trained and who would then go on to work in the press. But what they learned there was communist language. It's true that there are now universities that teach students what working in the press means, but you will never get sports commentators and writers from that context. Sports writing and TV commentary are complicated jobs that can't be learned theoretically. They have to be acquired through practice. We should have to take elocution lessons, which, however, have always been lacking in these universities.

In the first issue of *Corner* I wrote an article about a video work produced by a Croatian artist Ana Hušman, who took elocution lessons to be able to commentate a football game. How did you prepare for assignments when you were a sports commentator?

> Firstly I did research. Back then it was not easy at all. There was no internet, no Google, and very rarely did I have access to foreign magazines. I read up on our national team, I had notes that I used; it was a complex process I had to undertake for each and every game. Every commentator had to prepare their own materials. Now it's relatively simple – you can find the information you need on Google or any sports-focused search engine, which really makes the commentator's job much easier.

Did you ever encounter any difficulties when commentating a competition live? It would be interesting to discuss a particular example.

> I've had many kinds of situations throughout my career... I some-

times meet young people who tell me they remember playing on the carpet and hearing my voice on TV or growing up with my voice. I get quite emotional when hearing such things.

There was one moment, my 'moment of glory', so to say, at the Romanian Cup finals in 1988, Steaua vs. Dinamo. At the end of the game there was a big argument – Steaua had scored a goal that was disallowed due to being offside. Valentin Ceaușescu motioned Steaua's players to leave the field. It was total confusion. The team left the field, nobody could understand what was going on, and I, who was commentating the finals, was supposed to explain what was happening – the players are leaving the field, they're out, they can't play anymore, they'll be sanctioned. I would have risked my whole career. That's when I think I made the smartest decision of my life: I kept quiet! The interruption took 4-5 minutes, during which I, who normally talked a lot, did not say a single word. I extricated myself from the problem without anyone noticing. It was easy to get yourself banned back then. The following day, Ceaușescu, who was a Steaua supporter, said the goal counted and that Steaua must get the cup. The day before, Dinamo took the cup and left with it after Steaua had left the field. When the players leave the field it means surrender. The situation was unseen in world football. After the Revolution, Steaua renounced the cup.

What do you think about the language used by football players then vs. now?

Footballers' language is increasingly elevated; the level of culture is visibly growing, even though Romanian teams are playing worse and worse. Some of the players that are interviewed think clearly and express themselves correctly – I am often pleasantly surprised. Back in my day it was hard to get a few sentences out of them. Now things have changed for the better – these are the effects of freedom of speech, of the democracy we are living in.

Is football important to the construction of local and national identity?

Sports in general and professional sportspeople contribute a lot to asserting the identity of the society and country they represent, without a doubt. In the communist years a lot of money was funnelled into sports, because they wished to demonstrate

Anca Verona Mihuleț

communism's superiority to other systems. This structure fell completely after the revolution – such large investments into sports stopped being made. Many countries continue to invest in sports (not Romania, sadly), as they are aware that by doing this they are also investing in the image and reputation of their country abroad.

Professional sportspeople are role models that encourage young people to take up sports. Professional sportspeople often risk their health; the usual *sports-are-health* story doesn't apply. Professional sports are not healthy, they are, on the contrary, a constant aggression against the individual's health, but they do create role models.

Sports are consumed through television, the internet, and various forms of celebrity culture.

Sports are really a high-profit industry, garnering billions worldwide. The sports industry is built on champions and comprises many components: equipment sales, marketing, stadiums, places for supporters, all working as a whole. There is also the flipside: amateur sports, which is also stimulated by champions.

Can the sports press influence the public's view on sports or even sportspeople's view on their art? Can we consider the sports press a kind of education?

The sports press does indeed have this power. It pains me to say it, but sometimes it influences it for the worse. Often the press aims for a certain direction, one that is not healthy and recommendable, going so far as to manipulate. The readers, viewers, or listeners are like pigeons waiting with their beaks open for food. They gobble up everything that's being fed to them. People have written extensive studies and debated questions regarding the role of the press, and these should be given due consideration. Talking about the sports press, we need to become more aware of the medium's implications. The monthly *Sport în România. Revistă de cultură și educație sportivă* [Sport in Romania. Magazine of Sports Culture and Education], edited by the Romanian Sports Press Association, has no connections to the tabloid press of nowadays. I feel disillusioned about the online world, and so I still buy newspapers. Even if I do use the internet, the way one reads there does not compare to the presentation and pacing of an article you can actually see.

Could you talk more about the Romanian Sports Press Association?

The Romanian Sports Press Association is celebrating its 90th anniversary on November 22nd this year, being the second oldest association in the country, after the Romanian Automobile Club. In 1927 our forefathers founded a union to protect their professional interests and help them develop as a unit. It is a public service association and is under the patronage of His Majesty King Michael I, a very meaningful title for us. The association has around 400 members. We publish the monthly *Sport în România. Revistă de cultură și educație sportivă*, a quality magazine that takes up a lot of our time. We have various other actions – we signed a cooperation protocol with the Ministry of Education towards organising a few events together with the aim of promoting sports in schools. The magazine also promotes some necessary restructuring towards the development of sports in Romania. Sports in Romania are in free-fall, and the only way to rebound is to change existing structures and rebuild things from the ground up. For a long time Romanian sports lived out of the communist heritage. This regime cultivated athletes in a certain context and to a certain degree that was not possible after the regime fell. The only viable formula is to return to school and university sports. We advocate this measure. Politicians need to understand that investing more in school sports is a must. Then we need to wait. Our future world champions and Olympic athletes are there right now. We can't really have expectations from anyone else. There are a few cases that would contradict what I just said, but they are isolated events. Sports are struggling to survive in our country. We lack investments and infrastructure. I am not an optimist and certainly will not be until we come to our senses.

The interview took place on October 3rd, 2017 at the main office of the Romanian Sports Press Association in Bucharest.
image: journalist Dumitru Graur interviewing canoeist Ivan Patzaichin at the Otopeni Airport as he was returning from the 1984 Olympic Games; courtesy of Dumitru Graur

Anca Verona Mihuleț

CAPRICORN

The financial system you fine-tuned with such great skill is about to be exposed. The loved ones, which you relied on, are no longer by your side. Everybody knows the money never went to the sick relatives, but was used for personal, evil purposes. Close the deal with the terrace as fast as you can before the new season starts. A great danger is hovering over you because of the planet Uranus which elicits an hypnotic state.

AQUARIUS

You postponed solving some health issues, it's about time you stop being such a day-dreamer. You are about to make a trip to an exotic place such as the police department no. 21. Great satisfaction will come to you from a mysterious person. A treatment with mud and leeches would be advised: a reward for the amount of work you put in lately while capturing the stickers of enemy gangs. Your charm is on the rise. Love? Nothing can affect you anymore, at least during the next stage.

PISCES

If the uncertainty from the betting house doesn't disappear from your conscience, then you should divert your attention. Be more aggressive, everybody treats you like a stooge. Some changes need to take place in your life: change your wardrobe. Try other colours, too. In this cold season watch over your health, drink more liquids, preferably warm and with a lot of syrup. A piece of advice for the ones in Ghencea: for too long you've fed your optimism with corn puffs.

ARIES

Mercury recommends that you collect objects from amateur clubs, they are of superior quality, you make a charitable gesture and, apart from that, they are much nicer. The indigestion you've had lately is from the sunflower seeds bought from Fox Tail. Popcorn is an antacid recommended sometimes even by doctors. Don't sell your phone, it's fitted with the best performing camera on the market. You are not the only one going through the dark phase of transfers.

TAURUS

The enemies from the terrace have anticipated your moves. The good news is that you will receive a sum of money and many pyrotechnic materials from a veteran dressed in red overalls. The relationship with a loved one is entering Sun in Cancer. Communicating your feelings has always been a problem which gave you headaches. Not for a short time you will meet new people willing to take risky actions. Our recommendation is to use only public transport.

GEMINI

You are seen everywhere there is smoke and huge tensions. For you the year has started under the sign of hate. The new team anthem and new equipment have caused true psychic storms. And it's also hate which will bring to your soul sweet vengeful satisfaction. You no longer have uncertainties. You are an adversary which many envy with admiration and terror. In the near future you might fall in love irreparably with a person with green eyes. Beware! Do not give in to temptation.

CORNER #2